VALUE, REALI1

Value, Reality, and Desire is an extended argument for a robust realism about value. The robust realist affirms the following distinctive theses. There are genuine claims about value which are true or false—there are facts about value. These value-facts are mind-independent—they are not reducible to desires or other mental states, or indeed to any non-mental facts of a non-evaluative kind. And these genuine, mind-independent, irreducible value-facts are causally efficacious. Values, quite literally, affect us.

These are not particularly fashionable theses, and taken as a whole they go somewhat against the grain of quite a lot of recent work in the metaphysics of value. Further, against the received view, Oddie argues that we can have knowledge of values by experiential acquaintance, that there are experiences of value which can be both veridical and appropriately responsive to the values themselves. Finally, these value-experiences are not the products of some exotic and implausible faculty of 'intuition'. Rather, they are perfectly mundane and familiar mental states—namely, desires. This view explains how values can be 'intrinsically motivating', without falling foul of the widely accepted 'queerness' objection. There are, of course, other objections to each of the realist's claims. In showing how and why these objections fail, Oddie introduces a wealth of interesting and original insights about issues of wider interest—including the nature of properties, reduction, supervenience, and causation. The result is a novel and interesting account which illuminates what would otherwise be deeply puzzling features of value and desire and the connections between them.

Graham Oddie is Professor of Philosophy at the University of Colorado at Boulder.

Value, Reality, and Desire

GRAHAM ODDIE

Clarendon Press · Oxford

OXFORD
UNIVERSITY PRESS

Great Clarendon Street, Oxford OX2 6DP

Oxford University Press is a department of the University of Oxford.
If furthers the University's objective of excellence in research, scholarship,
and education by publishing worldwide in

Oxford New York

Auckland Cape Town Dar es Salaam Hong Kong Karachi Kuala Lumpur
Madrid Melbourne Mexico City Nairobi New Delhi Shanghai Taipei Toronto

With offices in

Argentina Austria Brazil Chile Czech Republic France Greece
Guatemala Hungary Italy Japan South Korea Poland Portugal
Singapore Switzerland Thailand Turkey Ukraine Vietnam

Oxford is a registered trade mark of Oxford University Press
in the UK and in certain other countries

Published in the United States
by Oxford University Press Inc., New York

British Library Cataloguing in Publication Data
Data available

Library of Congress Cataloguing in Publication Data
Data available

Typeset by SPI Publisher Services, Pondicherry, India
Digially printed and bound in Great Britain by
CPI Antony Rowe, Chippenham and Eastbourne

ISBN 978-0-19-927341-6 (Hbk)
ISBN 978-0-19-956238-1 (Pbk)

1 3 5 7 9 10 8 6 4 2

for

JONATHAN, MIRIAM

and

JESSICA

ACKNOWLEDGEMENTS

THIS book, which first appeared in hardback in March 2005, is about value—whether value is real, what it is, whether we can know about it, and if so, how we can do so. I argue that there are facts about value; that value is mind-independent, irreducible, and causally networked; and that we can have knowledge of value by experiential acquaintance. The book is thus an extended argument for a robust realism about the good.

In the Acknowledgements to the hardback edition I thanked several colleagues, students, friends, and OUP editors, including: Christopher Shields, Michael Tooley, Paul Studtmann, Chris Kelly, Dan Demetriou, Risto Hilpinen, Alan Goldman, Harvey Seigel, Keith Lehrer, Christopher Swoyer, Pavel Tichý, Philip Catton, Christine Swanton, Michelle Montague, Jack Copeland, Philip Pettit, Roy Perrett, Peter Momtchiloff, Jacqueline Baker, Jean van Altena, and Rupert Cousens. To this list I need to add Catherine Berry and Cherry Brooker, the editors at the Press who have been extraordinarily helpful in producing this paperback edition.

Since publication I have received valuable and challenging criticisms from a number of philosophers, including reviewers. I am particularly grateful to Kevin Mulligan (Geneva University), who has not only made many interesting criticisms, but who organized the Values Colloquium at the ECAP conference in Lisbon (August 2005). And his colleague, Olivier Massin, organized a wonderful workshop on the Metaphysics of Value in November 2008, at which Alain Pé-Curto, Federico Lauria, and Jonathan Simon delivered interesting critiques of central theses of my book. I have also gained much from interactions with Toni Rønnow-Rasmussen and Wlodek Rabinowicz both of whom attended the Lisbon and Geneva workshops. And I thank David Robb and the philosophy faculty at Davidson College for a very fruitful two-day workshop on the book in July 2008. Others with whom I have profitably exchanged views on these topics include Christoph Fehige and Daniel Friedrich.

It would be impossible to incorporate all the insights I have gained from these critics without writing a new work on value, and this volume is a paperback of the original work with only minor corrections. One feature of the original book that does stand in need of correction, however, concerns the history of the thesis which I dubbed "the experience conjecture", that our evidential access to value is through value-seemings and that desires are such value-seemings. To desire P is for P to seem, appear, or be experienced as, good. In his *Appearances of the Good* (2007) Sergio Tenenbaum also develops the thesis, which he first outlined in his 1999 article 'The Judgement of a Weak Will', that desires are appearances of the good. Tenenbaum argues, as I do, that such appearances contain a perspectival element, although our views on perspectivity are by no means identical. And Denis Stampe, whose views in his 1987 article 'The authority of desire' are very close indeed to mine, writes: "Desire is a kind of perception.... To desire something is to be in a kind of perceptual state, in which that thing seems good..." (Stampe, 1987, 359). Although Stampe does not develop the perspectivity of desire, he does argue for another distinctive thesis presented here—namely, that desires are ideally caused by what they are perceptions of. He writes: "...the sensitivity involved in desire is a matter of such states being produced by a mental mechanism that is activated, ideally, by and only by the apparent goodness of a state of affairs...." (p. 360). (I would say "actual goodness" rather than "apparent goodness".) Regrettably I was unaware of Tenenbaum's and Stampe's work when I wrote *Value, Reality and Desire* and I want to take the opportunity here to apologize for that, and to acknowledge the priority of these two papers. As a realist, however, I do derive some compensatory satisfaction from the fact that different philosophers, working essentially independently, converged on really rather remarkably similar views. Maybe that is evidence, however slight, that we are actually converging on the truth.

Finally, I want to thank the artist Melanie Yazzie, whose works give us direct experiential access to the good, for her permission to use "Silent Moments" on the cover.

CONTENTS

List of Figures   xiii

List of Tables   xv

1.   **Reality and Value**   1
1.1 Realism   2
1.2 Propositional Content   3
1.3 Presuppositional Fulfilment   8
1.4 Mind-Independence   14
1.5 Irreducibility   17
1.6 Causal Networking   19
1.7 A Schema for Degrees of Realism   22
1.8 An Overview of the Book   23

2.   **Judgement and Desire**   28
2.1 A Puzzling Asymmetry   28
2.2 An Internalist Explanation of the Puzzling Asymmetry   29
2.3 The Queerness Argument   30
2.4 Independence   32
2.5 The Judgement–Desire Gap   36
2.6 The Merit Connection   38
2.7 The Experience Conjecture   40
2.8 Moore's Paradox and its Shadow   43

3.   **Desires as Value Data**   47
3.1 The Necessity for a Source of Value Data   47
3.2 Experience and Belief: The General Case   50
3.3 Experience and Belief: The Case of Value   54

3.4	The Problem of Bad Data	58
3.5	Perspectivity	60
3.6	Satan's Injunction	63
3.7	Disappointment	67
3.8	The Value of Desire	70
3.9	Emotion	73
3.10	The BAD and the SAD	78
3.11	The Lure of Idealism	80
4.	**Value as Refined Desire**	**82**
4.1	Categorical and Dispositional Idealism	83
4.2	The Web of Desire	87
4.3	Refining First-Order Desires in the Light of Second-Order Desires	92
4.4	Reflexive Higher-Order Desires	96
4.5	Convergence in Higher-Order Desires	97
4.6	Instant Refinement	99
4.7	Connectedness Guarantees Agent-Neutrality	100
4.8	The Nature of this Ideal	102
4.9	The Attractions of Refinement Idealism	104
5.	**Value Beyond Desire**	**107**
5.1	Egoism	107
5.2	Altruism	113
5.3	Infatuation	116
5.4	Partiality	117
5.5	Hatred	120
5.6	Perversity	125
5.7	What Desire Can Do for Value	131
5.8	The Value of Refinement	136

6.   **Irreducible Value**   141

6.1   Three Stories   143

6.2   Reducibility   144

6.3   Supervenience   146

6.4   Avoiding Reduction by Going 'Fine-Grained'   148

6.5   Avoiding Reduction by Denying Boolean Closure   151

6.6   Properties as Convex Conditions   152

6.7   Value Properties   158

6.8   Convexity and the Natural Basis of a Value Property   162

6.9   The Evaluative Transformation of the Natural   166

6.10 Conceptual Expansion   172

6.11 Nature and Value   175

6.12 The Problem of Causal Networking   180

7.   **Value as Cause**   181

7.1   The Argument from Explanatory Idleness   182

7.2   The Argument from Causal Exclusion   187

7.3   Determinables, Determinates, and Causation   191

7.4   Mental Causation   195

7.5   Causation by Values   198

7.6   Causation and Convexity   203

7.7   Causation and Properties   206

7.8   Towards a Robust Value Realism   210

8.   **Value, Judgement, and Desire: Bridging the Gaps**   211

8.1   The Gappiness of Realism   211

8.2   Bridging the Gaps   214

8.3   Perspective, Location, and Distance in Value Space   218

8.4   Value Distance and Second-Order Desires   226

8.5   Knowledge of the Good by Direct Acquaintance   233

Appendices

1. A Refutation of Independence 240

2. Seemings as Evidence 241

3. The BAD Paradox 243

References 244

Index 249

LIST OF FIGURES

1.1	*A schema for degrees of realism*	23
4.1	*A web of second-order desire*	90
4.2	*Minimal care for others*	101
5.1	*Romeo, the egoist infiltrator*	110
5.2	*A pair of egoists*	112
5.3	*Pure obsessive altruists*	114
5.4	*Pure altruists branch*	116
5.5	*Romeo and Juliet are infatuated*	117
5.6	*Ostracized egalitarian*	119
5.7	*Two hate Romeo*	122
5.8	*Appropriateness of strength of desire*	135
5.9	*Appropriateness of strength of desire: the general case*	136
5.10	*Appropriateness of desire for valueless N*	137
6.1	*The temperature space*	153
6.2	*Three temperature conditions*	153
6.3	*The weather space*	156
6.4	*Region corresponding to cold if and only if dry*	157
6.5	*Region corresponding to cold or drizzly*	158
6.6	*Two-dimensional natural space involving pleasure/pain and desire/aversion*	164
6.7	*Region corresponding to: Y's response is appropriate*	165
6.8	*Region corresponding to: Y's response is totally inappropriate*	166
6.9	*Region corresponding to: Y's state is somewhat bad*	167
6.10	*Points assigned values*	169
6.11	*A transformation of the natural space*	170
6.12	*Region corresponding to: Y's response appropriate (good)*	171
6.13	*The combined natural-value space*	174
6.14	*Projection of D on to natural subspace*	178
6.15	*Projection of D on to value subspace*	179

8.1	*The gaps in the realist's universe*	212
8.2	*The gaps in the value realist's universe*	212
8.3	*Bridging the gaps*	214
8.4	*The experience conjecture*	215
8.5	*The causal networking thesis*	216
8.6	*The desire contribution thesis*	216
8.7	*Desires as value data*	217
8.8	*Desires influence value judgements*	217
8.9	*Judgements influence desires*	219
8.10	*The gaps bridged*	219

LIST OF TABLES

2.1	*Moore's paradox and the puzzling asymmetry*	45
4.1	*First-order (base) desires:* D_1	88
4.2	*Second-order desires:* C_1	91
4.3	*Revised first-order desires:* $D_2 = C_1 D_1$	93
4.4	*Twice revised first-order desires:* $D_3 = C_1 D_2$	94
4.5	*The ideal limit of* C_1 *and* D_1: $C_1 D_n \rightarrow D_\infty$	95
4.6	*Revised higher-order desires:* $C_2 = C_1 C_1$	98
4.7	*Minimal care for others*	100
4.8	*Romeo alone revises*	103
5.1	*Higher-order matrix for psychological egoism:* I	108
5.2	*The egoist infiltrator*	109
5.3	*The limiting distribution for the egoist infiltrator*	110
5.4	*A pair of egoists*	113
5.5	*Limiting desires for a pair of egoists*	113
5.6	*Pure obsessive altruists*	114
5.7	*Pure altruists branch*	115
5.8	*One egalitarian*	118
5.9	*The ostracized egalitarian*	119
5.10	*Limiting desires: ostracized egalitarian*	119
5.11	*Two hate Romeo*	123
5.12	*Limiting higher-order desires: two hate Romeo*	123
5.13	*Base desires for two hate Romeo*	123
5.14	*Limiting desires: two hate Romeo*	124
5.15	*Two hate each other*	124
5.16	*Limiting higher-order desires: two hate each other*	125
6.1	*A numerical assignment to the natural states*	169
8.1	*James and John*	227
8.2	*James's and John's first-order desires track their own happiness*	227

8.3	*Second-order desires of James and John*	228
8.4	*First-order desires after refinement*	228
8.5	*Care matrix:* C_1	229
8.6	*Distance matrix corresponding to* C_1	230
8.7	*Revised first-order desires = revised localized goods*	232
8.8	*Limiting first-order desires = limiting localized goods*	232
8.9	*The puzzling asymmetry*	235
8.10	*Moore's shadow*	235
8.11	*A weak asymmetry*	235

I   REALITY AND VALUE

THE world presents a sensible being—like you or me—with an astonishing array of objects of every variety of shape, colour, texture, and composition. Mostly we take these objects of experience for granted. We take it for granted that they are part of the world; that they have both sensible features and features which lie below the surface of appearance; that they have both kinds of features independently of our sensing them as such; and that their having these features produces various tangible effects, including our experiences of them. To abandon some of these beliefs is to abandon an aspect of realism. Most of us, however, are reasonably robust realists about the sensible world.

The world also presents a sensitive being—like you or me—with a rich array of values. It is a world replete with goods and evils: pleasure and pain, joy and misery, kindness and callousness, graciousness and greed, the beauty of Bach and the banality of Britney Spears. The value of some of these—like the value of pleasure, or of kindness—forces itself upon us. Their value lies on or near the very surface of appearance. The value of others—like the putative value of forgiving those who have harmed you—may be not so easily discerned. They may lie some distance from the surface, to be discovered only through close attention or the acquisition of specific skills. But whether they lie on the surface of appearance or below it, they are there, whether or not some particular person notices or knows of them. Questioning the reality of the sensible world is largely a philosopher's pastime, but philosophers are by no means alone in questioning the reality of the valuable.

What is at issue between a realist and an antirealist about value? An unflinching realist about value will affirm those same theses of the valuable that we are all naturally disposed to affirm of the sensible. There are genuine claims about value, and these claims are true or false. The true claims—the *facts* about value—have a certain ontological robustness. They are mind-independent—they are not reducible to desires or other mental states. Nor are they reducible to any other purely non-evaluative facts. Finally, these mind-independent, irreducible value facts are not idle bystanders, but are fully paid-up contributors to the causal network. Values can affect us, causally, and it is through their causal impact on us that we have knowledge of value.

These are not particularly fashionable theses, and taken as a whole they go somewhat against the grain of quite a lot of recent work in the metaphysics and epistemology of value. They constitute a robust realism about value. This book is an extended argument for robust realism about value. There are, of course, troubling arguments against each of the claims made by the realist. In the course of showing how and why these arguments fail, I outline the components of a version of robust value realism which is as coherent, attractive, and every bit as believable as any of its antirealist rivals.

I.I Realism

Wherever there are interesting entities, there realists and antirealists will gather: the physical world, the phenomenal world, minds, universals, particulars, God, the past, the present, the future, theoretical entities, causation, chance, mathematical objects, logical objects, and (last and foremost) the good. In each such case there is an *existence* question, and the posing of this question predictably spawns its realists and antirealists together with a lively debate between them. Do these debates have something in common, or is it rather a case of overlapping family resemblances? What exactly does a realist affirm and her antirealist opponent deny?

It is often suggested that there is no single doctrine of realism, but rather that it comprises a bunch of different strands: truth-aptness, mind-independence, existence of truth-makers, causal or explanatory power, and so on. A realist might pick out one strand, her antirealist opponent another, and with each tightly clutching her own strand, they will almost certainly end up talking past one another. Despite the appearances of chaos and confusion about the commitments of realism, a fairly simple order is discernible in these debates. We can distinguish five realist tenets—concerning, respectively, *propositional* content, presuppositional fulfilment, mind-independence, irreducibility, and causal networking—and in each of these debates these tenets define a series of increasingly realist stances. Realism thus admits of degrees, and the five tenets yield six degrees of realism. *sub degrees?*

Applying this schema to the case of value, the tenet of propositional content maintains that evaluative judgements involve the expression of genuine propositions about value, propositions which are apt for classification as either true or false descriptions of reality. The tenet of presuppositional fulfilment maintains that not only are such value propositions *apt* for classification as true or false, they do not lack actual truth values through unfulfilled presuppositions. (How a proposition may be apt for classification as true or false, without actually being true or false, we will soon see.) The mind-independence tenet denies that truths about value are simply congeries of facts concerning desires or preferences, or other such attitudes. Irreducibility denies that truths about value are congeries of any other non-evaluative facts. The last of the five tenets—that of causal networking—is the most controversial. It is one thing to claim that facts about value are irreducible, quite another to claim that they play an active role in the causal network. Ever since the Eleatic Stranger's remarks in Plato's *Sophist*, however, *power* has been taken to be a mark of the real. Further, it has also been thought to be essential to the knowability of the associated facts. How could we know anything about good and evil if they never played any role in shaping either the world or our responses to it? *Maybe follows if I./ /are true*

These five tenets give rise to a unified and orderly hierarchy of theses of increasing strength, each successive thesis bringing with it a deeper commitment to realism. At one end of this sequence we have extreme antirealism, and at the other, robust realism. The robust realist is thus committed to the five tenets of propositional content, presuppositional fulfilment, mind-independence, irreducibility, and causal networking.

1.2 Propositional Content

That there are connections between reality and truth seems just obvious. So there should be some connection between realism and truth. In his map of the realism debate in ethics, for example, Sayre-McCord maintains that 'what marks off some particular terrain as the realist's remains the same: over and over, it is the view that some of the disputed claims literally construed are literally true' (1988: 5). *That there is a truth of the matter*—this is surely on the right track, but it needs some refining. There are, in fact, two important connections between realism and truth which need to be distinguished: the first concerns the content of value judgements, and the second concerns the presuppositions of those propositional contents.

The most basic component of realism about some domain is that the judgements about the domain are what they give every appearance of being—they are genuine claims *apt* for evaluation as correct or incorrect, true or false. They possess *truth conditions*. They have, as their contents, propositions about the way things stand. Briefly, they have truth-evaluable propositional content. This claim is fundamental to realism, and its denial constitutes the most extreme antirealism.

It will be instructive throughout this exposition of the five tenets of realism to use illustrations from sundry debates about the real. The scientific realist, for example, thinks that typical scientific judgements (that the earth rotates on its axis, that there are electrons and forces, that the mechanism for the inheritance of traits crucially involves DNA molecules, that electrons are made of quarks, etc.) are truth-evaluable. A prominent alternative to scientific realism is *instrumentalism*: the view that scientific theories are not attempts to describe a hidden reality behind the phenomena, but are simply more or less useful tools for categorizing and systematizing—*saving*—the phenomena.

Or consider theological realism. Take a typical theistic judgement—for example, the eschatological claim that *God repays the virtuous with everlasting happiness and the vicious with everlasting suffering*. According to the theological realist, this expresses a genuine, truth-evaluable proposition. A theological antirealist of the instrumentalist variety notes that language can be used for all sorts of purposes other than fact-stating, and that religion is a particularly rich source of examples of such: praying, exhorting, blessing, forgiving, promising, marrying, and so on. Suppose Simon makes the eschatological claim cited. The theological antirealist says that Simon should not be construed as expressing a belief in a proposition about the existence of a superior being who takes a lively interest in dispensing just deserts. Rather, he should be construed as engaging in some other kind of speech act—perhaps that of exhorting people to be virtuous and discouraging them from being vicious.

Realism about value, of any variety, endorses the claim that value judgements—judgements about what is good and bad and better than—have propositional content. The realist about value holds, *inter alia*, that a judgement such as *it is better that the virtuous be happy rather than miserable* expresses a proposition, one which can be classified as true or as false. The most extreme antirealist about value denies that value judgements have such propositional content.

Extreme antirealism about value is the position known as non-cognitivism, the two main traditional versions being emotivism and prescriptivism. According to both, value judgements are not really expressions of propositional belief. Rather, they are expressions of quite different attitudes, and the appearance of propositional content is illusory. Thus emotivism (characterized by Iris Murdoch as that 'puerile attempt to classify moral statements as exclamations or expression of emotion' (1970: 49)) holds that value judgements function to express attitudes of approval and disapproval, desire and aversion When Simon says that it is better that the virtuous are happy rather than miserable, he is not, contrary to appearances, expressing a belief in a proposition about betterness, virtue, and happiness. Rather, Simon is simply expressing his desire that the virtuous be happy rather than miserable. Although the desire may involve a proposition (viz. that the virtuous are happy and not miserable), and that proposition may be either true or false, what Simon expresses by his value judgement is his desire, and a desire cannot be judged to be true or false in the way a belief can be so judged. Prescriptivism assigns a different force to evaluative judgement. When Simon says that it is better that the virtuous be happy rather than miserable, he is really issuing a command—perhaps *Make it the case that the virtuous are happy!* Again, although this command is associated with a proposition (that *the virtuous are happy*), the command itself cannot be endorsed as true or criticized as false.

Recently, a much more subtle and interesting version of non-cognitivism has gained popularity. It is a halfway house between traditional non-cognitivism and the most antirealist of the cognitivist theories. Non-cognitivism is a sparse theory, unencumbered by embarrassing entities like value propositions, value properties, and value relations. Someone sympathetic to this economy, but desiring the logical benefits conferred by entities that are truth-apt, would welcome entry to the alethic paradise without paying the ontic entry fee. Maybe there is such a way. The new-wave non-cognitivist claims that we can achieve this just by talking. The approach can be articulated and motivated in various ways, and what follows is both highly compressed and something of a hybrid.[1]

tis appealing

New-wave non-cognitivists typically draw inspiration from a disquotational conception of truth. We start with the idea that truth is a feature not of propositions but of syntactic items: sentences. A sentential theory of truth will endorse all instances of Tarski's celebrated T-schema, the hackneyed example of which is:

'*Snow is white*' is true if and only if snow is white.

Suppose that such instances of the T-schema are all that a theory of sentential truth needs to account for the phenomena associated with truth. If so, then the only function of the truth predicate is to 'remove quotation marks'. That, in a nutshell, is *disquotationalism.* Now suppose that propositional truth talk is really just elliptical for sentential truth talk. So *it is true that snow is white* is really elliptical for '*Snow is white*' is true. And *it is true that two plus two is four* is elliptical for '*Two plus two is four*' is true. These considerations apply as much to value talk as to number talk or snow talk.

Suppose one who likes the virtuous being happy expresses this sentiment by endorsing a value judgement: *it is good that the virtuous are happy.* Then he is committed to endorsing a sentential truth claim: '*It is good that the virtuous are happy*' is true. And this is elliptical

---

[1] The basic idea has received several different articulations, notably in the works of Simon Blackburn (see his (1993) for example), and Allan Gibbard (1990). My exposition is inspired mostly by the very clear account of *quasi-absolutism* given by Gilbert Harman in Harman and Thomson (1996: ch. 3). (Harman does not claim any originality for the idea.)

for the propositional truth claim: *it's true that it's good that the virtuous are happy*. So, by simply expressing likes and dislikes in value judgements, one is *thereby* committed to endorsing the *truth* of those judgements. But instead of concluding that one should *refrain* from expressing likes and dislikes in value judgements, our new-wave non-cognitivist concludes that one is fully entitled to endorse the *truth* of claims about value. Such claims must thus be truth-apt. Since expressing likes and dislikes surely does not commit one to a hefty ontology of propositions about value, truth-aptness by itself carries no ontic freight. Not even endorsing the *truth*—let alone the *truth-aptness*—of the judgement that *it is good that the virtuous are happy* commits one to a genuine talk-independent proposition about *goodness*.

The disquotationalist could also take a different tack here, urging instead that all there is to the existence of propositions, properties, and relations is the appropriateness of making truth-apt utterances. But such a stance is not easily intelligible. Better, then, to construe the disquotationalist as denying the ontic commitment while affirming truth-aptness. *Agreed*

Once we grant truth-aptness, we have all the logical benefits of propositional content: embeddability in truth-functional compounds, validity and invalidity, and so on. So if the new-wave non-cognitivists are right, just by talking *as if* there were such properties as *virtue* and *goodness*, we can have all the logical benefits of postulating such things, minus the ontological costs. Nice work (if you can get it). *To whats the owth...*

New-wave non-cognitivism is an attempt to construct a halfway house between old-wave non-cognitivism and the next stop on the road to realism: the error theory. It fully acknowledges that value talk looks and sounds for all the world like ordinary truth-apt chatter, but claims that we can unabashedly indulge in such chatter to our heart's content while denying any embarrassing ontological commitments to which the chatter might be thought to commit us. For our purposes we can conveniently bundle together both old-wave and new-wave non-cognitivists. What is common to, and important to, both is that they reject genuine propositional content. The most fundamental tenet of realism about value, then, is that value judgements have truth-evaluable propositional content.

1.3   Presuppositional Fulfilment

A body of theory is true if it gets everything right, and it is close to the truth if it gets a lot right. Sometimes the truth, or closeness to truth, of current theory has been thought to be an important component of realism—especially of scientific realism. I take this to be a mistake as it stands, but it is on to something important.

Suppose you are inclined to accept scientific realism. One day one of your favourite bits of science is refuted. In fact, it is shown to be badly false. Are you now obliged to abandon scientific realism? Hardly. On the contrary, the fact that our theories occasionally bump up against reality in this way is grist to the realist's mill. Likewise, a theological realist of the Christian persuasion, say, would not be obliged to abandon realism on matters theological if she came to believe, perhaps through a striking and unexpected announcement from the Pope, that Muslims are right, and the doctrine of the Trinity is not just false but blasphemous. So a realist can quite easily countenance the possibility that her views, even the ones dearest to her heart, might turn out to be wrong, perhaps very wrong.

Despite this, there is an important point lying obscured here. Consider two theological realists, one a Muslim and the other a Christian. They have an ongoing and lively dispute about the number of persons that constitute the Deity. This dispute will appear quite different to an out-and-out atheist. The atheist will think that this dispute about the number of persons constituting the Godhead is a complete waste of time. If they turn to her and ask the question, 'So, how many persons do *you* think there are in the Godhead?', she is likely to be most reluctant to proffer any answer. Not even the answer *zero* will express her view of the matter. She thinks that any definitive numerical answer to this question is misguided. For her, the question simply does not arise, because she thinks the question has an unfulfilled existential presupposition—that God exists. To cite *any* number, even zero, in answer to the question would be to endorse that existential presupposition, a presupposition she rejects. For the atheist, typical God talk embodies a presupposition which makes the whole discourse radically defective, despite the fact that it is clearly cognitively significant.

Often a body of discourse contains substantive presuppositions, and in order for a typical claim within that body of discourse to be *either* true *or* false, those presuppositions have to be true. Call this *presuppositional fulfilment.* Realism about a domain is committed to presuppositional fulfilment. The value realist is thus not committed by his realism to any particular body of substantive value judgements, but he is committed to the presuppositions of value talk, and in particular to its existential presuppositions. Just as typical God talk presupposes the existence of God, typical value talk presupposes the existence of a range of entities—the properties of *goodness* and *badness* and the relation of *better than*, to name a few.

Those who affirm propositional content but deny presuppositional fulfilment are known as *error theorists.* The atheist, for example, is an error theorist about God talk. John Mackie (1946, 1977) is usually cited as the pre-eminent exponent of an error theory in the domain of values. For the error theorist, value judgements express genuine propositions about value, and those propositions presuppose the existence of a range of evaluative entities—value properties, relations, and magnitudes (degrees of goodness). The error theorist thinks that value judgements are systematically defective. Since the existential presuppositions fail, there are no true value judgements. If we identify facts with true propositions, then the error theory about value can be characterized thus: *all value judgements are incorrect, because there are no facts about value.* The error theory of value, broadly construed, has been defended under a number of names. The nihilist can be construed as endorsing an error theory, and recent *fictionalist* accounts of various kinds of discourse also seem to be straightforwardly error theories.

In his earlier days, Mackie was wont to say that all moral propositions are *false.* But this formulation faces a logical difficulty. If the claim that *it is good that the virtuous are happy* is false, then the negation of this—*it is not good that the virtuous are happy*—is true, and it is a claim about goodness. The thesis that all value claims are false thus flies in the face of the elementary logical fact that the negation of a false proposition is true. In his later writings, Mackie was wont to say that value judgements are *not true.* The earlier and later positions would be equivalent if every proposition that is not true is false—that is to say, if we assume the law of excluded middle. But if there can be truth–value gaps, then the early and late positions are distinct, and the late position would not be subject to this objection. This is where the theory of presuppositions proves useful, for truthvaluelessness is inevitable if some propositions have substantive presuppositions which have to obtain before the question of truth and falsity of the proposition at issue even arises. If value judgements harbour such presuppositions, then such judgements could all fail to be true—in conformity with the later formulation—without any of them being false—contradicting the early formulation.

We still have a related problem though, albeit at a different level. If the error theory entails that there are no true propositions about value at all, then it is apparently self-defeating. For what about *that very claim*? If the error theory is cognitively significant, then, being a *proposition about value, it must be false by the error theorist's own lights.*

Consider the atheist again. She will typically take the following claims to have propositional content and an unfulfilled existential presupposition:

> *God will reward the virtuous and punish the wicked.*
> *God is three persons. God cares about the fall of every sparrow.*

Not all God-talk, however, needs to be construed like this. Consider:

> *The existence of God is incompatible with the existence of evil.*
> *A being has to be perfect in order to be God.*
> *God cannot be both one person and three persons.*

These are examples of claims about God which the atheist will happily endorse, and may even use in what she takes to be sound arguments for another claim about God that she wants to endorse: that *God does not exist.* Characteristically, these latter kinds of claim about God do not have the irksome existential import. They do not presuppose the existence of God. There are, of course, a number of theories of what God claims are about, but one thing is clear. These latter kinds of claim cannot be about an exalted *individual*, because to assume that they are begs a question which these claims clearly leave open—viz. the very existence of a supreme being. So what are they about? We could construe the term 'God' as a disguised description, and adopt something like Russell's theory of descriptions. Then God claims would not be about any particular individual, but would rather be about the constellation of properties that define the concept of God. On a closely related view, God claims are about a certain *role*, a role an individual can play, a role defined by that same constellation of properties—the God role (Tichý 1978*b*). The second collection of claims would be true or false regardless of whether or not the God role is actually played by any individual.

In explicating the theory of presuppositions, this role theory turns out to be rather illuminating. Certain claims about the role presuppose that the role is filled—they cannot be true or false if the role is empty. Others do not. The medieval *de re–de dicto* distinction is suggestive here (Tichý 1978*a*). The claims about God which can be true or false only if the God role is filled by some individual, we can call, rather naturally, *de re* claims about the role. Claims about the God role that can be true or false even if the role is not occupied we can dub *de dicto*. *De dicto* claims effectively attribute various *role* features—features which roles may have or lack—to the role itself: for example, that it cannot be occupied in a world full of evil, or that nothing imperfect could occupy the role while remaining imperfect, or that the role is not occupied in fact. *De re* claims also tell us something about the role, but typically they attribute *occupant* features to the presumed but unspecified occupant of the role. That is why they presuppose that the role is filled: for example, the claim that the occupant of the God role (whoever that happens to be) cares about sparrows falling.

According to the atheist, there are *de dicto* theological facts all right—the role has plenty of interesting features—but there are no *de re* theological facts. *De re* talk about God fails, through failure of the role to have an occupant. *De re* God-claims have truth conditions, they express propositions; but those propositions are neither true nor false, because the role is not occupied by anyone. They lack a truth value because of presuppositional failure.

Unlike the non-cognitivist, the error theorist construes value judgements as *de re* value talk with propositional content. Further, he holds that *de re* claims carry various existential commitments. But, I submit, he should think of these commitments as *presuppositions* of first-order, *de re* value talk, presuppositions that he thinks fail.

How might this apply to evaluative claims? The claim that *it is good that the virtuous are happy* presupposes that there is a property of goodness. If there is no such property as goodness, then the claim (although *apt* for bearing a truth value) fails in fact to bear a truth value. The question of its truth or falsity simply does not arise.

That the law of excluded middle has something to do with realism is a natural enough thought. We need to be careful, however, to distinguish different possible sources of truth–value gaps. The possibility of gaps arising from presuppositional failure should not be confused with the possibility of such gaps arising from a positivist identification of *truth* with *provability* or *verifiability*. Recent versions of verificationism have indeed emphasized the connection between antirealism and truth–value gaps, and verificationism bears strong historical and conceptual connections to a familiar version of antirealism: namely *idealism* (Dummett 1978). Idealism, although undoubtedly a species of antirealism, is, however, less radical than nihilism. Idealism has its place, but it is not here. We return to it below.

According to the error theorist, *de re* value claims carry substantive presuppositions to the effect that there really are value properties and relations—like *good*, *bad*, and *better than*. Since these things don't exist, these propositions turn out to be truthvalueless.

It is worthwhile to briefly clear up one possible objection to this view. If there really are no such properties and relations as *goodness*, *badness*, and *better than*, then isn't value talk really just *gibberish*? If these terms don't pick out *anything at all*, then the claims we formulate in those terms fail even to be truth evaluable. If such claims have any force at all, it will thus have to be a non-cognitive one. If this is right, we haven't really carved out a distinctive position.

Here again, however, we can draw an analogy with the role construal of God talk. To push through the analogy with value, 'good' would not single out a particular property, just as 'God' does not single out a particular individual. Rather, both single out a role. In the case of *God*, it is a role for an *individual* to play. In the case of the *good*, however, it is a role for a *property* to play. The term 'God' singles out a genuine role for an individual to occupy, but, according to the atheist, no individual actually occupies the role. Similarly, the term 'good' singles out a genuine role for a property to occupy, but according to the error theorist (the nihilist, the fictionalist), no property actually occupies it.

If 'good' denotes a property role, rather than a particular property, then we should be able to find a description which specifies the role: what it would take for a property to be *the good*, to occupy the *goodness role*. Interestingly, Mackie supplies us with just such a description in the following oft-quoted passage:

> Plato's Forms give a dramatic picture of what objective values would have to be. The Form of the Good is such that knowledge of it provides the knower with both a direction and an overriding motive; something's being good tells the person who knows this to pursue it and makes him pursue it. An objective good would be sought by anyone who was acquainted with it, not because of any contingent fact that this person, or every person, is so constituted that he desires this end, but just because the end has to-be-pursuedness somehow built into it. (Mackie 1977: 40)

Mackie's claims here suggest the following account: goodness is that property such that apprehension or knowledge of it would engage one's desires in a characteristic way. That is, apprehending that something is good would necessitate one's desiring it, perhaps in direct proportion to its degree of goodness. Suppose we do take this characteristic to be the essence of goodness, and turn it into the following definition:

> goodness $=_{df}$ that property ϕ such that, necessarily, for any state P whatsoever, if one believes (alternatively: apprehends, judges, knows) that P has ϕ, then one desires that P.

Thus if there is a (unique) property ϕ such that desiring P just *is* believing that P has ϕ, then ϕ would have what it takes to be *goodness*—ϕ would occupy the *goodness role*. According to Mackie, there is no property like this, and so the role goes unoccupied. This account would explain much in Mackie's theory that is otherwise opaque. Consider:

> It is good that the virtuous are happy.

On Mackie's account, understood according to the role theory, this has a perfectly obvious propositional content, and it is tantamount to the proposition:

> That *the virtuous are happy* has that property ϕ such that necessarily, for any state P whatsoever, if one believes (alternatively: apprehends, judges, knows) that P has ϕ, then one desires that P.

If the goodness role is empty, then this proposition has an unfulfilled presupposition, and so fails to have a truth value, as does its
negation. Other *de re* value propositions, like those that follow, will
suffer the same fate:

> *It is not good that the virtuous are miserable.*
> *It is bad that the vicious are happy.*
> *It is better that the virtuous are happy than miserable.*

On the other hand, consider:

> *Goodness does not exist.*
> *The apprehension of goodness would immediately engage the will.*
> *If it existed goodness would have to be a very queer property indeed.*

These are all *de dicto* judgements which attribute role features to
the role itself. The first—to the effect that the role is empty—is, by
Mackie's lights, perfectly true. The second—to the effect that for
some property to occupy the role, it would have to have a very
interesting feature—is, like the first, also true according to Mackie.
The third—to the effect that any occupant of the role would have
to be what Mackie calls *queer*—Mackie also holds to be true.
Indeed, Mackie thinks that goodness is so queer that it follows
that the role is *guaranteed* not to have any occupant.

This, I submit, is how we should understand the error theory of
value. Provided we understand value-talk according to the role
theory, Mackie can state his error theory without endorsing claims
which that very theory deems false. The error theory is not a false,
or truth-valueless, *de re* claim about something that does not exist.
Rather, it is a *de dicto* claim about the goodness role itself—a claim
which, if Mackie is right, is a truth about goodness.

1.4   Mind-Independence

Traditionally, the main rival to realism has been idealism, and the
hallmark of idealism is *mind-dependence*. Certain entities are
claimed to be nothing over and above the mental. Idealism is
thus a species of reductionism, but it is such an important species
in the history of realism–antirealism debates that it deserves its
own privileged niche.

First, exactly what is reduction? Take two kinds of entities, type-A entities and type-B entities. Although reduction is a contested notion, here is an undeniably *sufficient* condition for the reducibility of type-A entities to type-B entities: every type-A entity is *identical* to some type-B entity. This is the paradigm exemplified by the Russell–Frege reduction of numbers to classes. It is also what the early identity theorists wanted for the reduction of the mental to the physical.

Idealism is a species of reduction—reduction of the physical to the mental. According to Bishop Berkeley, the claim that *there is a tree in the quad* has a genuine propositional content, and the proposition in question may well be true. What is characteristic of Berkeleian idealism is that it denies the mind-independence of trees and quads. Trees and quads just *are* congeries of mind-dependent sense perceptions, as are their physical relations (like *being in*), as well as the physical facts consisting of physical objects standing in physical relations.

There is, of course, an alternative interpretation of Berkeley, according to which he is an error theorist about the physical. Berkeley himself went to some pains to repudiate that interpretation, insisting that his theory accords with the ordinary, everyday chatter of the folk. He insists that it is his opponents, physical substance theorists, who espouse an error theory of sensible trees and quads.

Outside certain interpretations of quantum mechanics, Berkeleian idealism about the physical world does not currently enjoy much of a following. Idealism in a variety of other fields is, however, a perennial temptation to philosophers. Idealism about mathematical objects has been something of a favourite, as has idealism about causal connections, and while idealism about God is not rated highly by philosophers, it is rather popular amongst theologians struggling with the ontological burden of their claims realistically construed. Of course, varieties of idealism about value are rife.

Strict idealism about physical objects entails the following determination principle: fix all the mental states of the observers of physical objects, and you thereby fix the distribution of physical properties of those objects. That is, there can be no difference in the state of the physical world without some difference in the state of at least one observer. The mental determines the physical. This determination principle may not be sufficient to characterize idealism, but it is certainly necessary. Realism about the physical world, by contrast, holds that the total state of the physical world could transcend the perceptual states of observers. That is to say, different distributions of physical properties are compatible with one and the same total mental state of observers. For example, even if there were no observers at all, there would be a myriad of different distinct possible distributions of physical properties. But clearly there is only one possible total perceptual state for an empty class of observers (viz. a null state) and consequently, for the idealist, just one physical state for physical objects (some corresponding null state) compatible with that.

The idealist may well find this consequence unpalatable, and, to block it, might extend the class of states that count in the determination of the physical states. Berkeley extended the class by adding an omni-observer, someone who can keep an eye on things: God. A different expansion moves beyond actual, categorical perceptual states to various potential perceptual states. Some physical differences which go undetected would be *detectable* by observers under suitable conditions. So the idealist could include those *counterfactual* perceptual states in the reduction base—what observers *would* perceive if they were suitably placed. This is the move from Berkeleian idealism to phenomenalism. Also, faced with the fact that observers have various cognitive shortcomings which should not be allowed to determine what is really there, together with the fact that sometimes observers are in error, the idealist will want to tidy up actual and potential perceptual states in various ways. Hence the physical state of the universe is determined not so much by what is actually perceived by actual observers, or even what *they* would perceive if they were suitably placed, but by what *would* be perceived or thought by various idealized observers. A physical object is a congeries not so much of actual perceptions, but of perceptions which ideal observers would have if ideally placed. Hence, amongst the variations on the basic idealist theme of mind-dependence we have various versions of positivism, certain *response-dependence* theories, *ideal limit* theories, and variations on these like so-called *internal realism*.

Application of idealism to the case of value seems straightforward. The sort of properties which are claimed, by the value idealist, to be mind-dependent will be the normal evaluative properties (like *goodness*), relations (like *better than*), and magnitudes (*degrees* of goodness). Let's settle on some objects as the bearers of value—say they are states of affairs. Then the simplest version of value idealism would be a straightforward analogue of standard idealism. It would posit perceptions or experiences of value (or some analogue of experience) and maintain that the goodness of a state consists in the fact that some suitable collection of valuers experience (or, under suitable conditions, would experience) it as valuable. Candidates for the value analogues of percepts might be any of a number of different mental states: love, approval, or desire, for example. The mind-dependence of value requires only that evaluative properties and relations reduce to congeries of such attitudes. A specific version of mind-dependence—like *desire*-dependence—requires that evaluative properties reduce to congeries of desires. However it is to be cashed out, we will have the result that there can be no difference in the distribution of goodness over states of affairs without a difference in perceptions of value. Sameness of perception of value guarantees sameness of the distribution of value properties over states of affairs.

1.5 Irreducibility

The term *reduction* is more than a little suggestive of diminished ontological status. A complete but succinct inventory of the universe need not make reference to them at all. Reduced entities lack ontological independence. It is often said of reduced entities that they are *nothing over and above* the entities to which they reduce. But reduction is not elimination. Reduction is the débutante's ball for aspiring entities, allowing them an entrée into respectable society. Reduced entities are genuine entities all right—their reduction gives them a pass into the realm of the real—but *something* is lost. Like the débutante who makes a successful match, they forfeit their names, they have an adjunct status, their identity is absorbed, and thereafter they are rendered virtually invisible.

Philosophers are fond of reducing things, and I have to confess that I share that fondness (Oddie 2001d). There is no shortage of reductionist accounts of this or that. As we have seen, idealism about the physical world is a species of reductionism—the reduction of the physical to the mental. This once popular doctrine has recently been usurped by its opposite—the reduction of the mental to the physical. The paradigm of this version of reductionism is the mental–physical identity theory—that all mental items (properties, events, states, etc.) are identical to some physical items (properties, events, states, etc.). Other examples of reductionism abound. Behaviourists claim that mental states reduce to dispositions to behave. Regularity theorists claim that the causal relation reduces to regularity, or to a species of regularity. Logicists claim that numbers reduce to sets of sets of particulars. Nominalists claim that properties reduce to particulars, and so on.

The idea that what is fully real enjoys an irreducible and independent ontological status is a deep and compelling one. (For example, it motivates Spinoza's doctrine that there is only one genuine being, one substance—God-or-Nature—because only God-or-Nature enjoys a totally independent existence.) That which is reducible is less real than that to which it reduces. The irreducibility doctrine maintains that for an entity to be fully real, it must not be reducible to anything ontologically more basic.

Naturalism about value I take to be the broad claim that value is nothing over and above the natural, that the value realm reduces to the natural realm. Old-style moral naturalism, which claims that moral properties are identical to non-moral properties, is clearly a species of reduction of the moral. And many of the candidates for identification with the good (happiness, pleasure, desire satisfaction, and so on) look very much as though they are, in addition, versions of the mind-dependence of value. The naturalist about value, however, can happily repudiate idealism. The non-value properties to which value properties reduce may turn out not to be congeries of mental states. The core of value naturalism is that the natural world just *is* the world. There are no properties, relations, and magnitudes *over and above* the natural properties, relations, and magnitudes. A complete, accurate, and succinct conceptualization of the universe thus need not trouble itself with propositions, properties, relations, and magnitudes other than the natural ones. A robust realist about value will thus deny naturalism.

There is a special problem for any version of non-naturalism about value. Value supervenes on nature. There can be no difference in value features without some difference in natural features. This is the well-known feature of the universalizability of value, a species of determination of value by nature. The universalizability of value amounts simply to this: any two objects with the very same natural properties must have the very same value properties. There can be no difference in value without some difference in nature. Articulating a notion of determination which does not entail reducibility has turned out to be rather difficult. There are proofs that any notion strong enough to yield the kind of determination required by universalizability entails reducibility (starting with Kim 1978). If these proofs are correct, then the non-naturalist is faced with a deep problem. An essential feature of value (universalizability with respect to the natural) entails the reduction of value to nature. It appears, then, that any realist (notoriously, G. E. Moore) who wants to eschew naturalism will have also to eschew universalizability (Moore 1960; Dreier 1992). That's a tall order.

Not many philosophers have had the courage to deny universalizability. Some have argued for a doctrine of particularism which appears to deny universalizability, and which would thereby be incompatible with supervenience.[2] That is a path that I, for one, would hesitate to take. Naturalism would be preferable to robust realism if one could accept robust realism only at the cost of jettisoning universalizability. The most plausible defence of non-naturalism, then, will show how and why universalizability does not entail the reducibility of value to nature.

1.6   Causal Networking

In Plato's Sophist, the Eleatic Stranger makes an intriguing suggestion:

My notion would be, that anything which possesses any sort of power to affect another, or to be affected by another, if only for a single moment,

---

[2] Dancy (1993) may be a case in point. See also Hooker and Little (2000).

however trifling the cause and however slight the effect, has real existence; and I hold that the definition of being is simply power. (Plato 1953:
246–7)

Call the claim that the Stranger seems to be suggesting—namely,
that causal power is the hallmark of existence—*the Eleatic Principle*
(Oddie 1982). It is the Eleatic Principle which will guide us in
elaborating the final tenet of full-bodied realism.

What principle is the Stranger adverting to here? Let's say that
something is *causally networked* if and only if it participates in a
causal network—it has the power either to affect something else or
to be affected by something else. The first part of the Stranger's
claim suggests that he takes being causally networked to be sufficient for real existence. The second, however, suggests that he takes
it to be necessary as well as sufficient. We could call these the *weak*
and *strong* Eleatic Principles respectively.

If we adopt the weak Eleatic Principle then showing something
to be causally networked is to show that it has 'real existence',
that it is fully real. But showing that it is not causally networked,
so far as the weak principle is concerned, does not tell us that it is
not fully real. On the strong principle, however, showing that
something is not causally networked is sufficient to banish it
from the realm of the fully real. (Note that on either principle
the power to be affected without the power to affect is sufficient
for being causally networked, and hence sufficient for robust
reality.)

The Stranger's suggestion has enjoyed something of a renais-
sance in recent metaphysics, either explicitly—notably in the work
of David Armstrong—or else implicitly—in all those 'causal theories' of this or that. Armstrong (1978) has wielded the strong
principle against numerous abstract entities from ontology: numbers, sets, possible worlds, to name a few. Given the strong principle, if values fail to be causally networked, then they will have to
be consigned to the realm of shadows and fictions.

There is a link between the strong Eleatic Principle and recent
arguments for the mental–physical identity theory based on the
causal exclusion principle. These attempt to show that we are
committed, by certain well-regarded principles, to a dilemma:
either mental states are identical to physical states, or else the

mental is not causally networked with the physical. One problem with the second horn of the dilemma is not just that it would conflict with the apparent truism that the mental *is* causally networked with the physical—philosophers have been prepared to jettison that. Rather, it would condemn the mental to the shadowy realm of the not fully real.

Robust realism about value is, finally, committed to value bearing the Stranger's mark of being. Value is robustly real if and only if it participates in the causal network.

A realist might well affirm the irreducibility of his favoured entities without thereby being committed to their participation in the causal network. A realist about numbers, for example, might hold that numbers aren't reducible to anything ontologically more basic, but hold that they lie beyond the causal network. Kant may well have held something like this position about noumena. (As is usually the case with Kant, it isn't easy to tell.) David Lewis held such a position on possible but non-actual worlds: they are real, but each is causally isolated from every other. (He did not hold this on non-actual *possibilia* generally, since they may well interact causally with other possibilia within their own worlds.) An apt label for the position which combines non-reductionism with a denial of participation in a causal network is not in common usage. Because such entities are held to transcend the causal network, I will co-opt the term *transcendentism.*

Examples of non-reductionist realism about value which subscribe to the participation of value in the causal network are rare, but they do exist. Plato sometimes seems to be a robust realist on this score, although the Neoplatonists developed the idea more explicitly. Variations on Neoplatonism have emerged quite recently. For example, Iris Murdoch (1993) appears to ascribe some kind of active power to the Form of the Good, although it has to be confessed that, as marvellous as her prose is, she does not make it quite clear what she is arguing for. Even more radically, albeit more perspicuously, John Leslie (1979) has defended a new kind of cosmological argument—that the only way to explain the existence of the world is in terms of its goodness. That which is good has, *ipso facto*, not just a claim to exist, but also a primitive *tendency* to exist, a tendency proportional in strength to its goodness. This tendency to exist is not something endowed externally by a contingent causal or probabilistic connection between goodness and existence. For the goodness of the causal structure itself is what explains the existence of a world with that causal structure. The tendency is thus supposed to be a purely internal, primitive feature of goodness.

As interesting as these claims may be, they will strike many as a bit outlandish. If the thesis that value is causally networked requires apparently extravagant theses of this sort, then it seems just plain implausible. It becomes even less plausible once we concede the supervenience of value on the natural. For surely (one might argue) the natural features of objects are all causally explicable in terms of other natural features of objects. And since the valuable supervenes on the natural, on pain of causal overdetermination, it must be the natural features which do all the real causal work. Hence not only is there no need for us to postulate value properties over and above natural properties, there is a positive reason for us *not* to do so. The principle of inference to the best explanation, together with principles of simplicity and parsimony, will force us to forgo value in our deepest understanding of the world.

1.7   A Schema for Degrees of Realism

We now have a set of five questions we can ask about a domain of discourse which gives the appearance of being about some range of entities.

1   *Propositional content*: Do the statements of the discourse really express genuine propositional content?
2   *Presuppositional fulfilment*: Are the existential presuppositions of typical *de re* statements in the domain actually fulfilled?
3   *Mind-independence*: Are the entities which satisfy these existential presuppositions (call these the *characteristic entities*) mind-independent?
4   *Irreducibility*: Are the characteristic entities irreducible to any more basic category of entities?
5   *Causal networking*: Are the characteristic entities appropriately causally networked?

These five questions, asked and answered in sequence, generate a hierarchy of six degrees of realism about value, depicted in

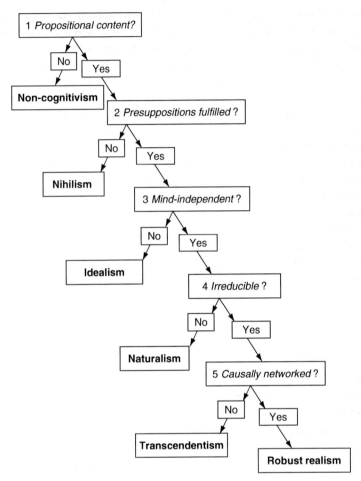

Fig. 1.1   *A schema for degrees of realism*

figure 1.1. At the top of the figure we have extreme antirealism, and
at the bottom we have extreme realism.

1.8   An Overview of the Book

The rest of this book is a stroll down the chart.

In Chapter 2, I outline two problems of knowledge which any cognitivist about value faces. One is the familiar problem of the motivational inertness of bare facts, and the knowledge of such facts. Evaluative facts, on the other hand, would be queer because they would violate this general inertness. The other is the much less familiar problem of value data. A realist who does not want to embrace scepticism will have to posit some kind of value data. But what, exactly, are the value data? Where do they come from? The inertness problem can be approached through a puzzling asymmetry in value judgements, an asymmetry which can easily be explained by the internalist thesis that value judgements are special in being intrinsically or necessarily motivating. Internalism and non-cognitivism dovetail very nicely—they seem almost made for each other—and so the non-cognitivist has a ready explanation for the puzzling asymmetry. The cognitivist can also embrace internalism, but then he is in danger of also embracing something apparently rather queer: that certain beliefs—beliefs about value—would necessitate certain desires. I argue that there is a natural way for the cognitivist to explain the puzzling asymmetry, and it is one which simultaneously solves the problem of the missing data. The explanation appeals to two rather radical ideas. First, experiences of value are necessary, though not sufficient, for us to have knowledge of value. Second, desires are experiences of value. I call the conjunction of these two theses *the experience conjecture*, and I show how it explains, *inter alia*, the puzzling asymmetry.

In Chapter 3 I argue more extensively for the experience conjecture, and tackle some of the fairly obvious objections to it. Other objections have to wait for aspects of realism to be developed before they receive adequate treatment.

The realist thinks that the world enjoys a certain independence from experience which the idealist denies. She thinks that our experiences do not, all by themselves, determine the shape of reality. The value realist, likewise, thinks that value enjoys a certain independence from our experiences of value—our desires, if the experience conjecture is correct. And the value idealist denies this. Something about value idealism has proved perennially attractive. There is something compelling about the idea that value is, at least in part, the product of our experiences of value. I like skiing, and you like swimming. That seems to make it more valuable for me to go skiing while you go swimming, than for me to go swimming while you go skiing. The value idealist thinks that this is the essence of the relationship between value and desire—that desires, taken collectively, fully determine the shape of value.

In Chapter 4 I do a considerable amount of spadework on behalf of value idealism, by developing a promising reduction of value to desire. The guiding idea is a fairly familiar and popular one. It is not the simple idea that the valuable is what we *happen* to desire in fact (that is, perhaps, a value analogue of Berkeleian idealism), but the more sophisticated and plausible idea that the valuable is what we *would* desire were we to *refine* our actual desires into a completely coherent set (a value analogue of phenomenalism). I develop a novel way of articulating such a refinement theory with some precision, and show how it provides a map of value that is remarkably close to that of the realist—much closer, I think, than either idealists had hoped for, or their realist opponents had realized possible.

The refinement theory that I develop embodies important lessons which a realist can happily appropriate. And it helps to clear up some of the outstanding objections to the experience conjecture left over from Chapter 3. But the thoroughgoing idealist cannot deliver a totally satisfactory account of the valuable. The map, while surprisingly accurate, is not quite accurate enough. In Chapter 5 I show where a refinement theory and a realist theory have to part company. The idealist cannot explain every truism about our experiences of value. To get an adequate explanation, we are compelled to postulate a desire-independent value residue.

Of course, one could be a reductionist about value without being an idealist. One might be a naturalist. The reduction of value to nature is also an attractive programme, one that has an enormously powerful line of argument going for it. The universalizability of value with respect to the natural seems undeniable: no difference in distribution of value without a difference in distribution of purely natural (or non-evaluative) features. Now, there are a number of well-known arguments that this kind of determination of one domain by another entails reduction of the one to the other, and the reduction of the valuable to the natural is precisely what the naturalist demands. Naturalism is a kind of realism—it is closer to the bottom of figure 1.1 than to the top. But it is a modest kind of realism. In Chapter 6 I present a general theory of properties, based on the notion of convexity. This general theory, together with some facts about additivity and organic unity, yields the irreducibility of the valuable to the natural.

The irreducibility of value saddles the realist with a compulsory question, one that she has to answer adequately in order to complete and pass the final exam: *Where does value fit into the causal network?* This question is not just an optional extra. It matters how the realist answers this one, because the answer is relevant to the issue of scepticism. It is difficult to see how irreducible entities that are also transcendent—that is to say, entities that do not participate in the causal network of which we, and our experiences, are a part—could be *reliably* connected with our experiences of them. We can certainly *have* experiences of entities that do not cause those experiences (we can dream, we can hallucinate), and such experiences may even end up being veridical. But their being so might be just a matter of luck. If there is good reason to think that our experiences of irreducible values are not causally networked with the values themselves, then that will be a reason for being a value sceptic. Briefly, if values were completely transcendent entities, they would not be causally connected with our experiences of value, and so (barring some version of idealism) those experiences would not yield knowledge. For experiences of value to be reliable indicators of value, the experiences have to be appropriately causally networked with the values themselves. I argue for the causal networking of value in Chapter 7.

In this first chapter I have given a map of the territory in which the varieties of realism and antirealism are located. I hope it is a good guide to the terrain; but even if it is, it is clearly not the only way of drawing the map. In the final chapter I offer a different and complementary take on the nature of realism and antirealism, one which has a clearer application to value when our journey is almost over than it would have here just as we embark.

Briefly, realism can be characterized as the affirmation of three important logical gaps, each gap being associated with what is often regarded as a kind of shortcoming, a defect. But they can also be viewed as inevitable consequences of our being the kinds of beings we are. First, there is the gap between appearance and reality—the logical gap which constitutes the possibility of illusion or distortion. Second, there is the gap between reality and belief—the logical gap which constitutes the possibility of error. And third, there is the gap between appearance and belief—the logical gap which constitutes the possibility of incoherence between percept and concept. Various versions of antirealism try to close these gaps, thereby handily blocking the possibility of a certain kind of shortcoming.

Given the experience conjecture—that desires are experiences of value—we can see how value realism also affirms three gaps that various versions of antirealism deny. First, corresponding to the appearance–reality gap, there is the *desire–value gap*—the possibility that our experiences of value (our desires) may be out of kilter with actual value. Second, there is the *value–judgement gap*—the possibility that our judgements about value, perhaps even those that seem most thoroughly justified, might be out of kilter with the value facts. Third, corresponding to the gap between appearance and belief there is the *desire–judgement gap*—the possibility of our value judgements being out of kilter with our desires. The realist affirms the existence of all these gaps—the associated limitations are, after all, genuine. But if it is content with simply affirming the gaps, realism courts scepticism. Reasonable realists would like to bridge the gaps (not close them), and I attempt to do so by drawing together the connections between value, desire, and judgement which are laid bare in the course of this inquiry.

2 JUDGEMENT AND DESIRE

THE value realist is, minimally, a cognitivist, holding that value judgements have propositional content, rendering them apt for evaluation as true or false. The best-known, and most discussed, charge against realism is that such propositions would be queer. The charge can be elucidated by means of a puzzling asymmetry in judgements about value and desire. The asymmetry is easily explained by a version of internalism, the thesis that value judgements are intrinsically motivating. But whereas it is an easy and natural step for a non-cognitivist about value to embrace internalism, for the cognitivist internalism may be something of an embarrassment. It does not sit happily with otherwise sensible views about knowledge and belief. At least, that's the charge. Let's see whether it can be made to stick.

2.1 A Puzzling Asymmetry

Millions of people suffer from conditions—like blindness-inducing glaucoma—that would take only a few dollars to cure. You know that. And as you cast your eye over my assets, you may notice that I actually have a surplus which I am not sending to charities. In that case it would not be odd for you to affirm:

> The best thing he could do with his surplus income would be to donate it all to charity. But he has little or no desire to do that.

If cognitivism is right, then there is a perfectly good pair of propositions which serve as the propositional content of these two utterances of yours: one about the value of an action of mine and the other about my desire to undertake it. I can grasp these propositions and see their logical independence. Now suppose that, when faced with the choice between donating surplus dollars to an organization that would deliver cures to the afflicted and spending those dollars on some treat for myself, I find myself desiring the treat more. Then it seems that I might well be inclined to agree with you, and affirm the following:

> The best thing I could do with my surplus income would be to donate it all to charity. But I have little or no desire to do that.

This sounds a little odd. And there is something a little bit odd not only about a public affirmation of it on my part, but even of a private acknowledgement. If cognitivism is right, however, then the same propositions which serve as the propositional content of your utterance also serve as the propositional content of mine. So why should *my* affirmation of this pair of propositions sound odd, whereas *your* affirmation of the same pair not sound odd? This is the puzzling asymmetry.

2.2 An Internalist Explanation of the Puzzling Asymmetry

The internalist has a nice explanation of the puzzling asymmetry. Suppose that to endorse a value judgement involves being moved to behave or respond appropriately in the light of it, and being moved to behave involves having appropriate desires. To summarize:

> *Judgement internalism.* Necessarily, one who endorses a value judgement possesses the corresponding desire to act or respond appropriately.

Given judgement internalism, the oddness of my affirmation is laid bare. That I endorse the value judgement necessitates my possessing the appropriate desire—the desire to donate my surplus income to charity. So by expressing my endorsement I commit myself to the existence of that desire. But straightway I go on to deny the existence of that very desire. So the oddness of my utterance consists in a kind of contradiction—between what I imply by affirming the value judgement (viz. that I have a certain desire) and what I imply by affirming the non-value judgement (viz. that I lack that very desire). *Your* utterance, however, does not commit you to any kind of contradiction. By endorsing the very same value judgement you affirm *your* desire that *I* donate my surplus income to charity. Your affirmation of that is quite compatible with your subsequent denial that *I have the appropriate* desires. Internalism thus provides an apparently neat explanation of the puzzling asymmetry.

Internalism also flows rather naturally from a non-cognitivist analysis of value judgements. It's a platitude that one can express attitudes other than belief by uttering a declarative sentence. If I say to someone 'I hate Bush!', I don't merely express my *belief* in the proposition that I hate Bush, as someone else might do by saying while pointing at me, 'He hates Bush'. Rather, what I express is *hatred* for Bush. So an apparently declarative affirmation can be used to express an attitude, like hatred. Some uses of evaluative language not only play that kind of expressive role, but may play only that kind of role. When, after surveying the range of available flavours of ice-cream at the ice-cream counter I exclaim 'Pistachio is the best!', am I sincerely expressing belief in a proposition about the value of that flavour? Isn't it more likely that what I am expressing is not a belief, but rather a desire for pistachio ice-cream? In order to explain my affirmation, there is no real need to postulate the existence of a relation of *betterness*, or the truth-evaluable propositional content *that pistachio ice-cream is better than all other kinds of ice-cream*. Now, suppose that all evaluative language is simply the expression of desires, and that endorsing a value judgement, *that such-and-such is good*, is just a way of expressing the associated desire for such-and-such. Then internalism flows naturally from that brand of non-cognitivism. To endorse a value judgement is just to express a certain desire. To endorse a value judgement *sincerely*, it would seem that you must *have* the desire the possession of which you are thereby expressing. Thus, sincerely endorsing a value judgement entails possession of the corresponding desire. The non-cognitivist can thus happily appropriate the internalist explanation of the puzzling asymmetry. Internalism and non-cognitivism fit like hand and glove.

2.3　The Queerness Argument

The realist is also free to explain the puzzling asymmetry by embracing internalism. But internalism does not bond so easily

and freely with cognitivism as it does with its rival. Internalism is
not just an additional commitment for the realist, but a rather
embarrassing one.

The realist is a cognitivist, holding that standard value judgements possess propositional content. It is natural for the cognitivist
to go on to hold that value judgements share standard features with
other judgements: that a typical affirmation of a value judgement is
just like the typical affirmation of any other judgement. Typically,
to sincerely affirm a judgement with propositional content is to
express one's belief in that proposition. Thus, typically, to sincerely
affirm a value judgement is to express one's belief in a proposition
about value. At least, that does not seem obviously false. If this
assumption is embraced along with internalism, however, then the
realist will be committed to queer propositions. (This kind of
argument has become closely associated with John Mackie, who
seems to have first employed the term 'queer' in this context.[1])
Propositions about value are queer, according to this line of reasoning, because grasping or believing them violates a doctrine
(*intellectus nihil movet*) which can be traced back to Antiquity, but
which receives its authoritative modern statement in the writings
of David Hume:

> Reason is, and ought only to be, the slave of the passions, and can never
> pretend to any other office than to serve and obey them. (1955: 415)

We have already quoted Mackie's summary of the queerness argument (in section 1.3). Here is a recent spelling-out of Mackie's
line of argument, offered by Michael Smith.

> [T]he idea of a moral judgement thus looks like it may well be incoher-
> ent, for what is required to make sense of such a judgement is a queer sort
> of fact about the universe: a fact whose recognition necessarily impacts
> upon our desires. But the standard picture tells us that there are no such
> facts. (1991: 402)

(Smith talks of moral judgements, but the argument will apply
equally to value judgements.) The standard picture adverted to
here is just the Humean, or neo-Humean, account of motivation—
that motivation involves desires as well as beliefs, and that beliefs
alone do not, indeed cannot, motivate. What the standard picture

---

[1] See Mackie (1977: esp. 15–49).

requires is that there be two broad classes of mental states: beliefs and desires. Furthermore, beliefs and desires satisfy an independence thesis:

> *Independence*: For any belief B and any desire set D, the possession of belief B is logically compatible with both the possession and the non-possession of desires in D.

For the moment, grant that this independence thesis is true. Internalism tells us that the endorsement (or sincere affirmation) of a particular value judgement is necessarily accompanied by the appropriate desire. Cognitivism tells us that the sincere affirmation of a value judgement just is the expression of a belief. And the independence thesis tells us that the mere having of a belief does not entail the having of any desires at all. So the triad consisting of judgement internalism, cognitivism, and independence threatens a contradiction—something has to go. Consequently, if the realist wants to embrace internalism, she will have to reject the independence of belief and desire—and that's queer. (Is the argument valid? Probably not as it stands; but whether or not it is valid, it will prove worthwhile to take a close look at the assumptions.)

Notice that this reconstruction of the queerness arguments is all about *beliefs* about value, rather than *facts* (true propositions) about value. The assumption that there are facts about value is not, strictly speaking, required to generate this contradiction. Still, one could easily use the above argument to smear the putative value facts with the same stain. If there were true propositions about value, then either those propositions could be the objects of belief or they couldn't. If they could be the objects of belief, then (given internalism) those beliefs would necessarily impact on desire. In that case value facts would share the queerness of value beliefs. If they couldn't be the objects of belief, then that in itself would also be queer, albeit in a different way.

2.4 Independence

Smith cites two arguments in favour of the independence thesis. First, there is the direction-of-fit argument. Beliefs purport to represent the world as it is, and a belief is faulty to the extent that its content fails to represent the world accurately. Briefly, beliefs are required to fit the world, and they can be justly criticized if they fail to fit the world—if they are false. Desires, on the other hand, do not purport to represent the world, and are not usually said to be true or false. The content of a desire may be true or false, just as the content of a belief is either true or false. But it is clear that a desire cannot be criticized *merely* by pointing out that the content of the desire is not the case. In that sense, the content of a desire does not have to fit the world, or fit the world now, for it to be a perfectly defensible desire. Rather, the world is in some sense 'defective' for not matching the content of one's desires. Beliefs have to fit the world, but the world has to fit desires. There are thus two classes of mental states, characterized by different 'directions of fit', and (perhaps because they are orthogonal dimensions) beliefs and desires are independent.[2]

The direction-of-fit metaphor may be unnecessary here. Smith spells out the essential contrast between beliefs and desires directly in terms of rational criticizability.

Since our beliefs purport to represent the world they are subject to rational criticism: specifically they are assessable in terms of truth and falsehood according to whether or not they succeed in representing the world to be the way it really is. Desires are unlike beliefs in that they do not even purport to represent the world as it is. They are therefore not assessable in terms of truth and falsehood. Indeed, according to the standard picture they are at bottom not subject to any rational criticism at all. (Smith 1991: 400)

Or, as Hume puts it:

'Tis not contrary to reason to prefer the destruction of the whole world to the scratching of my finger. 'Tis not contrary to reason for me to chuse my total ruin, to prevent the least uneasiness of an Indian or person wholly unknown to me. (1955: 458)

The claim that desires are not subject to any rational criticism is rather implausible, at least without hefty qualifications. First, a combination of desires may be logically inconsistent in the sense that they cannot all be jointly realized. (I want to be the richest man

---

[2] Anscombe (1957); Smith (1987); and Humberstone (1992).

in the world, but I don't want everyone to be poorer than me.) Such combinations of desires are clearly rationally criticizable. Secondly, even if not *logically* incompatible, desires may not be jointly realizable given my beliefs. (I want to go to the concert and I also want to go to the lecture, but I believe they are being held at the same time.) Admittedly it is the total package of belief and desire which is here irrational and criticizable. But if the belief component is rationally impeccable, it is the desires which must then suffer reason's censure. Thirdly, desires may also be based on irrational belief. (I desire to leap out of a tenth-floor window because I have a more basic desire to arrive safely on the ground floor, and a belief that jumping out of tenth-floor windows is an efficient way of achieving my basic desire. The derived desire is rationally criticizable because the belief which mediates between the basic and the derived desire is crazy.) Smith acknowledges this third caveat: 'desires are subject to rational criticism, but only insofar as they are based on beliefs that are subject to rational criticism' (Smith 1991: 401). There are other objections to the claim that desires are not rationally criticizable. As we will see in Chapter 4, desire sets may embody a certain incoherence the elimination of which reason demands.

Here's a more promising argument for independence. Belief and desire suffer from the standard state–content ambiguity which afflicts all our talk of the mental. By *belief* one might mean the propositional *content* of a belief—the proposition believed. As in 'It was our belief that Bush would easily win the election'. The thing which characterizes both beliefs is one and the same propositional content. Alternatively, one might mean the mental *state* of believing that propositional content. As in 'Your belief that Bush would easily win the election made you happy, but my belief that Bush would easily win the election made me depressed'. What has differential effects here is not the common propositional content of the belief—how could it?—but rather the numerically distinct belief states. Similarly, by *desire* one might mean the content of a desire—*what* is desired—or else one might mean the mental state of *desiring* that thing.

In the content sense, beliefs are clearly logically dependent on other beliefs, because beliefs (in this sense) just *are* propositions which stand in relations of logical dependence. But in the state sense, beliefs seem just as obviously to be logically independent of each other: the having of one belief does not, by itself, necessitate the having of any other belief, even when the content of the first belief necessitates the content of the second. (People can be illogical.) Now, if belief states are logically independent of one another, how unlikely that any given belief state should entail a desire state. In the state sense, then, beliefs and desires are obviously logically independent. Being in some belief state does not entail that one is any particular desire state.

This argument is, perhaps surprisingly, fallacious. There are, in fact, purely logical reasons why belief states cannot be totally logically independent of one another as demanded, and for the same reason belief states cannot be totally logically independent of desire states. The reason is that there are vastly more propositions than there are possible situations, and as such there are too many propositional objects of belief and desire for there to be enough room in logical space to combine any old belief with any old desire set. There are just not enough possibilities to underwrite the logical possibility of all the different combinations of belief and desire required for the independence thesis to be true.[3]

This rather abstract refutation of independence is based on the Cantorian fact that a power set is always of greater cardinality than the set itself. If propositions are classes of possible worlds, then the set of propositions has a higher cardinality than the set of possible worlds. So there are more propositions than there are possible worlds, and hence more belief–desire pairs than there are possible worlds. If propositions are more fine-grained than sets of possible worlds, then there are even more propositions. In appendix 1 I exhibit a particular concrete proposition-pair that it is not logically possible to embrace as belief and desire.

Here is a rather more direct and down-to-earth counterexample to independence involving particular beliefs and desires. Suppose that to be in pain is to experience a very unpleasant sensation, and suppose the unpleasantness of a sensation consists (at least in part) in the strong desire to be rid of the sensation. So, to be in pain is *ipso facto* to desire that the painful sensation cease. Suppose, further, that one cannot be mistaken in one's pain beliefs—that is to say, of necessity, if one believes that one is in pain, then one is in pain.

---

[3] See Tichý (1988): ch. 6 and Oddie (2001*d*).

It follows that a certain kind of belief (the belief that I am experiencing pain) necessitates a desire (the desire for the painful sensation I am experiencing to stop). So a typical pain-belief necessitates a desire—the desire for a certain sensation to cease.

The weakness in this refutation is, of course, the claim that pain beliefs are infallible. While it would certainly be an odd kind of cognitive defect to believe one is in pain without being in pain, it is not an unimaginable defect. People can certainly have false beliefs which are just as odd. Still, the Cantorian argument outlined above, as well as the argument in the appendix, are each sufficient to show that this quite general independence thesis fails, and with it the premiss of one kind of prominent argument against realism.

2.5   The Judgement–Desire Gap

Even if one grants these or other limitations on the general independence thesis, a friend of the queerness argument could always retreat to a more local and plausible principle, one which would do the job. Isn't it just downright *implausible* that having the particular belief that P is good *necessitates* having the desire for P? Are we not familiar with lots of cases in which that claim is obviously false? Isn't denying judgement internalism a much more plausible escape strategy for the cognitivist?

Clearly judging that something is good does not always go hand in hand with an *overriding* motivation to pursue that good. Something judged to be good may be just one such thing amongst several competitors only one of which can be pursued. Pursuing something judged to be good, even judged to be the best, may be rather risky, and unlikely to succeed. Pursuing what you judge to be best may run a high risk of landing something you judge not to be very good at all—the best can be the enemy of the good—and that may be enough to drain you of all enthusiasm for pursuing the best. Further, pursuing what you judge to be best, all things considered, may conflict drastically with what you judge to be in your own best interests, and your interests may channel your desires in their direction. Finally, you may judge something to be the best, all

things considered, and even compatible with your own best interests, but you simply lack sufficient desire to pursue it. That's not
logically impossible. So, the apparently conflicted self with whom
we opened the chapter is not really so exceptional after all. I have
company amongst the lazy, the self-interested, the risk-aversive,
and the akratic. But the phenomenon is more widespread than this
gallery of rogues might suggest. Quite generally, we do not think it
particularly exceptional to find gaps, often small but sometimes
very large, between our value judgements and our desires.

So believing something is good does not entail an overriding
motive to pursue that good. Still, the queerness advocate might
grant this and insist that a value judgement necessitates *some* degree
of motivation, *some* desire, and that is enough to contradict independence.

Gaps come in different sizes. A gap may be small, or it may be
large. In the case of desire and value judgement, the gap will be
large if the value attributed is large while the corresponding desire
is small. The larger the gap, the more out of kilter one's desires are
with one's value judgements. Suppose we grant the possibility of a
gap here, and that it can vary in size. By continuity, there seems to
be nothing to block the logical possibility that one have a maximal
degree of belief that something is good, yet have the absolutely
minimal corresponding desire. If this is right, then the cognitivist
should eschew any version of internalism which entails that a
maximal belief–desire gap is not even possible.

Cognitivism is well-equipped to account for these gaps—for the
various ways in which one's value judgements can come apart from
one's desires—even without a generalized thesis of independence of
belief and desire. By contrast, simple versions of non-cognitivism,
like expressivism, seem badly placed to save the phenomena. If a
value judgement is *simply* the expression of a desire, rather than an
expression of a genuine belief, then it is a mystery how one can
sincerely make such a judgement and fail to have the appropriate
desire. In such cases the expressivist will have to deny that the
judgement is sincere, or heartfelt, or something like that. If one
makes a show of endorsing the judgement, it may be an attempt to
deceive some audience into believing that one has desires which one
in fact lacks, perhaps an audience consisting of oneself. But, as a
general rule, that seems far-fetched. The phenomena at issue here,

the gaps between one's desires and one's judgements of value, are just too familiar to all of us.

2.6   The Merit Connection

If a cognitivist eschews judgement internalism, what can he then say about the puzzling asymmetry? What is the connection between value and desire that explains why it is odd for me to affirm the following judgement even when the propositions expressed are true?

> *P is really very good, but I don't desire P at all.*

Here's a possibility. Many value theorists with a realist bent have suggested variants of a thesis about the relation between value and desire which I will dub the *merit connection*. Briefly, the thesis is that the good is what *merits* desire. Given that something is good, it is appropriate, or fitting, to desire it. Variations on this theme can be stated using closely related attitudes like approval and love. This thesis, broadly construed, can be found in Aristotle (1962), Franz Brentano (1969), Alexius Meinong (1972), Max Scheler (1973), C. D. Broad (1930), and Roderick Chisholm (1986), and more recently Kevin Mulligan (1998) and Mark Johnston (2001). C. D. Broad stated the merit connection in this way:

> I'm not sure that 'X is good' could not be defined as meaning that X is such that it would be a fitting object of desire to any mind which had an adequate idea of its non-ethical characteristics. (Broad 1930: 283)

The right-hand side might be necessary and sufficient for the left, and if so, we can treat the right-hand side as a definition of *good*. But even if we do treat it as a definition, it is clearly not a definition of *good* in non-evaluative terms. The term *fitting*—like the terms *merit*, *worthy of*, and *appropriate*—is clearly evaluative. And as evaluative terms go, *fitting* seems a lot less basic than *good*. It would be much more natural to define what it takes for a desire to be fitting, or appropriate, in terms of the far more fundamental notion of goodness. But we can put to one side the issue of definition and reduction, and simply note that the thesis posits a necessary connection between value and desire. We can state the thesis in a way which allows for degrees of goodness:

> *The merit connection*: P is good just to the degree that P merits being desired (or just to the degree that it is appropriate for P to be desired) by anyone with an adequate idea of P's non-value characteristics.

Given the merit connection, and given that it is a matter of necessity, the following also holds of necessity:

> P is very good if and only if P is worthy of being strongly desired by anyone with an adequate idea of its non-value characteristics.

But then someone who utters

> P is very good, but I don't desire P at all,

is obliged to accept:

> P is worthy of being strongly desired by anyone with an adequate idea of its non-value characteristics, but I don't desire P at all.

Something may be found jarring here. In the first clause I assert that P is worthy of being strongly desired by anyone with an adequate grasp of P—implying, of course, that I myself have such an adequate grasp—but then I go on to note that I myself don't desire P at all.

There is a tension here, but is the tension more obvious here than in the original? Perhaps it's a *little* more obvious. Both clauses now make explicit claims about desire, but note that the first clause isn't a claim that the second clause repudiates. The first clause is about the *value* of a certain desire, and the second clause about the *non-existence* of that desire. The tension between acknowledging the value of desiring P while at the same time acknowledging the actual lack of desire for P is rather *like* the tension between acknowledging the value of P while at the same time acknowledging my actual lack of desire for P. In both cases, I acknowledge that I am not responding appropriately to value, but the *oddness* of that acknowledgement has not really been explained.

2.7   The Experience Conjecture

There is another thesis about the connection between value and desire which explains the asymmetry rather more naturally. Here I will state the thesis with a minimal defence, and show how it explains the asymmetry. In the next chapter I will give it a deeper defence and reply to some objections.

Consider the normal relation between experience and belief. When I have a visual experience of a bright red rose, say, the rose presents itself to me as bright red. It *seems* or *appears* bright red to me, in that sense of *seems* which is tied to perceptual presentation rather than to belief. Normally, of course, the visual experience of a bright red rose—that is to say, the rose's appearing bright red to me—gives me a reason to believe that the rose really is bright red. But it is a defeasible reason in the sense that any number of conditions might crop up which might indicate that, despite its appearance, the rose is not really red after all. Conditions may not be ideal for seeing, or my visual apparatus may be in an impaired condition, or I may be on drugs, or whatever. If I discover any of these defeaters, I may well believe that the rose is not bright red after all, or not nearly as red as it seems, despite the appearances and despite the fact that the rose persists in appearing bright red to me. If the rose can seem to me (be experienced by me as) bright red, even though I believe it not to be bright red, then there must be seemings which do not entail believing. I can also have the belief, of course, without the seeming. P's seeming to me to be the case (in this sense) and my believing P to be the case are thus logically independent. That is what I mean by the non-doxastic sense of *seems*.

Suppose, now, that there are *experiences* of value—value seemings. If there are genuine experiences of value, they could stand to values as ordinary perceptual experiences stand to the objects of perceptual experience. An experience of the goodness of P, say, would be the state of *P's seeming (appearing, presenting itself as) good*, where this seeming is an experiential, non-doxastic take on the value of P. If there is such a state as the experience of the goodness of P, then, by analogy with the perceptual case, it would give me a reason to believe that P is good. But, again by analogy, it would be a defeasible reason, in the sense that the totality of information available to me might indicate that P is not good, despite its seeming to me to be good. Either conditions may not be favourable for my experiencing P's value, or my ability to experience value might be impaired in some way. If I uncover any such defeaters, I may well come to the conclusion that P is not good after all, or not nearly as good as it seems—despite both the initial appearances and the fact that P may persist in seeming good to me.

I suppose we could postulate such experiences, call them 'intuitions of value' to mark them off from other more familiar states, and appeal to a special 'faculty' which would be exactly the right kind of thing to deliver such intuitions. But those are not particularly happy things to have to do. Russell famously quipped that postulation has all the virtues of theft over honest toil, but it isn't clear that he was right about this. If you steal something, then you have something in your possession without having to do any more work. Unlike theft, however, postulation leaves you empty-handed unless you follow it up with some hard work. If you postulate 'intuitions' as states which play a certain sort of role in a theory of beliefs about value, then the term 'intuition' is really just a place-holder for any state satisfying the demands of that theory. We could of course leave things there, and be a bit mystified, or else we could do some work—that is to say, we could rummage around in the collection of perfectly familiar mental states, and see whether any of them fit the characterization.

Instead of postulating intuitions, let's stick with our simple characterization of *experience of value* and rummage around for a fitting candidate. There may be more than one—for example, approvals, emotions, feelings, or maybe combinations of these with other states—but consider desires. When I desire that P, P has a certain magnetic appeal for me. It presents itself to me as something needing to be pursued, or promoted, or embraced. Now the good just *is* that which needs to be pursued, or promoted, or embraced. So my desire that P involves P's *seeming* good (seeming to be worth pursuing). So the desire that P looks as though it just *is* the experience of P as good.

The desire that P is not the *belief* that P is good (just as the experience of the rose as red is not the belief that the rose is red). Nor does my desiring P—my experiencing P as good—entail that I have the belief that P is good, any more than my experiencing the rose as bright red entails that I believe it to be bright red. The belief that the rose is bright red is something which one could have without experiencing the rose as bright red, and something which one might not have even if one were having the experience of the rose as bright red. Similarly, the belief that P is good is something which one could have without experiencing P as good, and something which one might not have even if one were experiencing P as good.

Let's gather these two theses (that there are experiences of value which can serve as reasons for evaluative beliefs, and that desires are such experiences) into the following conjecture:

> *The experience conjecture*: The desire that P is P's seeming good (or P's being experienced as good).

If the experience conjecture is right, then experiences of value are not exotic states which some otherwise mysterious faculty of value intuition delivers. They are mundane states with which we are totally familiar—desires.

I have said that desires are experiences of value. It does not follow that experiences of value are all and one desires. Are they? I want to leave that open here. Maybe all experiences of value are either desires or contain a desiderative component. Alternatively, however, desire may be just one way of experiencing value, as visual experiences are just one way of experiencing shapes. (One might have a tactile experience of a shape or even an auditory one—witness bats and dolphins.) It is quite possible that *value experience* is a determinable of which *desire* is a determinate. I myself think that desires stand to the goodness of *states of affairs* as visual experiences stand, not to *shapes*, but to *colours*. Visual experiences are the standard and paradigmatic way of experiencing colours of objects (although one might dream up other ways of doing so). Likewise, desires are the way we experience the value of states of affairs. The value of other categories of object (persons, or works of art, for example) might demand a different determinate realization of value experience. It may be that the way in which one experiences the value of a person is through *loving*; or of a work of art, through *liking*. I leave this possibility open.

The experience conjecture will be developed and defended in depth in later chapters. My main purpose here, though, is to put the conjecture to work to explain the puzzling asymmetry. The point is really quite a simple one. While the belief that P is good does not necessitate the desire that P, there is clearly a connection between the belief and the desire, which typically makes it a bit odd to espouse the one with having the other. The oddness can be explicated as an instance of what I will call 'the shadow of Moore's paradox'.

2.8   Moore's Paradox and its Shadow

We start with the well-known paradox, discovered by G. E. Moore, which bears a superficial similarity to the asymmetry problem. Consider the following schema:

Q is true, but he does not believe that Q.

There are many instances of this schema that someone could truly utter while pointing at me (viz. most of the true propositions can be substituted for Q). Further, it is entirely unproblematic for you to point at me and affirm of some particular proposition that it is true, but that *he does not believe it.* It is, however, highly problematic for me to affirm:

Q is true, but I don't believe that Q,

even while I can happily concede that almost all true propositions are such that I don't believe them.

A fairly good explanation of this asymmetry involves the notion of conversational implicature. When I assert Q, I not only affirm Q itself, but I thereby express the proposition that *I believe Q.* Although in affirming Q I do not explicitly *say* that I believe *Q*, I do thereby express the fact that I believe Q. It is not an implication of *what* I affirm that I believe Q, but it is an implication of my *affirming* Q. By affirming Q, I *conversationally* imply that I believe that Q, because the proposition that X affirms Q sincerely does entail that X believes Q. So in my original affirmation, what I say *implies* that I don't believe Q, and *conversationally implies* that I do believe Q. That's why it is odd.

Let's now turn to a related phenomenon, which as far as I know has not been discussed. It is the shadow of Moore's paradox. You can assert, unproblematically, the following of me:

Q is true, although Q doesn't seem true to him.

It does, however, sound a bit odd for me to say:

Q is true, although Q doesn't seem true to me.

Now this utterance isn't as obviously paradoxical as the Moorean assertion. But in typical circumstances there is something a little bit odd about it.

This oddness can also be explained by the notion of conversational implicature. When I assert, under typical conditions, that Q is true, there is a conversational implicature that I believe that Q is true (Moore's insight), but there also seems to be some sort of *presumption* that I have evidence for Q (typically I do not assert things for which I have no evidence), and one standard source of such evidence is Q's seeming true to me. Of course, even if Q seems to me to be true, this is still only a defeasible reason for believing Q to be true. I can see a rose as bright red even though it is not (I might be looking at a white rose through red-tinted glasses). And I might not see it as bright red even though it is (I might have blue-tinted glasses on). In the latter case I might well affirm an instance of the odd-sounding schema above. For the most part, however, I base my beliefs about the visual properties of things on the way they present themselves to me in experience, and so, absent odd conditions, an assertion like 'the rose is bright red but does not seem at all bright red to me' is a little bit jarring. The asymmetry between the first- and third-person assertions in this case is not nearly as pronounced as it is in Moore's paradox. Hence my designation of it as the 'shadow of Moore's paradox'.

Substitute *P is good* for Q in the schema, and abbreviate *P is good is true* to *P is good*:

P is good, but P doesn't seem good to him.

That's a claim you might assert unproblematically of me. But it sounds a bit odd for me to say:

P is good, but P doesn't seem good to me.

When I assert that P is good, the standard conversational implicature is that I believe P is good. But if P does not *seem* good to me, then I don't have a, perhaps the, standard reason for believing that it is good. So much simply lies in Moore's shadow.

Now let's add the experience conjecture to this. My desire that P just is P's seeming good to me. So the above is equivalent to:

P is good, but I don't desire that P.

Whatever oddness attaches to this can be explained in terms of the oddness of the proposition above which (according to the experience conjecture) is necessarily equivalent to it: namely, *P is good, but it doesn't seem good to me.* The utterance is an acknowledgement that my experience of goodness (how good things seem to me) and my evaluative beliefs (how good I believe things to be) have come apart. That's not impossible, of course. Indeed, it is not so very unusual. But acknowledging a belief that something is the case, while also acknowledging that things don't seem that way to me, does require a bit of explaining. Table 2.1 summarizes the explanation of the puzzling asymmetry.

The experience conjecture thus has at least one attractive consequence: it enables the cognitivist to explain the puzzling asymmetry without violating independence. If desires are experiences of the value of states of affairs, then it follows immediately, even on the standard Humean account, that *experiences of value* are intrinsically motivating. The experience of P as good would necessarily motivate one to promote, pursue, or embrace P, because it would simply *be* the desire that P, and desires are intrinsically motivating. It is not the evaluative belief that P is good that is intrinsically motivating, hence the independence of belief and desire is not threatened. There is, however, an internal connection between a

TABLE 2.1. *Moore's paradox and the puzzling asymmetry*

	Not odd	Odd
Moore's paradox	Q, but he doesn't believe Q.	Q, but I don't believe Q.
Moore's shadow	Q, but it doesn't seem that Q to him.	Q, but it doesn't seem that Q to me.
Substitute *P is good* for Q	P is good, but P doesn't seem good to him.	P is good, but P doesn't seem good to me.
Substitute *X desires that P* for *P seems good to X.*	P is good, but he doesn't desire P.	P is good, but I don't desire P.

desire and an evaluative belief. The desire that P is the experience of P's being good. An experience should not be confused with a belief, not even with the belief that the experience would, under normal circumstances, give one some reason to adopt. But if desires are experiences of value, then that would also explain why value judgements—which clearly involve beliefs about the good—do not typically float entirely freely of motivation.

In the next chapter we turn to a more thorough defence of the experience conjecture.

3   DESIRES AS VALUE DATA

A web has both an internal structure and external connections. Both internal structure and external connections help to shape and maintain the web. It is this two-fold feature of a web that sustains the metaphor of the web of belief. The internal structure of the web of belief is provided by reason—the logical and probabilistic relations between the propositions that form the nodes of the web. The external connections, on the other hand, are provided by experience—that implacable source of the data which tether our beliefs to the world outside the mind.

Our value judgements, according to the cognitivist, are also beliefs with propositional content, and they form a web within the web of belief. The role of reason in shaping and maintaining the web of judgement has been heavily explored in the philosophical canon, but there is not nearly as much about the necessity for, and nature of, experiences of value. Any cognitivist about value who does not want to end up in scepticism must face the problem of value data. In the previous chapter I investigated the queerness objection to value facts, and in response to it I floated the experience conjecture—that desires are experiences of value. This conjecture, if correct, entails that we have a rich source of value data. But the conjecture cries out for further elucidation and testing.

3.1   The Necessity for a Source of Value Data

Any cognitivist will agree that value judgements should satisfy the constraints of reason, and that an adequate epistemology of value must give reason a large and legitimate role. Minimally, our beliefs about value should be logically consistent. But that's a very weak demand, and even pure reason may impose more interesting constraints. Perhaps pure reason can claim the principle of the universalizability of the evaluative with respect to the non-evaluative. After all, if some version of the universalizability principle is true, it should be true of necessity, and necessary truths are in the domain of pure reason. Maybe there are further constraints of pure reason, like the transitivity of the *better than* relation.

Much of what passes for rational inquiry in the domain of value can be explained rather easily by reason's demand for consistency. Argumentation about value often involves drawing out consequences from one's own settled value commitments, or embarrassing one's opponents with unwelcome consequences of their value commitments ('twitting one another with inconsistencies', as C. D. Broad once put it). Still, suppose these were the only constraints on our value judgements. The class of logically consistent theories of value, even those satisfying universalizability and transitivity, is vast, and nothing is easier than to construct such a theory (e.g. the nihilist's theory that *nothing has any value*, or the closely related theory that *everything is of equal value*). So, with only these demands to constrain us, the range of viable theories of the good would be almost unlimited.

Not only is reason too weak to provide the content of a theory of the good; it is too pale to deliver knowledge with the right kind of motivational force. This is the kernel of truth in Hume's claim that 'reason is, and ought only to be, the slave of the passions, and can never pretend to any other office than to serve and obey them' (1955: 415).

To see this, imagine a pure intellect—a ratiocinator—a clever being capable of performing any feat of reasoning that we might contemplate. Such a being might be able to derive, by pure reason, a large collection of truths about goodness. There would, of course, be a long list of relatively uninteresting tautologies about goodness. But there might be more than this. He might be able to reason that value is transitive, that the value of a lottery is the expected value of winning, and so on. These a priori truths by themselves, however, would be incapable of *moving* the pure ratiocinator, since, as a pure ratiocinator, he traffics only in beliefs. He has no desires, and so nothing he learns from his ratiocination will be of the least importance to him. His knowledge of value, even if it gives him some definite direction to move in, will lack any motivational power. If this is right, then pure reason doesn't seem quite the right way for a person to come to a practical knowledge of value.

Or again, consider an enhanced pure ratiocinator, one who is hooked up to a device which gives him information about purely natural (non-value) states. Imagine that perception and ratiocination exhaust his mental life. So he surveys the world and all it contains dispassionately. He doesn't *care* about anything, because that would be an additional element in his mental life. He just records the facts and deduces various consequences. Again, nothing would *matter* to him. He would not form views about the goodness or badness of the states he records, and he would be totally unmoved by what he discovered.

Finally, imagine that somehow we feed the enhanced ratiocinator some extra, non-tautologous beliefs about the good—propositions like *it is bad that the virtuous are miserable while the vicious are happy*. Even if the ratiocinator takes up these beliefs and incorporates them into his belief set, not only is it doubtful that these will constitute genuine *knowledge* for the ratiocinator, but it is not clear how they could engage his will. Somehow, the source of knowledge of the good must occur closer to the source of motivation.

There is, of course, an intentional defect in these thought experiments. Perhaps the ratiocinator or his enhanced counterparts are not really *doing* anything at all. Perhaps they are really just non-conscious automata. But if so, it is not clear that they *know* anything or that they are genuinely *deriving* propositions. If, however, they are conscious agents who are genuinely engaged in the activities of observing and reasoning, then it seems that they would have to care a little bit about doing *that*. They would have to have something like the desire to reason, to derive a priori truths, and to take some minimal interest in their observations. A perfectly desireless ratiocinating agent seems impossible. If he is genuinely *doing* the reasoning, then days when the reasoning doesn't go well, or what he produces is trivial, he will feel frustrated, perhaps disappointed with himself. He might think, 'Tomorrow, I hope to do better than that. The stuff I derived today is worthless.' Now, however, he is starting to look less like a *pure* ratiocinator. He is starting to look a bit more like a valuer. His desires and his value judgements are beginning to mesh, to interact.

He is still somewhat narrowly focused, but he is slightly more recognizable—at least to anyone who has visited a department of pure mathematics.

These thought experiments suggest that to acquire knowledge of value we need a source of value data, data which stand to beliefs about value as perceptual data in general stands to beliefs about the world. The data of ordinary perceptual experience give us reasons to accept certain low-level judgements about the world, judgements which have to be taken into the web and made to connect appropriately with other judgements. Experience provides reasons to adopt or change our beliefs, reasons which may, of course, be overridden in the light of other experiences, or of experience taken as a whole in the light of our best available theories. But often our judgements are reasonable in the light of experiences the evidential force of which is not overridden, at least not immediately, and that is what makes the growth of knowledge possible. Reports of experience, and even experience itself, can, of course, be theory-laden—that is to say, partly structured by the beliefs held by the one having or reporting the experience. For all that, novel experiences, those licensing judgements additional to or at odds with our current beliefs, do sometimes force themselves on us, and they are not always dismissed or suppressed simply because they are novel or recalcitrant.

The thought experiments suggest not only the necessity for value data, but also the inadequacy of motivationally inert data. The value data should infuse the value judgements they undergird with motivational force. One way to achieve this would be for value data to be closely connected to desire. An experience of the goodness of P should bear an appropriate and necessary relation to the desire that P.

3.2 Experience and Belief: The General Case

Perceptual data give us an epistemic handle on the world. Here I sketch a fairly familiar account of the relation between perceptual experience and belief. Obviously this is a controversial matter, and a lot more needs to be said. But what follows is an outline of a strong candidate for the truth.[1]

Suppose you are having a visual experience of a large red rose. Why does that experience give you reason to believe that there is a red rose there? One answer (that of the idealists and their cousins, the positivists) is that the facts about a red rose boil down to facts about red-rose experiences. Red roses are constituted of red-rose experiences. One problem with this is that there is clearly a logical gap between the proposition that there is a red rose in front of me and my having the experience of a red rose. And in any case, it is deeply implausible that the state of affairs consisting of a red rose being in front of me is constituted by my experiences of such. I can have all the red-rose experiences required by the existence of a red rose without there being a red rose there. (I might be a brain in a vat.)

One realist account of experience (perhaps David Armstrong's) turns idealism on its head and makes experience a species of belief. Instead of taking visible objects to be constituted by visual experiences, this view takes visual experiences to be constituted by beliefs about the visible. My visual experience of a red rose is a collection of beliefs which either contains or entails that there is a red rose there. But that doesn't seem right. I can have all the beliefs that we would normally think are justified by experiences of a certain sort, without having those experiences. Consider the phenomenon of blindsight, the strange ability to acquire accurate and detailed beliefs about visual objects without the accompanying visual experiences. Beliefs are not sufficient to constitute an experience. And whatever the actual truth about blindsight, we can imagine a being acquiring beliefs about the visible without that being having visual perceptions. Experience is more than belief.

A more tempting theory (perhaps Kant's, although that's always hard to tell) blends realism with idealism. According to a Kantian-style account, perceptual experience is a clever synthesis of percept and concept. Experience is definitely more than belief or judgement (there is more to it than the combining of concepts), but perceptual beliefs are somehow worked right into the experience by the mind, as it conjures experience out of the raw data of sensation.

[1] The details can be found in Huemer (2001: ch. 5).

Again, as with both the previous accounts, the problem of the gap between experience and belief is supplanted by the problem of no-gap. In seeing a red rose in front of me, *ipso facto* I judge or believe there to be a red rose in front of me. Typically, however, we *base* our judgements about the visual world on our visual experiences. We take a visual experience of a red rose to provide a reason for adopting the belief that there is a red rose there. This would be circular if the experience was itself partly _constituted by that very belief_. Kant elevated this circularity into a central tenet of his theory of knowledge—in his doctrine of synthetic a priori knowledge. If certain principles, like that of causal determinism, are an inevitable constituent of our mental make-up, they get impressed on all visual experiences, and as a consequence no experience would ever conflict with them.

All of these accounts seem susceptible to the charge of circularity. We do take our visual experiences to justify in some way our beliefs about the visible world, but not because those experiences are themselves bunches of beliefs or because the beliefs report no more than is already there in the experience. I can go on having the red-rose experience even if I do not believe that there is a red rose there. I might believe that there is no red rose there because I believe that I am hallucinating, or dreaming, or that it is all done by clever mirrors. And I can believe that there is a red rose there even though I am not there and have not visually experienced it.

Why is it so tempting to build beliefs into experience itself? There is an important relation between the visual experience of a red rose and the belief that there is a red rose there, and the relation is mediated by a proposition about a red rose. When a person has a visual experience of a red rose, it seems to him *that there is a red rose there*. The proposition which is the object of the belief (*that there is a red rose there*) is constitutive of the experience. The visual experience of a red rose has built into it not a *belief* about a red rose, but rather a *proposition* about a red rose. That the belief is not constitutive of the experience is evidenced by the fact that non-veridical perceptual experiences can be identified as non-veridical, and yet persist through such an identification. But what misleadingly suggests that the experience incorporates the belief is the well-known ambiguity in the notion of *belief*. By *belief* one can mean the act of believing, the affirming of a certain proposition (this is the *state* sense of belief); or one can mean the object of the belief—its content, or the proposition believed. In this latter, *content* sense, the belief that *there is a red rose there* is just the proposition that there is a red rose there, and of course that proposition is constitutive of the visual experience. But that proposition (the belief in the *content* sense) need not be believed by someone having that visual experience. In the state sense of belief, the belief is not a necessary part of the experience at all.

Perceptual experiences are, then, *essentially propositional.* A perceptual experience is necessarily connected to a proposition or possible state of affairs: the possible state of affairs which would obtain if this perception were true (veridical).

But why, exactly, do perceptual experiences give us *reasons* to believe the associated propositions? Doesn't that presuppose that experience is reliable, that the experience of its seeming that P is a reliable indicator of the truth of P? It's not just that we can't be *sure* that experience is an indicator of truth. Why should we place any trust at all in the reliability of experience? Is there any reason to think that *it seems that P* should raise one's confidence in P?

It is possible that we have reached bedrock here. We cannot justify everything, on pain of regress, and if we do not start with a presumption in favour of the appearances as some kind of guide to what's really there, then the threat of general scepticism is hovering over us. In fact, however, we can show that only a very weak presumption is required, a presumption which seems far more plausible and less dogmatic than its negation. All we need is a very modest *possibility thesis*: that it is at least *possible* that the appearances are a source of data. Given this weak possibility thesis, we can show that an appearance that P should boost one's confidence that P.

This modest possibility thesis can be fleshed out as follows: *there is a non-zero chance that seemings are evidence for the way things are.* What follows is that the appearances—seemings—can play a legitimate role in a theory of knowledge. That is to say, the information that *P seems to be the case* should boost one's degree of belief in P. (A proof of this can be found in appendix 2.) It does not follow, of course, that seemings inevitably boost confidence. It may seem to be the case that P, but we may have other information which undercuts the epistemic force of that appearance. (The stick may look bent, but it also feels straight—two seemings, each of which cancels out the epistemic force of the other.) Thus it is that our beliefs can sometimes be legitimately changed by the appearances, but at other times may remain stubbornly and rationally out of sync with the way things persist in seeming to us.

3.3   Experience and Belief: The Case of Value

What should a mental state be like if it is to count as an experience of value?

First, of course, we want states which are analogous to perceptual experiences. Value experiences should not reduce to value judgements, or congeries of judgements; rather, they must stand to judgements about value as ordinary perceptions stand to beliefs about the world. That is to say, experiences of value should be necessarily related to, and serve as defeasible reasons for endorsing, judgements of value.

Secondly, we want experiences of value to be connected appropriately not only with value judgements, by serving as defeasible reasons for those judgements, but also with motivation. They should help bridge the logical gap between value judgement and desire—bridge, but not close.

The state which mostly simply and naturally gives me a defeasible reason for believing that X has feature F is the state: *X seems (appears, looks) F to me.* Its seeming to me that X is F clearly bears an internal relation to the proposition that X is F. So, the simplest state which would give me a reason to believe that P is good is the experience of *P's seeming (appearing) good to me.* The passage from this experience of the good to the corresponding judgement about the good would thus be just like the passage from a perceptual experience to a belief about the world—even if that journey must sometimes be resisted for good reasons.

What are these value seemings, given that we will end up in circularity if they are beliefs or reduce to beliefs? The simplest hypothesis satisfying the first desideratum is the experience conjecture floated in Chapter 2: that my desire that P is the experience of P's seeming good to me. Here is the argument I gave there.

When I desire that P, P has a certain magnetic appeal for me. It presents itself to me as something needing to be pursued, or promoted, or preserved, or embraced. Now the good just *is* that which needs to be pursued, or promoted, or preserved, or embraced. So my desire that P certainly involves P's *seeming* good (seeming to be worth pursuing). It is but a small step from there to identifying the desire that P with the experience of P's seeming (appearing, presenting itself as) good. Further, if desires are experiences of value, it is easy to show that they also satisfy the second desideratum. They connect value judgements to motivation in a direct and immediate way.

Are desires sufficiently experience-like to do the job? Desires can be, and typically are, experienced. They have a phenomenology. Desires can be felt as more or less strong, mild as well as nagging. They come as aversions as well as attractions. They can be cold or hot, weak or strong. On the face of it, then, desires are, or at least can be, a certain sort of experience.

Do desires have a life below the threshold of conscious experience? Maybe. But this does not rule them out as sufficiently analogous to perceptual states. For there do seem to be subconscious perceptual states, or perceptual states on the periphery of consciousness. Subconscious desires, if there are such things, might be analogous to those. We would not want to deny that perceptual experience is a primary source of data about the world just because some perceptual states float below consciousness. Nor would we want to deny that subconscious perceptual states, if there are any, are perceptions of a certain sort.

The evidence for subconscious desires is not entirely unambiguous. You ask me whether I desire that my children's lives go well. I reply: Yes, naturally. You ask, did I have the desire fifteen seconds ago, or did it spring into existence when you asked me about it? Again, it might be fairly natural to think that I had the desire fifteen seconds ago, and that I was not at that stage conscious of it. But do I desire that my children's lives go well when I am in a deep dreamless sleep? Or suppose I am run over by a bus, and go into a coma, a fairly serious although not irreversible coma—a coma of the sort that I have a chance of emerging from psychologically intact. In that comatose state do I still desire that my children's lives go well? It seems rather a stretch to say that I really do desire that, while totally comatose. It seems much more plausible to say that when I am in a coma or asleep, what I have is some kind of ~~disposition to desire~~, a disposition that will be triggered by suitable conditions. If my character and personality have a chance of surviving through the coma, then there must be something like that disposition present there as well. So I have that disposition when in the coma, and when I am asleep. Don't I also have the disposition when I am not attending to the matter at all? Presumably. Now, since I have that standing disposition, do we really need to add that (when I am awake but not attending to the matter) I also have the fully-fledged desire? That seems otiose. The disposition to so desire when the matter is brought to my attention is sufficient to explain the phenomena.

On a dispositional theory of desire, desires are identified with dispositions which mesh with beliefs to produce actions (Pettit and Smith 1990; Smith 1995). The desire that my children's lives go well, according to the theory, is a disposition to do A, whenever I come to believe that A will enhance my children's prospects. So, on a dispositional theory the distinction between an actual occurrent desire and a disposition to so desire becomes blurred. Both are dispositions to cause actions. One (a desire) will mesh with a belief directly; the other throws up a state which meshes with a belief. Clearly, though, there are dispositions to desire which are not themselves desires. We do not want to attribute desires to the totally comatose man. The person in a deep coma doesn't really have any desires. We might ask, 'What would he want us to do in these circumstances?' But we would probably not ask, 'What *does* he want us to do in these circumstances?', and certainly not, 'What does he want *now?*'

If the desire that P just is the experience of P's seeming good to me, then it can serve as a reason, albeit in some sense defeasible or overridable, for thinking that P is good. But why should a thing's appearing good be *any* kind of evidence at all for believing that it is good? Doesn't that simply beg a huge question: the question about the reliability of my desires, not just as appearances, but as genuine indicators of the good? Wouldn't the realist be taking a huge leap in affirming that value seemings track value? Here, however, we can appeal to the same justification as in the general case. We do not have to assume that value seemings are actually reliable indicators of the good. All we have to assume is that there is *some chance* that they are some kind of indicator of the good. It follows from that very weak possibility assumption that something's seeming good does, in itself, raise the probability that it really is good. Of course, additional information may undermine the probability of P's goodness. (I might desire that P and likewise desire Q, where Q is practically or even logically incompatible with P.) P may seem good to me (I desire that P), but, like its perceptual analogue, that constitutes a defeasible reason for endorsing the judgement that P is good.

Desires clearly have what it takes to connect value judgements with motivation. They do so immediately. If the data that give us the simplest kind of reason for judgements about the good come in the form of desires, then value judgements get hooked up with motivation at the ground level. But, despite this rather tight connection between the acquisition of beliefs about value through experience and the acquisition of the corresponding desires to act, the connection is not too tight. A perceptual warrant may be defeated before it is used in belief formation. Even when a perceptual warrant is not defeated, it may fail to support the corresponding belief in the light of the support that has already accrued to a multitude of other beliefs—it may simply be of insufficient weight to overturn or modify existing beliefs. And finally, even if a perceptual warrant does induce a belief, the belief can outlive its perceptual warrant. Analogues of these in the case of value judgement and desire would open several familiar gaps between belief and desire.

The hypothesis that desires are value data does not involve the postulation of a mysterious mechanism. We are perfectly familiar with our desiring this and desiring that. We don't need to postulate a faculty of value intuition, for example, one for which we have no independent evidence. Nor do we need to postulate experiences of a wholly different sort from anything else that we are familiar with, states which are only contingently linked to desires. The hypothesis that desires just are experiences of value seems to be the most economical one on offer.

It is time now to turn to some pressing objections to the conjecture.

3.4   The Problem of Bad Data

Consider what is perhaps the most obvious and serious objection to the thesis that desires are value data. Our desires are defective in various ways. If my desire that P is P's appearing good to me, how can my desires be for *bad* things, or for things which I take to be bad, or worse still, things that I *know* to be bad?

Here is a quick response. That we often have bad data does not entail that we never have any decent data. As we have noted several times, experience provides, at best, highly defeasible reasons for the associated beliefs, and the same goes for desires. There can be inappropriate and misleading desires, just as there can be inaccurate perceptions. Desires do not have to be a completely reliable presentation of the good in order to play the role of value data. Something can seem good to me even though it is not. Analogously, I can have perceptual experiences of things that are not there. There can be totally misleading desires, just as there can be totally misleading perceptual experiences.

This response is quick but dirty. It does not really address the pervasiveness of the problem, and it does not indicate how we deal with it. The worry here is that almost all the data are bad, that my desires are very far indeed from being a reliable presentation of actual value. To see this, note that different people's desires are often diametrically opposed. It is rare that something looks very red to you and very blue to me, but it is not uncommon for me to strongly desire P while you strongly desire not-P. Our different perceptual experiences seem to cohere more tightly than do our different desires. How can your desires and my desires *both* constitute reasons for belief about the good if they are so at variance?

The following is a statement—by Noah Lemos—of a closely related challenge to the thesis that one's desires give one reasons to endorse some value judgements rather than others:

The mere fact that *A* prefers, as such, *A*'s being happy and *B*'s being sad to *B*'s being happy and *A*'s being sad is no reason for *A* to think that the former state of affairs is intrinsically better than the latter's. ... More generally, it seems entirely possible to have no reason to believe that *P* is intrinsically better than *Q* and yet at the same time to prefer *P* to *Q*. (Lemos 1994: 193)

Lemos does not mention desires, but rather preferences. Nevertheless, we could think of preferences here as pairs of desires, and the point would be the same. Lemos gives a further argument for the claim that the desires yield no reason at all for believing something about the actual values.

> It seems possible that someone might know that two states of affairs are of equal intrinsic value and prefer one as such to the other without having any reason to think that either is better. James might know that his being happy is as intrinsically good as John's being happy, and yet James might prefer his being happy to John's being happy. On the view under consideration this would imply that James has some reason to think that his own happiness is intrinsically better than John's. (Lemos 1994: 194)

Given that James *knows* that the two states are equally valuable, his desires cannot be *any* kind of reason for him to believe that his happiness is better than John's.

The point can be cast in the terminology of *agent-relativity* and *agent-neutrality*. For the robust realist the value of a state of affairs is not relativized to individuals. States S and T can be compared for value without having to index the comparison to an individual. So the state T which consists in both John and James being miserable is (for the sake of the argument) worse than the state S which consists in John being happy and James being miserable. Admittedly S is better *for John* than T is, while S may be no better *for James* than T is, but for all that S is better than T *simpliciter*. That is the *agent-neutral* value-ranking of the two states. The realist does not have to make the error of denying that, in addition to the agent-neutral value-ranking there are varying agent-relative value-rankings (*better for John, better for James*), which rank the states differently. But the realist will deny that that is all there is to it. G. E. Moore did make that error, arguing that the agent-relative notion of goodness is contradictory. His argument is, however, demonstrably fallacious. (Fumerton 1990).

Real value, if it is going to be worth having at all, has to be an agent-neutral affair. Desires, on the other hand, present the good in a highly agent-relative manner. An answer to this challenge has to say more than that my desires can be, and sometimes are, unreliable presentations of the good. Any decent response has to do two things. First, it has to show how we could come to acquire accurate value judgements on the basis of what might appear to be *hopelessly* and *systematically* bad data. But, just as importantly, any purported solution to this problem will have to provide room for persistent and *legitimate* agent-relativity in desire, even after our agent-neutral value judgements have been perfected in the light of both experience and reason. Here I sketch one way of accommodating the agent-relativity of desire without impugning desires as value data.

3.5 Perspectivity

One way to bring out the problem of the agent-relativity of desire is by comparing the demands of the merit connection with the consequences of the experience conjecture. The merit connection, recall, says that the good is what merits desire. Presumably, then, if I were desiring properly or adequately or ideally, I would desire things just to the degree that they are good. But given the experience conjecture, that means that ideally I should experience value reality as it is in itself. Anything less than an isomorphism between value and desire would be a defect. And that seems rather far-fetched.

Consider two cases. Imagine I have a badly fractured limb caused by a skiing accident; part of the femur is protruding through the skin, and the thing is excruciatingly painful. A stranger skiing the same slope just behind me has suffered a similar fracture, and he is now lying in the snow alongside me, suffering what appears to be the same degree of pain. I would like his pain to cease, naturally, but I am even more desirous of the cessation of my own pain. When the stretcher team appears, it turns out that they have only one shot of morphine left. Since the relief of the stranger's pain is just as valuable as the relief of my pain, the merit principle demands that I be indifferent as to whose pain is treated. But I am not.

Or imagine I am in the unhappy situation in which my daughter is drowning a hundred yards from where some other girl is drowning, some stranger's daughter. As is the norm in such cases, I can't save both. I certainly would like to be able to save both, but I cannot do so, and not surprisingly I have a stronger desire to save my daughter while the other girl drowns, rather than to save the other girl while my daughter drowns. Now I know that, in all probability, my daughter's life is no more (or less) valuable than the life of the stranger's daughter, and that my happiness is no more (or less) valuable than the stranger's. But even though I know these things, I cannot desire to save the stranger's daughter as much as I desire to save my own daughter.

We face a dilemma here. Given the merit connection, I should be indifferent between saving my daughter and saving the stranger's daughter. If that's what value demands of desire, then it is a defect of me, as a valuer and a desirer, that I am not completely indifferent about who I save. And that seems wrong. On the other hand, if it is not a defect, then, following Lemos's line of thought, it is hard to see how my desires give me any reason at all for corresponding value beliefs. If it is quite in order for me to want to save my daughter (or to want my pain to cease) more than I want to save the stranger's daughter (or to want the stranger's pain to cease), even though the one is not more valuable than the other, how can my desires be construed as any kind of evidence of value?

In neither case does it strike me as at all plausible that I *should* be indifferent, that my desires (or the stranger's) *should* be proportionate to the actual values. Rather, it is perfectly in order for me to desire the cessation of my pain more than I desire the cessation of the stranger's equivalent pain. And it is also perfectly in order for me to desire to save my daughter somewhat more than I desire to save the stranger's daughter. In fact, I would be regarded as something of a monster if I had to toss a coin to decide which of them to save. And it isn't clear how I could have a pain just as bad as the stranger's, yet have identical desires concerning the cessation of both. If this is right, then there is something very wrong with the merit connection, at least as I have stated it.

Suppose desires are experiences of value, just as sensory perceptions are experiences of the material world. Suppose I look into the heavens at the setting sun and the rising moon. The sun is much bigger than the moon, of course, but the moon looks the bigger of the two. That's because the sun is much further away. Are my experiences here defective? Would my perceptual apparatus be better if it always yielded an appearance of the sun as vastly bigger than the moon, no matter which position I took up with respect to them? That doesn't seem right. I am having a perfectly apt experience of the two celestial bodies, given that I am located on Earth. That is exactly how one would expect those two bodies to look from Earth to a human being whose perceptual apparatus is in perfect working order. Clearly you cannot be expected to perceive things exactly as they are, no matter what your situation is with respect to them. Nor should you believe that things are exactly as you perceive them to be, no matter how you are situated with respect to them. The relation between experience and the world and one's beliefs is more complex and interesting than that.

If desires are experiences of value, and valuers are differently situated with respect to value, then we should expect something analogous to the phenomenon of perspective. And the two cases illustrate this. While my pain and the stranger's pain are equally bad, I am clearly situated very differently with respect to my pain than I am with respect to the stranger's. In fact, part of what makes pain bad is surely the fact that its bearer badly wants it to stop, and that is clearly not under any direct control. (That's why we need morphine.) I cannot be expected to detach myself from that desire and be indifferent between the cessation of my pain and the cessation of the stranger's pain. So, it is perfectly in order for me to want my pain to stop more than I want the stranger's pain to stop.

What about the drowning girls? Just as with pain, I am very differently situated with respect to my daughter and her survival than I am with respect to the stranger's daughter and her survival. I love my daughter, fiercely, in a way that completely precludes me from being indifferent between her death and the death of a stranger's daughter. And it would be absurd to demand that my love for my daughter not inform the strength of my desire for her to go on living.

It is not that I don't care about the stranger's pain, or the death of the stranger's daughter. I am not absolutely indifferent to either of them. I certainly believe them to be as bad, respectively, as my own pain and the death of my own daughter, and in addition, I do have a desire for their well-being. But given that I care about myself and my daughter more than I do about the stranger and the stranger's daughter, I cannot be indifferent as to where good and evil flow.

Consider size and perception of size again. An observer, even an ideal one, has to take up a wide range of different observation posts in the world, and his perceptual apparatus should be appropriately sensitive to variations in perspective. Even to an ideal observer in my current position, the sun should appear smaller than the moon, even if to an ideal observer equidistant from both, but within viewing range, they should look just the reverse. The moon should look bigger than the sun from the vantage point of Earth, and it is no defect of the observer that it appears that way to him.

So, even though the *facts* about size are observer-independent, *experiences* of size are appropriately observer-dependent, since they depend on the situation, point of view, or perspective of the observer. Analogously, even though facts about value are valuer-neutral, experiences of value can and *should* be valuer-relative, since they depend on exactly where the valuer is situated with respect to the objects of desire. In general, we do not require that a perceiver's experiences be isomorphic to reality for him to be perceiving appropriately. Analogously, we should not require that a valuer's desires be isomorphic to value for her to be responding appropriately. Now, if desire has a perspectival component—as the two examples suggest—then the merit connection, at least as it is formulated above, looks wrong. For if there is a legitimate perspectival component to desires, a person adequately responding to value need not desire things exactly to the degree that they are good.

If desires are experiences of value, and experiences of value not only can but should be perspectival, then this goes a long way to explaining away what is otherwise a deep problem for realism about value. We can embrace a world of agent-neutral value without condemning as defective or perverse the persistently agent-relative nature of desire. But also, the perspectival nature of value experiences no more undermines their claim to yield a glimpse of value, than the perspectival nature of ordinary perception undermines its claim to yield data about the material world. (A more detailed account of the perspectival nature of value experiences will be provided in the final chapter.)

3.6 Satan's Injunction

Milton's Satan issued an injunction to himself: 'Evil, be thou my good!' Does Satan's injunction raise a problem for the experience conjecture?

What exactly is Satan commanding here? Is it that from now on he desire evil? If he desires evil, then evil will, of course, seem good to him. Nothing in the experience conjecture rules that out, provided that desire is not an infallible indicator of goodness. If we allow that desires can go wrong, that they can misrepresent value, then the experience conjecture presents no conceptual obstacle to desiring evil.

But is Satan asking for something more—namely, that he desire something that he himself *regards* as evil? This time the experience conjecture does seem to be in danger of running afoul of folk wisdom. According to the conjecture, any state of affairs that is desired is experienced as good. So if the conjecture is true, how can one desire what one regards as bad?

Suppose I have had it drummed into me from an early age that it is always bad to steal other people's stuff, and as a consequence I do regard it as always and everywhere bad. On a lonely and abandoned street late one night, I pick up a wallet with both a considerable sum of money in it (say, $50,000) and the name and address of the owner. No one has seen me pick it up. I could easily pocket the money and throw away the wallet without being discovered. I need the money. Perhaps I even need the money more than the owner needs it. My desire to pocket the money is stronger, I find, than my desire to return the money to the owner. According to the experience conjecture, my desire to pocket the money just is its seeming good that I pocket the money. But how can that be, if I really regard stealing someone else's money as always and everywhere bad?

There is an ambiguity in the pivotal notion here. *Regarding* stealing as bad might be simply *believing* that it is bad, or it might be *experiencing* it as bad. Clearly the little scenario presents no problem for the experience conjecture if my regarding stealing as bad is interpreted as an evaluative belief. It is quite possible, although doubtless cognitively uncomfortable, to combine a value judgement (that stealing is always bad) with a value experience (the experience of pocketing the other person's 50K as good). There is, of course, a sense in which the experience is incompatible with the belief. I cannot both hold on to the belief and deem the experience a reliable one. Either the belief is false or the experience is misleading. But that is a contradiction between the content of the experience and the content of the belief. There is no contradiction between the two *states* involved—holding the belief while having the experience. That kind of conflict between a belief and an experience is not that uncommon in general (I see the stick as bent but believe it to be straight), and we shouldn't be surprised to find it occurring in the value realm.

There is a different worry here. The example suggests not only that desires might not always be good data, but that in the case of conflict one should defer to one's value judgement, not one's desires. But that is too hasty. We could as easily have considered an example of putative theft which leans in the other direction. Huck Finn, a believer in the common-sense morality of the day, believed that it was bad to help a slave escape from his rightful owners. He believed that it was theft of valuable property, legitimately purchased. But Huck found, to his surprise, that he liked Jim too much to turn him over to the bounty-hunters—he didn't want to hand him over, and he didn't do so. He allowed his desire to override his initial value judgement, and went on to heap some scorn on the latter. And just as well.

That desires are value data does not entail that they should always be trusted, or that in cases of conflict with judgement, it is the judgement that must surrender. As with perception and belief, sometimes a well-entrenched belief, well supported by theory and data, should overrule a recalcitrant datum that conflicts with it. But sometimes the recalcitrant datum really does tell us something new—as in the case of Huck.

Not all apparently problematic cases of desiring the bad can be explained as judgement–desire conflict. Some conflicts are more visceral than this suggests. There can be conflict among the appearances, the desires themselves. I am standing there with the wallet in hand. I want to return it, and I want to keep it. It may be that *stealing* the money does not attract me. I don't desire *to steal the money*. But I do desire *to keep the money*. Now, one might be tempted to say that, since the money belongs to someone else, to keep the money *entails* stealing it (just as *stealing it* clearly entails *keeping it*). So the contents of the two desires are, in the circumstances, logically equivalent, and so I have a contradictory pair of desires. Something appears to me to be good (keeping the money) while *the very same thing* (stealing the money) appears to me to be bad.

This diagnosis of this situation commits a rather common fallacy, one which David Stove (1972) has called *misconditionalization.* Suppose that A and B jointly entail C. The following is often inferred from this: *given that A is true, B entails C.* (Stove gives several common examples of this.) But the inference schema is invalid. A trivial counterexample: it is raining, and it is windy entails that it is raining. But consider: given that it is true that it is raining, the proposition that it is windy entails that it is raining. This is clearly false. That it is windy does not entail that it is raining, and *necessarily* there is no entailment here. The non-entailment is independent of any contingent facts. In particular, the entailment does not hold when it happens to be raining.

The argument for the conclusion that *keeping the money* is the very same state as *stealing the money* commits the fallacy of misconditionalization. That I keep the money and that the money belongs to someone else jointly entail that I steal it. But it does not follow that, given that it is true that the money belongs to someone else, keeping it entails stealing it. Stealing it is logically stronger. So there is no inconsistency in the pair of desires: I want to keep the money, and I don't want to steal the money. Of course, I know that the money belongs to someone else, and so, since I am not stupid, I know that to keep it I have to steal it. In light of my beliefs, fulfilling the first desire involves violating the second. I desire something (keeping) which I know involves something I don't desire (stealing). So something that seems to me good, in the circumstances requires something else that seems to me bad. This is a kind of conflict in desire, but it is not a pure conflict of desire. It is not one and the same thing seeming both good and bad.

Returning to Satan's injunction to himself, clearly, Satan can desire what is bad, and he can also desire what he himself judges to be bad. If that is what he is commanding, then to obey the command, he will have to be unbothered that the desires he acts on systematically run counter to his value judgements. There is, however, a more radical and problematic interpretation of his command. Is Satan commanding that he himself *desire* things which *seem* to him bad? In other words, to desire something in virtue of the bad that he experiences it as having. That does teeter on a contradiction. Satan not only knows that treachery is evil, he experiences it as such. But he wants to *desire* to be a traitor even while treachery *seems evil* to him. How can he manage that if the experience conjecture is right?

In fact he can. There is a contradiction in both desiring P and *not* desiring P. But there is no contradiction in desiring P and desiring *not*-P. Such a deeply conflicted desirer is in a bad way, and his desires can be criticized rationally, but such combinations of desire are possible. Perhaps to be such a desirer is what Satan wants. It is a perverse desire, to be sure, but not an unrealizable one.

3.7   Disappointment

Disappointment is a common enough experience and, on the face of it, not very difficult to analyse. To be disappointed, you need to have a desire, an expectation (at some level) that the desire will be satisfied, and then subsequent acquisition of the belief that the desire has not been, or will not be, satisfied. Call this the non-satisfaction account of disappointment.

Here is an unhappy episode from *Anna Karenina*:

That which for almost a year had constituted the one exclusive desire of Vronsky's life, replacing all former desires; that which for Anna had been an impossible, horrible, but all the more enchanting dream of happiness—this desire had been satisfied. Pale, his lower jaw trembling, he stood over her and pleaded with her to be calm, himself not knowing why or how.

'Anna! Anna!' he kept saying in a trembling voice. 'Anna, for God's sake....' But the louder he spoke, the lower she bent her once proud, gay, but now shame-stricken head, and she became all limp, falling from the divan where she had been sitting to the floor at his feet; she would have fallen on the carpet if he had not held her. (Tolstoy 2001: 149)

Vronsky's and Anna's all-consuming desire is fulfilled, but evidently they are not happy and satisfied. It would be something of an understatement to say that Anna is disappointed. The non-satisfaction theory doesn't explain Anna's distress. Can the experience conjecture aid in explaining disappointment upon desire-satisfaction?

Before we embark on that, let's dig a bit deeper to explain Anna's disappointment on the non-satisfaction theory. One explanation is that Anna's situation is a complex one, and as it happens, not all her desires really have been satisfied in this situation. She wanted to consummate her affair with Vronsky, yes, but she has other desires which make it an 'impossible, horrible' dream. That she would regard it that way is pretty much overdetermined. *Impossible*, because she desperately wants what she knows is (given the mores of the day) incompatible with this desire—namely, to continue having custody of her son. *Horrible*, because she knows she cannot live without her son. So it isn't clear that Anna *can* get what she desires. Given her situation, her desires are incompatible, and she knows that. All this is made apparent to her in her dreams:

But in sleep, when she had no power over her thoughts, her situation presented itself to her in all its ugly nakedness. One dream visited her almost every night. She dreamed that they were both her husbands, that they both lavished their caresses on her. Alexei Alexandrovich wept, kissing her hands, saying: 'It's so good now!' And Alexei Vronsky was right there, and he, too, was her husband. And marvelling that it had once seemed impossible to her, she laughingly explained to them that this was much simpler, and that now they were both content and happy. But this dream weighed on her like a nightmare, and she would wake up in horror. (Tolstoy 2001: 150)

   Evidently Anna is not a model of coherent desiring. She wants too many different things that are incompatible with what she knows to be the case. The question remains, however, whether a fully coherent desirer might still experience disappointment at the satisfaction of her desires. Surely one shouldn't be disappointed upon fulfilment of desire, if the non-satisfaction account is correct. And yet, disappointment attendant upon desire-satisfaction seems not only possible in the absence of irresolvable conflicts in desires, but something we are all fairly familiar with. Take the common phenomenon of buyer's regret. You experience a strong desire to purchase something, a desire that continues to nag away at you. You research the object, find out where it can be purchased most economically, dwell on it, turn it over in your mind, and so on. The desire keeps growing, and in the end you act on it. But when you bring the purchased object home and take it out of its box, suddenly it seems to lose its attraction. You have exactly what you wanted. But the object just sits there, unwanted now, rebuking you.

The experience conjecture is compatible with both realist and idealist theories of value. There is nothing in the idea that desires are experiences of value that prevents value from being *constituted* by desires—and in the next chapter I will spell out this idea in some detail. On such idealist theories the phenomenon at issue—disappointment upon desire fulfilment—is very hard to understand. I desire P. So P seems good to me, and what seems good to me (according to the idealist) is good for me. Then P is realized, I am aware that it is realized, and nevertheless I am disappointed.

Of course, when P is realized, I might have a much better idea of what P actually involves. Before I am plunged into the P state as a participant, I may not have an adequate grasp of it. My imagining of P may lack a lot of the detail that being immersed in P will provide. And I may not like P once I know all that. But disappointment still seems possible even when I am not provided with a more adequate grasp of P. Further, I may be disappointed not because P comes along with some other state Q, which I neither anticipated nor desired. Rather, I am disappointed in P *itself*. Seeing P realized, it no longer seems any good to me, I don't desire it any longer.

If we reject idealism, then the puzzle vanishes. All that disappointment entails is that one or other of those desires, the earlier or the later, is a misrepresentation of value. Either my initial desire indicating the goodness of P was misleading, or my current desire indicating P's lack of goodness is misleading. Further, if we combine this with the above sketch of perspective, then we also have the beginning of an account of what the difference might consist in. When P is realized, and I am immersed in P as a participant, my perspective on P changes. I am now much 'closer' to P. So it is perhaps not surprising that my experience of P's value changes. And, we should not be surprised, if the analogy with perception holds, that the closer view of P is more likely to be the more reliable one.

If desires are experiences of value, then the phenomenon of disappointment merely underlines that desires are not an infallible source of information about the good, and that one's experiences of value are likely to change as the relation between the object of experience and oneself changes. Realists won't be in the least disturbed by that. Rather, they will welcome it.

3.8   The Value of Desire

As I have noted on several occasions, idealist theories of value ground the good in desire and its fulfilment. The flip side is that the bad is grounded in the frustration of desires. Some versions of Buddhism apparently ground value in desire, and (according to Laurance Rosan) promote desirelessness as the most valuable state a sentient being can attain. There is a neglected argument for this (purportedly) Buddhist thesis that desirelessness is the highest good which is interesting and relevant in this context, because it takes as one of its two main premises an explicit statement of the experience conjecture. Here is Rosan's very clear statement of the thesis:

Now, to the extent that I desire anything, I must also regard it as desirable or good; that is, the very fact that something is the object of my desire means that it must have been able to attract my desire for it. At least it appears good to me, regardless of whether or not it is inherently good …. Thus, I could never desire anything which at the moment of my desiring would appear to be bad, but, rather, whatever I desire must always appear to be good. (Rosan 1955: 57)

Rosan combines this with a Platonic thesis. Plato claimed that what one desires is always what is not the case: 'he who desires something is lacking in that thing' (Plato 1958: 532). As Rosan puts it:

When I desire anything, the object of my desire must be something that I do not yet possess; if I already had it, it would be impossible for me to desire to obtain it. Although I may desire to retain something once it is already possessed, here the object of desire is the continuation of a present condition, so that it is a future condition which is desired, and this obviously cannot be possessed in the present. Therefore, desire always implies a lack of something which is not yet possessed. (Rosan 1955: 58)

Now for the core of Rosan's argument for the thesis that desirelessness is necessarily good (which, it has to be admitted, involves some fudging):

If … desire implies a lack of something which is not yet possessed and which must always appear to be good, desire must always imply the lack of an apparent good … To this extent it is the absence of good, the deprivation of good; in other words, desire must always be at least apparently evil. The object of desire is good, to be sure, but the desire itself cannot be good. (Rosan 1955: 58)

The fudging occurs on the border between appearance and reality (with the weasel words 'to this extent …' doing the work). An apparent good is not necessarily a good, and so the lack of an apparent good is not necessarily an evil. It is only an apparent evil. So even if desire does imply the lack of an apparent good, it does not imply the lack of a good. Still, it is not hard to patch up the argument to make the conclusion just as problematic. Suppose that you desire P—so P seems good to you. Suppose, further, that your desire is appropriate—P really is good. Given the Platonic thesis, P fails to be the case. Thus if you desire P appropriately, a good is missing from the world. So, necessarily, an appropriate or accurate desire entails an evil—that a certain good is lacking. All appropriate desires are thus bad. That's bad. If we add that inappropriate desires are bad in virtue of their inappropriateness, it follows that all desires are bad, and that desirelessness is good.

The argument clearly hinges on both the experience conjecture and the Platonic thesis that one can desire only what is non-existent or lacking. On the face of it, though, one can desire what is, just as one can desire what is not. Suppose my host asks me what kind of wine I would like, offering a range including a Pinot Noir. I decide on the Pinot Noir, and my host duly passes me a full glass. Do I still want it now that I have it? Well, suppose that my host were to whip it out of my hand. I would be surprised and disappointed, and my disappointment wouldn't be in any way assuaged if my host were to point out that once I had received the Pinot Noir I no longer desired it.

Plato anticipates this kind of objection and rebuts it by suggesting that if one desires the *status quo*, what one *really* desires is that the *status quo* persist into the future, something which it doesn't yet do.

And when you say, I desire that which I have and nothing else, is not your meaning that you want in the future what you have at present? He desires that what he has at present may be preserved to him in the future, which is equivalent to saying that he desires something which is nonexistent to him, and which as yet he has not got. (Plato 1953: 533)

Perhaps what Plato means here is that, once you get the glass of Pinot Noir, what you want is not that you *now* have a glass of Pinot Noir in your hand, but that you *will* have a glass of Pinot Noir in your hand in a moment's time; that is something that is 'nonexistent to you' now, and that is why you are disappointed by your host's swiping it.

This cannot be right either. Presumably a desire can be either thwarted or fulfilled only if one *has* that desire: the desire that P is thwarted if P is not the case, and fulfilled if P is the case. A desire can only be a fulfilled or thwarted desire if the desire is actually had. Even if Plato is right that what I want is *to have a glass of Pinot Noir in one moment's time*, then that desire is thwarted if *in one moment's time* I don't have the glass; and it is fulfilled if *in one moment's time* I do. Suppose I desire that P (that I will have the Pinot Noir in one second's time), and it is true that P (I will have the Pinot Noir in one second's time). Then I have a desire for something, P, that is in fact the case. Since my desire is for something that is the case, my desire is fulfilled, not thwarted.

Suppose that at noon I want to have a glass of Pinot Noir in my hand at 12.01 p.m. Maybe I don't *know* at noon that I will have a glass at 12.01, and, in that sense, at noon what I desire is 'nonexistent to me'. But then, if Plato has shown anything, he has shown only that one cannot have a desire for P and know that P is true. Or perhaps, that one cannot have a desire for P and believe that P is true. So one cannot have a desire that one believes to be fulfilled. In that sense I can only desire what is 'nonexistent to me'.

This modified Platonic principle would not, of course, mesh with the experience conjecture to produce the bad conclusion. For suppose I have a desire for P, which is appropriate, so that P is good. Then, according to the modified principle, that is quite compatible with P's being the case, and so the world is not necessarily deficient in a good even though I appropriately desire that good.

Finally, the experience conjecture sits very uneasily with the Platonic principle. If the desire that P is simply *P's seeming good*, then it is clear that there is absolutely no obstacle at all to desiring what is the case. For what is the case *can* clearly seem good to me even while I fully believe it to be the case. I have the glass of Pinot Noir in my hand now, I know I have the glass of Pinot Noir in my hand, and *that* fact really does seem good to me, *right now* (I really do want that glass in my hand, *now*.)

Far from supplying us with the conclusion that desires are necessarily bad, the experience conjecture suggests that appropriate desires are necessarily good. A desire has a two-fold nature—it is both a representation of an aspect of the world (its goodness) and a component of motivation. Desires necessarily prod us in the direction of their object. Suppose I desire that P (P seems good to me), and suppose further that my desire is an appropriate or accurate one (P really is good). Then *ipso facto* I am motivated to pursue (promote, enhance, preserve, or embrace) something good. Accurate desires thus tend to promote or preserve the good. A critic might claim that this establishes only that accurate desires are *instrumentally* good, but not that they are *intrinsically* good. But clearly, something that is *necessarily* an instrument productive of the good is itself necessarily a good. And what is necessarily good is (presumably) intrinsically good.

Of course this does not establish that desire-satisfaction in general is necessarily a good. If a desire is for something bad, then this argument does not establish its goodness. Rather, it suggests that both the desire itself and its satisfaction in such a case are bad. Whether the satisfaction of such a desire mitigates the evil desired is not yet settled. That possibility is something we will investigate in greater depth in the next two chapters.

3.9 Emotion

Most of those in the broad tradition in which this kind of account of value data is naturally placed (Brentano, Meinong, Scheler, Chisholm) nominate *emotions*—either particular emotions or emotions in general—rather than desires, as the experiences which give us access to value. According to Brentano (1969), for example, it is the emotions of *love* and *hate* which reveal the good and the bad. Chisholm (1986) takes as data the *appropriate taking of pleasure* or *displeasure* in various states. Meinong (1972) embraces emotional presentation in general, and Scheler (1973) the full complement of feelings and emotions.[2]

---

[2] Johnston (2001) argues that a certain sort of emotional state, which he calls 'an affective' desire, plays the role I have assigned to desire more generally. However, he also takes the term 'desire' much more broadly than I do, and so it may be that we are in rough agreement.

Theories of emotion typically attempt to reduce emotions to some more basic mental elements—typically, beliefs (non-evaluative beliefs as well as value judgements), desires, feelings (that is, raw feels)—together with sundry connections, causal and non-causal, between them. Theories run the gamut from the very austere (reduction to a single element) to the lavish (complexes of all these elements, dynamically interacting). Simple theories identify emotions either with feelings, or with beliefs, or with value judgements, or with desires. On the most inclusive theory, emotions are rich complexes of all these elements—non-evaluative beliefs, value judgements, desires, and feelings—dynamically interacting (Oakley 1992: 7).

Consider a simple theory that emotions are characteristic sensations ('affects') or bunches of such (James 1967: 15–17). Fear, for example, just is the complex of sensations caused by the rush of adrenalin which fearful situations produce. The sensation theory is sometimes called the *feeling* theory, but the term *feeling* is ambiguous. It can be used to mean either a sensation or an emotion. First, one can be experiencing an emotion without any accompanying bodily sensations at all. One might be mildly angry, for example, without any of the characteristic sensations of anger. Further, the very same sensations might accompany both fear and excitement, or both shame and guilt. What distinguishes fear and excitement, or guilt and shame, must be something other than sensation, something to do with the object of the emotion, perhaps a belief involving the object.

Certainly beliefs seem to be involved in some emotions. Consider joy, for example. An experience of joy is always joy about something, some state of affairs: that you have just won a Fulbright, that your spouse has just landed a great job, that the barbarians have lost the White House, or that the war is over. Now, you cannot be said to be joyful about winning a Fulbright, for example, unless you believe that you have won a Fulbright. To be overjoyed that P, you have to believe P to be the case. So, the emotion of joy is partly constituted by a non-evaluative belief about the obtaining of the object of the emotion. It is a *factive* emotion.

Not all emotions, however, are factive. Take fear. Often, perhaps typically, you fear things that you do not believe will come about. I fear that there will be a nuclear war within the next ten years. If someone asked me, 'Do you really *believe* there will be a nuclear war in the next ten years?', I would probably answer: 'No, I actually think there is only a one in a thousand chance of it, but that's scary enough.' It would be irrational to fear nuclear war if you thought there was absolutely no chance of it occurring—so rational fear does impose some constraints on believing. But an emotion can clearly fail to be rational in this sense. People fear things they may not believe have *any* chance of occurring. They may also know that the fear is irrational, but they still experience it. (Is irrational joy— joy without belief in the accompanying proposition that it presup- poses—also possible?)

It is certainly not sufficient for joy that you have the accompany- ing belief. You can believe that you won the Fulbright without being joyful about it. Somehow the goodness of winning factors into the emotion. According to another simple account, an emotion is noth- ing more or less than a value judgement (Solomon 1981). Guilt is the value judgement that I have done something bad. Anger is the value judgement that some injustice has been perpetrated against me. The difference between fear and excitement can thus be distinguished by the implicit judgements involved—one positive, one negative.

If a value judgement is just an evaluative belief, then this theory would be very simple indeed. The problem is that an evaluative belief by itself does not seem to entail any particular emotion. Clearly, joy at winning the Fulbright does involve the judgement that winning the Fulbright is a very good thing. But endorsing the judgement that P is a very good thing does not entail that you experience joy that P. You might hear the news that your colleague won the Fulbright instead, and you might judge that it is a very good thing that he won it, since he was clearly an excellent candidate and deserved to win, and so on. But you experience no joy at his winning. You may be envious of his winning, and that is entirely compatible with your judging it a very good thing that he won. For you to experience joy at the news, it seems clear that you have to *welcome* the news. You have to welcome it warmly. And you welcome it warmly not just in virtue of judging it, coldly, to be a good thing. It has to be something you *desire*. To be joyful thus entails desire.

On the fully inclusive theory, your joy about your winning a Fulbright is construed as a highly complex state constituted by your belief that you have won the Fulbright, your desire to win, the value judgement that the win is a good thing, together with the fact that this belief–desire complex causes you various pleasurable feelings. But this is a rather hefty theory of emotion, and at least some of these elements look redundant. Certain emotional states do not require sensations. Others do not require beliefs. While a value judgement is involved, it is not sufficient, and (as we will see) the endorsement of the value judgement is not necessary either. The only element that seems essential so far is a desire.

Certainly desires seem necessary to emotions. Imagine, if you can, becoming completely desireless, losing all desires and aversions, for any state whatsoever, while retaining all of your evaluative beliefs. Such a drastic transformation would be very odd for the reasons spelled out in the previous chapter; but it should be possible, if some strong but plausible version of the thesis of the independence of belief and desire is correct. It is difficult, however, to imagine a being, stripped of all desires, continuing to experience emotions. How could you experience *shame*, for example, if you didn't desire that your wrongdoings not be publicly exposed? How could you experience anger over an unjust slur if you had no desire to be treated with appropriate respect? How could you be in love with someone if you were absolutely indifferent to their well-being?

According to the experience conjecture, the desire that P is just the state of its seeming that P is good. If emotions necessarily incorporate desires, then the experience conjecture explains the temptation to include the associated value judgements in the emotions, or even to identify the value judgements with the emotions. But the experience conjecture also explains why it is unnecessary to add the value judgement as a component. Desires are directly connected to value judgements, but having a desire does not entail endorsing the associated value judgement. If an emotion involves a desire, then an emotion incorporates an experience of value, and thus like a desire stands to a value judgement as a perceptual experience stands to a belief. The emotion can serve as a reason for endorsing the judgement, but without containing the judgement as a component.

Perhaps emotions can, then, be simply identified with a certain sort of desire.[3] On the desire theory, fear might be a desire to flee a

---

[3] Maybe this theory can be foisted on Hume or Spinoza. See Hume 1955: II, ii, 6; Spinoza 1955: III, xl. xxxii–xlviii.

threat, and courage the desire to stay and face the threat. And as we will see in Chapter 5, a case can be made that love and hate are a species of higher-order desiring. Love might be the desire that the desires of one's beloved be satisfied; hate, the desire that the desires of one's enemy be thwarted.

I hesitate, however, to give a uniform, general account of the emotions, since emotional states are rather diverse. It may be that some emotions can be identified with desires, while others involve richer complexes involving beliefs and sensations as well as desires. But it is plausible that emotions all have a desiderative component; so the theory of value experience I am advocating here can happily appropriate the insights of the broad tradition which identifies particular emotions, or emotions in general, as a source of a value data.

Finally, when I introduced the experience conjecture, I was careful to state it in the following way: a desire is an experience of the value of a state of affairs. This is important, because it leaves open the following possibility. *Experience of value* may well be a determinable of which there are various different determinates selected by various different categories of object. *Desire* would then be that determinate of this determinable which is selected by the category *state of affairs*. But objects other than states of affairs can have value, and not all such objects are the objects of desire. Other kinds of object may be experienced as valuable without being desired. Both persons and works of art have value, for example, but it seems a bit strange to say that one experiences the value of a work of art by *desiring* it, and very odd to say that of persons. (The most natural interpretation of the claim 'I desire that painting' is that I want to own it, and while that desire may follow upon experiencing the painting's value, it need not.) Experiencing the value of a person might take the form of *loving* rather than desiring (although, as we will see, the nature of love might be analysed in terms of desire). Experiencing the value of a work of art may be different for different kinds of art, since different kinds of art may belong to different ontological categories. Some works might be best regarded as physical objects, others as properties of physical objects, and still others as roles that a physical object might play. And so it may be that different kinds of value experiences are appropriate to each. Of course, one might try to reduce the experience of the value of the work of art to a desire for a state of affairs which involves the work (just as one might try to reduce love to a species of desiring). One candidate is the desire *that the work of art exist.* It is, of course, controversial what the ontological categories of different kinds of works of art are. If the work is a property or a role, then the existence of the work would be the realization of that property in a particular, or the occupation of the role by a particular. So there may be ways of extending the experience conjecture beyond states of affairs, but nothing I say need be taken to imply that all experiences of value are desires.

3.10   The BAD and the SAD

David Lewis has exposed a paradox at the heart of a thesis he calls 'Desire-as-Belief'—or DAB, as it has come to be dubbed in the literature. DAB is a version of judgement internalism—the thesis that beliefs about goodness necessarily motivate. According to DAB, such beliefs necessarily motivate by playing the same role in one's motivational structure as desires themselves. A stark version of this is the thesis that a desire just *is* a belief about goodness. An alternative formulation is this: a belief about goodness just *is* a desire. So we could also call it the *belief-as-desire* thesis, since the claim is that a certain sort of belief—an evaluative belief, a value judgement—necessarily plays the same role in motivation as a desire. Then the doctrine has the happy acronym BAD. Whatever acronym we settle on (I'll call it the BAD thesis), Lewis's proofs, and subsequent refinements, have sought to show that there is something fundamentally problematic about the thesis, because it conflicts with the basic tenets of rational decision theory. We could call this the BAD paradox.

   At first glance the BAD paradox (which I will summarize in a moment) does not bear on the experience conjecture, since this latter does not say that a *belief* is a desire, but rather that a certain sort of experience—an experience of goodness, or *seeming* goodness—is a desire. *P's seeming good* is *the desire that P.* We could call this the SAD thesis (with SAD an abbreviation for *seeming as desire*). On the face of it, while there is a superficial connection between the BAD and the SAD, there is no obvious deep connection between them. It isn't hard to unearth a connection.

Lewis states the desire-as-belief thesis as follows: one desires A just to the degree that one believes A to be good. It thus involves a systematic correlation between belief (or *degree* of belief) and desire (or degree of desire). The following suggests itself as a possible explication of this idea: the strength of one's desire for A is equal to the strength of one's belief in the proposition that A is good.

Let $D(A)$ be the *strength of desire for A*; let $P(A)$ be *degree of belief in A*; and let $\mathring{A}$ (which is read 'A-halo') be the proposition *that A is good*. Then we can state the BAD thesis rather succinctly thus:

Belief-as-desire: $D(A) = P(\mathring{A})$.

This is indeed a simple formula, and one might wonder whether it really is the correct explication of belief as desire, characterized as *desiring A just to the degree that one believes A to be good.* The italicized phrase is unfortunately ambiguous. Does *degree* attach to the *strength of the belief* or to the *amount of goodness A is believed to possess?* If we adopt the former reading, we get: *desiring A to the same degree as the degree of belief in the proposition that A is good.* If we adopt the latter, we get: *desiring A to the same degree as the degree of goodness one believes (estimates) A to have.* These are two quite different explications, and our simple formula here settles firmly on the former. But the latter reading seems just as natural, if not a good deal more so. For suppose one is pretty near certain that A is better than so-so, but not that it is thoroughly good. Then one invests o probability in the proposition that A is (thoroughly) good. But one's desire for A may not be o.

Still, the former reading is the one which Lewis (and others) have adopted, and it is this formula which clashes with decision theory—in particular, that one updates one's beliefs by conditionalization, and that degree of desire obeys the standard formula for subjective expected utility. (A simple proof of the incompatibility of BAD with these two tenets of subjective decision theory can be found in appendix 3.[4])

---

[4] See Oddie (1994) for a detailed analysis of the BAD paradox in Lewis (1988). Lewis's original proof is unnecessarily complicated, as he acknowledged in his (1996). Unfortunately my 1994 analysis can be circumvented by the much simpler proof I give

Suppose that we think of *seemings* as coming in different degrees. Then one might think it natural to simply identify *strength of A's seeming to be the case* (abbreviated: Seems(A)) with *degree of subjective probability* (P(A)). Something seems to me to be the case just to the extent that I find it probable.

Seeming-as-belief: Seems(A) = P(A).

If both desire and seeming come in degrees, then that suggests a generalized version of the experience conjecture (or SAD): the degree to which I desire A is the degree to which it seems to me that A is good.

Seeming-as-desire: D(A) = Seems(Å).

If we put *seeming as desire* (i.e. the experience conjecture) together with *seeming as belief*, we get the BAD principle: the degree to which I desire A is my degree of subjective probability for the proposition that A is good.

Belief-as-desire: D(A) = P(Å).

And that leads to contradiction with decision theory (see appendix 2).

It isn't hard to pinpoint the culprit here. It is the thesis that seemings are best construed as a species of *belief*—here interpreted as degrees of subjective probabiltiy. We can read the SAD paradox as an argument for the view that experiences are *not* beliefs, even if they ground the rationality of belief. It is thus a novel route to the thesis of the so-called non-conceptual content of experience, a thesis which others have argued for both in value contexts and in non-value contexts.[5]

3.11   The Lure of Idealism

Suppose that we both posit experiences of value and admit that desires are ideal candidates for such experiences. Then idealism

in the appendix 3. But in any case, it turns out that BAD is not a good explication of any version of internalism (see Oddie 2001*b*), and given an adequate explication, the paradox can be defused provided we adopt the kind of causal decision theory espoused by Lewis himself in his (1981*a*), supplemented by the Principal Principle—see Lewis (1986) and also Oddie and Menzies (1992).

[5] See Mulligan (1998) for an extremely clear exposition of the argument for so-called non-conceptual content.

about value becomes a tantalizingly economical option. Why not simply reduce value to value experiences, to desires? Tempting perhaps, but not easy. The hard task facing the value idealist is that of constructing a common, non-perspectival, agent-neutral world of values out of the vast collection of apparently inconsistent, highly perspectival, agent-relative desires. That's the task to which I now turn.

4 VALUE AS REFINED DESIRE

THE realist posits an external world which impinges on us through our experiences of it. The idealist finds the implicit mind–world gap both mysterious and irksome, and to remedy this posits a mind-dependent world, one which consists simply of congeries of the experiences themselves. In the last chapter I embraced experiences of value as part of a response to the queerness argument. For those who are willing to embrace such value experiences but who are also ontologically abstemious, it will be tempting at this point to take the idealist tack with respect to value. That is to say, it is tempting to take value to consist in, or reduce to, congeries of value experiences. In a nutshell, that is idealism about value. If we combine value idealism with the experience conjecture—the thesis that desires are experiences of value—then what we have is close to the rather familiar thesis that value reduces to desire.

As attractive as the idealist project at first appears, however, reducing value to desire is a rather tall order. Desires can be a motley, incoherent bunch, and at first blush they seem an unpromising basis for value. It is hard enough to read a consistent evaluative scheme off *one* person's set of desires, let alone to integrate the rabble of conflicting desires experienced by different desirers at loggerheads with one another. One promising response for the idealist to this motley incoherence of actual desires is to spurn those desires in favour of suitably refined desires. That is to say, the idealist might hold that the valuable is not just what is desired in fact, but rather what *would* be desired were we to *refine* actual desires into a harmonious and coherent collection.

In this chapter I will do a considerable amount of spadework on behalf of value idealism by developing what appears to be a really quite promising articulation of this refinement approach to value. What is really quite remarkable is that the map of value which this refinement account delivers is surprisingly close to the realist's map over large stretches of the terrain—much closer, I think, than realists would have believed possible, or their antirealist rivals could have reasonably hoped for. Value idealism is thus a much more promising programme than many realists would like to concede.

In Chapter 5 we will in fact discover that this promising programme does not quite deliver all the requisite goods—that there is what we might call a *desire-independent value residue*. Still, it behoves a serious realist to determine exactly how much of value the idealist can extract from desire before declaring that there is something about value that outstrips even our most refined desires.

4.1 Categorical and Dispositional Idealism

It can be instructive to compare idealism about the valuable with idealism about the material. Categorical idealism about the material world—Berkeley's thesis—maintains that to be is to be perceived. Categorical idealism about the valuable maintains, by parity, that to be valuable just is to be experienced as valuable (viz. desired). But surely I can fail to desire the valuable, and what I desire in fact may not be valuable.

Related defects in categorical idealism about the physical—for example, that there are no unperceived physical objects—elicited the phenomenalist response. The phenomenalist agrees with the idealist that the real reduces to perception, and with the realist that the tree in the quad exists unperceived. His solution is to resort to counterfactual perceptions (dispositions to perceive, or 'permanent possibilities of sensation' (see Oddie 2000)). The tree exists unperceived provided we would have tree-in-the-quad experiences given suitable conditions. Analogously, dispositional idealism about value holds that something is valuable, even when not desired, if we would desire it under certain suitable conditions (Lewis 1989). Unlike categorical idealism, dispositional idealism provides a sufficient gap between value and desire to accommodate the possibility of inappropriate desires. If conditions for valuing are not suitable or ideal, then one may desire what isn't valuable, or fail to desire what is.

David Lewis (1989) has argued for a dispositionalist idealist account of value. According to Lewis, the valuable is what we would value under ideal conditions. He argues, first, that valuing is not a species of believing—for example, believing that something is valuable. If it were, it would not have the right purchase on our motivations. Rather, it must be a species of desiring. Is valuing something simply desiring it, then? No, says Lewis. The nicotine addict might want to smoke a cigarette but not value doing so, so valuing cannot just be the same as desiring. Following Frankfurt, Lewis argues that the valuing here is a second-order desire. A desire to smoke is a first-order desire—it takes as its object some state of affairs that does not itself 'involve' a desire. Desiring not to desire to smoke is a second-order desire—it takes as object a desire, the desire to smoke. So the conflicted addict desires to smoke, but also desires to desire to not smoke (or desires to not desire to smoke). The latter, according to Lewis, is what we mean by saying that the conflicted addict values not smoking. So on this view, I value what I *desire to desire*.

The account provides a gap between valuing and desiring, and that may be right. There are cases in which what one values comes into conflict with what one desires. You might value being generous, say, but nevertheless find yourself acting on an ungenerous desire. But if you value something and your values are in the driver's seat, then your first-order desires will line up with your values, and you will act on those.

Lewis goes on to define *value* as what one would value under ideal circumstances. Ideal circumstances involve 'full imaginative engagement'. If we take C. D. Broad's tentative definition of good, and substitute second-order for first-order desire, we end up with something rather close to Lewis's account:

> X is good = X is such that it would be a fitting object of (second-order) desire to any mind which had an adequate idea (as delivered by full imaginative engagement) of its non-ethical characteristics.

The account has some attractive features, but it can be broadened. As it stands, it is somewhat solipsistic. I desire P, but that desire has not necessarily been refined. It is raw data, but it needs to be tested and sifted. So I ask myself, do I also desire to so desire? Suppose the answer is Yes. Then I not only desire P but value P. But is P really good? That is a further question, as it should be.

To determine this, I consider P under conditions of full imaginative engagement, and if, after this demanding exercise, I *still* desire to so desire, then P really is valuable.

What if *you* perform the demanding imaginative experiment on P and find at the end of it that you do not desire to so desire? Then, according to the account, P is not valuable. So we have a contradiction. Lewis concedes this and retreats to a version of agent-relative value. Value is tacitly indexed—it is value *for us*, where the *we* here is the largest group of valuers who agree with me on second-order desires, after we all engage imaginatively. If no one else agrees with me, then the *we* shrinks to a singleton.

This is not really a happy outcome even for an idealist about value. The raw material out of which value emerges—desires—are admittedly highly agent-relative, highly perspectival. But the challenge for idealism, whether of the physical or of the valuable, is to deliver a unique, non-perspectival, agent-neutral world which both transcends and incorporates the highly agent-relative raw data with which we begin. If refining the raw material of individual experience merely yields something just as perspectival, just as agent-relative, then the process has brought us no closer to real value. As Michael Smith puts it, in a discussion of whether or not dispositionalism leads to relativism (read: agent-relativity of values) or realism (read: agent-neutrality of values) the fundamental question which the dispositionalist account of value raises is this:

Is it plausible to suppose that there are some desires that all subjects would converge upon if they had desire sets that are maximally informed and coherent and unified? Many will insist that there are no such desires (Sobel 1999). If they are right then we must conclude that realism is false. … My own view, however, is that this is all far too quick. It is unclear whether there are any desires that all subjects would converge upon if they had desire sets that are maximally informed and coherent and unified, but it is equally unclear that there are no such desires. It therefore seem to me best to suppose that the debate between realists and irrealists is yet to be resolved. (Smith 2002: 343).

It might be useful to climb down from these peaks of abstraction and consider a homely example. I want my daughter to learn the violin, say, but I wonder whether it would really be valuable for her to do so. I desire to desire her learning, so there is no conflict between my first-order and second-order desires—I value her learning. But is it really valuable for her to learn? I have read the dispositionalists on value, and so now I try to imagine her learning to play the violin in some detail, and I find I desire to desire her violin learning. So my first-order desire is endorsed by a second-order desire, and my second-order desire survives the fire of imaginative engagement. Maybe that is enough to settle whether *I* value her learning the violin, but is it enough to settle whether it is *valuable* for her to do so? Surely one thing that needs to be considered is whether my *daughter* desires to learn the violin. Suppose she has little or no desire (or little or no desire to desire, or little or no disposition to desire) to learn the violin, but I *still* like the idea of her learning. Doesn't that suggest that I haven't put enough weight on her desires? If I *care* about my daughter at all, then I will try to ascertain whether she has any desire to learn the violin (or at least the potential for so desiring). I don't simply want the people I care about to play the appropriate role in what I would like to happen. Rather, I have at least some desire that they play an appropriate role in what they desire. Caring for another clearly involves some desire for *their* desire satisfaction.

The dispositionalist might reply that *full* imaginative engagement will take into account the desires of others, *via* my desire for their desire satisfaction. This may be true, but we need to make it explicit that there is this interaction, not only between my second-order desires and my first-order desires, but between *my* second-order desires and *their* first-order desires.

Of course, I don't just care about my children. I love them. Loving is a species of caring—a particularly intense kind—and what loving shares with the other members of the genus is a second-order desire that certain first-order desires be satisfied. This holds whether it is oneself or another one cares about. There may well be more to loving and caring than this, but there is certainly not less. Loving, whether love of self or love of another, involves desiring the good of the other, and (since the other's good presumably depends upon the satisfaction of her desires) it involves desiring her desire satisfaction. This is the essential insight of all those accounts within the Aristophanean tradition according to which the essence of love is the *taking on board* of the interests of the beloved.[1] Through a process of reflection on, and refinement of, one's own desires for another's first-order desire satisfaction, there is a sense in which the beloved's desires become *one's own*.

It's plausible that all these desires—first-order, second-order, and maybe even higher-order—have something to do with the actual shape of value, and that successive refinements of this complete set of desires will yield closer approximations to the shape of value. But if value takes its shape from desire, then it must be sensitive to the way in which these desires intersect and overlap. We are nodes in a complex web of desire—desires for this or that, desires for our own desire satisfaction, but also desires for the desire satisfaction of others we care about, some of whom in turn care about us and our desire satisfaction, some who don't, and some who care about others for whom we couldn't care less. If value hangs by threads of desire, then it hangs by threads suspended from nodes all over the intricate web of desire, not just from the one thin thread hanging from the node where *I* happen to be located.

4.2 The Web of Desire

The web of desire is complex, and to understand its role in shaping value, we have to disentangle it. In particular we have to disentangle first-order desires for this or that outcome from the second-order desiring involved in loving and caring about ourselves and others. This will, at the outset, involve simplification and idealization, but in the end we will see how these different elements recombine and meld together in a natural way.

Let's work with a simple concrete situation involving both first-order and second-order desires. Romeo has various first-order desires, desires for this and for that, which will make him happy, say. But Romeo also has some second-order desires. He does want his first-order desires satisfied—he cares about his own desire satisfaction—but he also cares about Juliet. In fact he loves her.

---

[1] Plato (1980); Solomon (1981); Nozick (1989); and Lehrer (1997). See also Frankfurt (1999).

Whether or not Juliet is satisfied is rather important to Romeo too. He wants her to have what she wants. Romeo doesn't care one whit about Lady Capulet or the old Nurse. Juliet reciprocates Romeo's love, but, unlike Romeo, she also cares about her old companion, the Nurse. Her Nurse's happiness does mean something to her, although not nearly as much as Romeo's does. Everyone is looking out for number one to some extent, but Lady Capulet is unusually self-centred. Mostly she cares only about herself, getting what she wants, although she does spare a little care for her daughter.

These desire sets do not mesh happily together. For example, Romeo wants Juliet to be happy, and that's important to him, but he doesn't care one whit about her old Nurse. Juliet, however, does care about the Nurse; the Nurse's happiness does mean something to her. To make his desires fully coherent, then, Romeo would have to revise them to incorporate some concern for the Nurse. Romeo is not alone in having a less than fully coherent desire set. As we will see, all of the protagonists in this story suffer from incoherencies in their desires.

We start, then, with some first-order desires which we assume to be entirely self-regarding—an assumption which will turn out to be inessential but is useful for purely illustrative purposes. Call these (somewhat pejoratively) *base* desires. Each person may, for example, have a base desire for (his own) pleasure, happiness, fame, fortune, or whatever. It doesn't really matter what it is for. Consider a sample of possible distributions of desire satisfaction over our small population (1 is for complete desire satisfaction, and 0 for complete dissatisfaction, but we could contemplate degrees of satisfaction between 0 and 1).

In table 4.1 S_1 is thus the state in which all four have their base desires satisfied; S_2 is the state in which Romeo, Juliet, and the

TABLE 4.1. *First-order (base) desires*: D_1

	S_1	S_2	S_3	S_4	S_5	S_6	S_7	S_8
Romeo	1	1	1	1	0	0	0	0
Juliet	1	1	1	0	1	0	0	0
Nurse	1	1	0	0	1	1	0	0
Lady Capulet	1	0	0	0	1	1	1	0

Nurse are satisfied, but Lady Capulet is not; ... S_8 is the state in which none of them is at all satisfied. The fact that the rows are all distinct indicates that these first-order desires are agent-relative, perspectival. Romeo, for example, is the only one who is happy in S_4, and the only one who is not happy in S_5. If the rows were all the same (that is, each column contained the same number all the way down) we would have an *agent-neutral* desire matrix.

We are not, however, simply self-regarding beings. Or even if we are, it is at least possible that we not be such. People care not only about the satisfaction of their own desires, they also care about others, particularly those whom they love and cherish. Caring about another involves desiring, to some extent, what the other desires, giving her desire satisfaction some weight. This caring for another can be regarded as a species of second-order desiring— desiring, *to some degree*, that the other's desires be satisfied. (You might object here and say: no, caring is desiring that the person gets what is actually *good* for them, regardless of their desires. But we are engaged in the idealist project here of constructing the good out of the desired, and the idealist is not entitled to assume the good, even the good for a person, at this stage.)

The structure of second-order desires in our little scenario can be depicted with a simple graph where an arrow from X to Y represents the fact that X desires Y's desire satisfaction to some positive degree, and a double-headed arrow represents mutual care (see fig. 4.1). Caring admits of degrees. It can be small, or (as in the case of love) large. That a person's carings involve second-order desires which both range over the first-order desires of the members of a group to which they belong and admit of degrees, enables us to utilize a matrix representation like that developed by Lehrer and Wagner (1981) in their theory of epistemic consensus (see also Lehrer 1997). (Their theory is, in turn, an application of the theory of Markov Chains (Kemeny and Snell 1967).) According to Lehrer and Wagner, people not only believe this and that to certain degrees. They also place weight on the opinions of others as well as themselves. Those they think of as experts, they place a high weight on. Those whose opinions they discount, they place a zero weight on. One can and perhaps should revise one's own opinions in the light of the opinions of others, giving each other person's opinion its due weight by one's own lights. While I draw

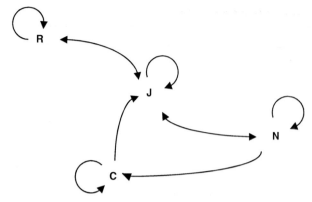

FIG. 4.1   *A web of second-order desire*

heavily on the Lehrer–Wagner model of belief revision, I don't wish to imply that my interpretation of the matrix apparatus always coincides with theirs. I take it out of the belief realm into the realm of desire.

Let c_{XY} be the *degree* of care which individual X invests in individual Y—how much X desires Y's desire satisfaction. c_{RJ} measures the degree of Romeo's desire for Juliet's desire satisfaction; c_{RN} of Romeo's desire for the Nurse's desire satisfaction, and c_{RR} of how much Romeo invests in his own desire satisfaction. This measure of degree of care can clearly be *normalized*. We can sum up the different degrees and divide by the total, so that once normalized the different components (c_{RR}, c_{RJ}, c_{RN}, c_{RC}) sum to 1. Normalized c_{RJ}, for example, is a measure of the *proportion* of his total caring that Romeo invests in Juliet's desire satisfaction. Juliet also cares about herself (c_{JJ}) and cares quite a lot for Romeo (c_{JR}), a little for the Nurse (c_{JN}) and a little for her mother (c_{JC}). The individual proportions of Juliet's total space of care also have to sum to 1. For the sake of concreteness, let us suppose that the second-order desires in our little example, once normalized, are as shown in table 4.2. The Romeo *row* details the proportional strengths of Romeo's desires for the desire satisfaction of each member of the group—including, of course, himself; the Juliet row details the strength of Juliet's second-order desires, and so on. That the second-order desires of the protagonists in our story are (like their

TABLE 4.2.   *Second-order desires*: C_1

	Romeo	Juliet	Nurse	Lady Capulet
Romeo	0.7	0.3	0	0
Juliet	0.3	0.5	0.2	0
Nurse	0	0.1	0.8	0.1
Lady Capulet	0	0.1	0	0.9

base desires) heavily agent-relative is transparent—it is reflected in the fact that the rows differ from each other. Again, if the rows were all the same (that is, each column contained the same number all the way down), we would have an agent-neutral desire matrix. Note that in the web of desire there is an arrow going from X to Y just in case c_{XY} is a non-zero entry in the second-order matrix.

So much for the second-order desires. The base, first-order desire matrix and the second-order, care matrix are both clearly agent-relative affairs. If we think of desires as experiences of value, then there are considerable differences in the value experiences of the protagonists. They see the value of states quite differently, and as well they see the value of the good of others quite differently. There is not only tension between the different desires of the different desirers. More interestingly, there is a kind of tension between these two agent-relative matrices. Take any one of these protagonists, Romeo say. His first-order desires are not in equilibrium with his second-order desires. There is a kind of tension between them.

To see in what the tension consists, suppose Romeo compares his attitudes to states 1, 3, and 4. At the first-order level he is currently indifferent as to which is realized. Now, since he doesn't care about either the Nurse or Lady Capulet, it is reasonable to take his indifference between states 1 and 3 to be justified, since those states differ only with respect to the desire satisfaction of people for whom he cares nothing. But recall that his own base desires are not the only ones that he wants satisfied. He has a strong second-order desire for Juliet's first-order desire satisfaction.

4.3   Refining First-Order Desires in the Light of Second-Order Desires

Since Juliet's base desires are satisfied in state 3 but not in state 4, and Romeo wants Juliet's desires satisfied, Romeo's desires would be internally more coherent if he desired state 3 more than he desired state 4. His second-order desires are thus somewhat out of kilter with his base, first-order desires. To lessen the tension, he would have to revise his desires, and assuming that he really does care about Juliet, his second-order desires should be given priority over his first-order desire. So, ideally he should revise his initial base desires in the light of his own second-order desires.

Suppose Romeo could revise his first-order desires. He considers each person he cares about and weights their desire satisfaction in each possible state S. His revised desire for state S is then naturally taken to be a *weighted average* of the degrees of desire satisfaction, in S, of each participant, where the weight is given by the amount Romeo cares about the person in question.

> *Strength of Romeo's revised desire for S*
>   = amount Romeo cares for Romeo × Romeo's degree of desire satisfaction in S
>   + amount Romeo cares for Juliet × Juliet's degree of desire satisfaction in S
>   + amount Romeo cares for Nurse × Nurse's degree of desire satisfaction in S
>   + amount Romeo cares for Lady C × Lady C's degree of desire satisfaction in S.

Somewhat more succinctly, let the strength of Romeo's initial desire for $S = \mathbf{D}_1^R(S)$ and let his revised desire for S be $\mathbf{D}_2^R(S)$. Then the above can be summarized:

$$\mathbf{D}_2^R(S) = c_{RR}\mathbf{D}_1^R(S) + c_{RJ}\mathbf{D}_1^J(S) + c_{RN}\mathbf{D}_1^N(S) + c_{RC}\mathbf{D}_1^C(S)$$

Strength of Romeo's revised desire for both S_1 and S_3

$$= 0.7 \times 1 + 0.3 \times 1 + 0 \times 0 + 0 \times 0 = 1.$$

Strength of Romeo's revised desire for S_4

$$= 0.7 \times 1 + 0 \times 0 + 0 \times 0 + 0 \times 0 = 0.7.$$

After revising his first-order desires in the light of what he cares about, his second-order desires, Romeo is still indifferent between states 1 and 3, but now his desire for both is stronger than is his desire for state 4.

As noted, everyone in our story suffers from the same lack of internal equilibrium between their own first-order and second-order desires. Maybe they should all revise them in the way Romeo has done. Juliet should revise her first-order desires in the light of her second-order desires, as should the others. What we get from a systematic revision is another first-order desire matrix. Mathematically, it is simply the product of the initial cares and the initial base desires:

Revised desires = product of care matrix and initial desires:
$$D_2 = C_1 D_r.$$

Suppose all have revised their base desires in the light of their cares (table 4.3). As he surveys this new distribution of desire, Romeo notices that he is indifferent between states 1 and 3, but that in state 3 Juliet's first-order desire satisfaction is less than it would be in state 1. So, given that he cares about Juliet, Romeo shouldn't now be indifferent between states 3 and 1. So maybe he needs to revise his desires again in the light of his desire for Juliet to have her desires satisfied (table 4.4).

You will notice that a really quite remarkable thing is happening. Not only are the agent-relative desires changing, *but they are starting to harmonize.* Disagreements between these desires are becoming smaller. In D_1 the difference between Romeo's and Juliet's desire for state 4 is maximal (that is =1). In D_2 the difference is reduced to 0.4, and in D_3 it is 0.22. In D_1 both Romeo and Juliet are first-order indifferent between states 6 and 7—in both of

TABLE 4.3. *Revised first-order desires*: $D_2 = C_1 D_1$

	S_1	S_2	S_3	S_4	S_5	S_6	S_7	S_8
Romeo	1	1	1	0.7	0.3	0	0	0
Juliet	1	1	0.8	0.3	0.7	0.2	0	0
Nurse	1	0.9	0.1	0	1	0.9	0.1	0
Lady Capulet	1	0	0.1	0	1	0.9	0.9	0

TABLE 4.4.   *Twice revised first-order desires* : $D_3 = C_1D_2$

	S_1	S_2	S_3	S_4	S_5	S_6	S_7	S_8
Romeo	1	1	0.94	0.58	0.42	0.06	0	0
Juliet	1	0.98	0.72	0.36	0.64	0.28	0.02	0
Nurse	1	0.83	0.17	0.03	0.97	0.83	0.17	0
Lady Capulet	1	0.19	0.17	0.03	0.97	0.83	0.81	0

which neither he nor Juliet is happy. In D_2 Juliet desires state 6 to some extent because the Nurse, about whom she cares, is happy. Romeo is still first-order indifferent. In D_3, however, he slightly prefers state 6 because Juliet's D_2-desire for state 6 over state 7 has now impacted on Romeo's first-order desires.

We can now see exactly what it takes for Romeo's second-order desires (or cares) to be out of harmony with his first-order desires. It is that revision of his first-order desires on the basis of his second-order desires would lead to a *different* first-order desire distribution. More generally, second-order desires (C) are *out of harmony* with first-order desires (D) just in case the first-order desires would be different if revised in the light of the second-order desires: $CD \neq D$. Conversely, C and D are *in harmony* just in case revision of D by C would change nothing: $CD = D$.

The revision procedure can, of course, be repeated indefinitely, and we obtain a sequence of first-order desire matrices: D_1, D_2 ($= C_1D_1$), D_3 ($= C_1D_2$), ..., D_n ($= C_1D_{n-1}$). Thus if at each stage $C_1D_{n-1} \neq D_{n-1}$, then C_1 and D_{n-1} are in some tension. If we keep revising, the product matrix C_1D_n in this case converges to a limiting desire matrix, D_∞. Furthermore, this limiting matrix, unlike D_n, is in perfect harmony with the original care matrix: $C_1D_\infty = D_\infty$. Finally, in D_∞ all the rows are identical (see table 4.5). In the limit of this revision procedure, everyone in the group would agree on the strength of their desires for all states. This, despite the fact that they start out with very different conflicting first-order and second-order desires. D_∞ is the agent-neutral *ideal limit* of C_1 and D_1. (We might also call it the *harmonious refinement* of D_1 by C_1.)

What is the connection between the original base desires in D_1 and the perfectly refined desires in D_∞? Don't the original individual base desires lose their significance in the ideal limit? Not at

Table 4.5. *The ideal limit of* C_1 *and* D_1 : $C_1 D_n \to D_\infty$.

	S_1	S_2	S_3	S_4	S_5	S_6	S_7	S_8
Romeo	1	0.75	0.5	0.25	0.75	0.5	0.25	0
Juliet	1	0.75	0.5	0.25	0.75	0.5	0.25	0
Nurse	1	0.75	0.5	0.25	0.75	0.5	0.25	0
Lady Capulet	1	0.75	0.5	0.25	0.75	0.5	0.25	0

all. In the ideal limit each person would desire states solely on the basis of the total amount of original base-desire satisfaction. In the end, the greater the base-desire satisfaction in S, the more S is desired by everyone. The original agent-relative base desires have been transformed by degrees into an agent-neutral desire distribution, *but one which is nevertheless highly sensitive to the satisfaction of the original base desires.* Thus, from purely self-regarding first-order desires, together with fairly unexceptional second-order desires, we have extracted by successive refinement impartial, agent-neutral desires, simply by having each individual refine her desires, always in the light of her very own second-order desires.

The coherence of the ideal first-order desires with the second-order desires is revealed by the fact that $C_1 D_\infty = D_\infty$. With D_∞ we have attained perfect harmony between first- and second-order desires, and revising further in the light of those second-order desires would change nothing. The limiting first-order desires are thoroughly in harmony with everyone's initial second-order desires.

We may not always attain agent-neutrality in the limit. But whether or not we have convergence, the limiting matrix, whether agent-neutral or agent-relative, represents desires to which each one would be drawn by their initial first-order and second-order desires if each refined their own desires to perfect harmony. The first-order desires given by D_∞ are those that each would, in the ideal limit, endorse if all could systematically refine their own first-order desires in the light of their own second-order desires, remembering that those second-order desires range over the first-order desires of others as well. So these limiting first-order desires, the product of <u>successive refinement</u> in the light of all the second-order desires, are naturally identified with what the individuals would desire in the limit under ideal circumstances. So if the

dispositional theory of value is correct, these limiting desires reveal
real value itself.

4.4   Reflexive Higher-Order Desires

I introduced c_{XY} as the degree to which X cares about Y. I have
been treating c_{XY} as a measure of X's second-order desires concerning Y's first-order desire satisfaction. But surely X's desire for
Y's *second*-order desire satisfaction plays a role in X's caring for Y?

Lehrer and Wagner, in their treatment of epistemic respect,
distinguish respect for another as a judge of some matter concerning the world (call that *level-one respect*), from respect for another as
a judge of other people's epistemic worthiness (call that *level-two
respect*). For example, someone might invest tremendous epistemic
respect in Einstein when it comes to judgements about the physical, but give him a relatively low weighting when it comes to his
judgements of the trustworthiness of other physicists. (Apparently
Infield, who co-authored an introduction to physics with Einstein,
suffered directly from this phenomenon. Despite—or maybe because of—the fact that Einstein wrote him glowing references, he
couldn't land a decent job.) We can clearly iterate the ascent here.
At some level, Lehrer and Wagner argue, the weights will be the
same for two adjacent levels, and in their multi-levelled theory
they investigate the conditions under which stable consensus opinions (limiting probabilities) emerge.

In the case of genuinely *caring* about others, it is not so obvious
that we can sustain a *rational* distinction between the levels. It is, of
course, conceivable that Romeo desires Juliet's first-order desires
be satisfied, but does not care at all about her second-order desires.
That might occur where the latter diverge sharply from his own
second-order desires—say, where Juliet loves a Capulet whom
Romeo loathes. (Loathing generates its own problems, to which
I return below.) If the idea that caring goes hand in hand with a
desire for desire satisfaction is right, then to the extent that Romeo
genuinely cares about Juliet, he must care about her desire satisfaction quite generally. He must take seriously the whole gamut of her
desires, including her desires concerning desire satisfaction itself.

There is no compelling reason to restrict his caring about Juliet to caring about her first-order desire satisfaction alone.

This view gains support from the considerations in favour of Frankfurt's thesis that it is one's second-order desires which define one's identity. It is one's deep desires which are constitutive of one's *deep self* (Susan Wolf's apt phrase). So caring about *Juliet* is surely bound up with desiring her deep desire satisfaction, not just her superficial desire satisfaction. So caring requires, quite generally, higher-order desires which can be regarded as *reflexive*—desires which range over desires which *include those very desires*. Allowing higher-order desires to be reflexive in this way in no way undermines their role in correcting first-order desires. It simply opens up the possibility of using those desires to *refine themselves*.

4.5 Convergence in Higher-Order Desires

Any desires can be revised in the light of one's own higher-order desires, including those higher-order desires themselves. If Romeo cares about Juliet's desire satisfaction, and she cares about the Nurse's, then *ipso facto* Romeo has a reason to care about the Nurse's too. If he doesn't do so, then the way in which Romeo distributes his cares is in tension with his overall distribution of care—i.e. with itself. The same goes for each of the others. In other words, when $CC \neq C$, we know that C is not internally harmonious. The initial distribution of higher-order desires recommends that it itself be revised—and by what, if not by itself?

Consider C_1: if all revise, what we get is a new set of second-order desires (see table 4.6):

$$C_2 = (C_1)^2 = C_1 C_1.$$

Romeo's desire for the Nurse's desire satisfaction is positive in C_2, and his desire for his own desire satisfaction has shrunk. C_2 is in tension with both C_1 and with itself, and revision is again self-recommended. This can be done in one of two ways. Each person could use their original desires in C_1 to update C_2 to C_3 ($C_3 = C_1 C_2$), and repeat to obtain C_4 ($C_4 = C_1 C_3$). Call this procedure (for reasons that will become obvious) the *slow method of desire*

TABLE 4.6.   *Revised higher-order desires*: $C_2 = C_1 C_1$

	Romeo	Juliet	Nurse	Lady Capulet
Romeo	0.58	0.36	0.06	0
Juliet	0.36	0.36	0.26	0.02
Nurse	0.03	0.14	0.66	0.17
Lady Capulet	0.03	0.14	0.02	0.81

revision. Under favourable conditions this sequence will converge to an agent-neutral desire matrix C_∞, a harmonious refinement of the original collection of higher-order desires. The entry in column i in matrix C_∞ is the degree to which all would end up desiring the desire satisfaction of person i if all revised their second-order desires in the light of those very second-order desires.

There is, however, something philosophically unsatisfactory about the slow method of desire revision. Suppose all revise their initial desires (C_1) in the light of those desires, so that their new higher-order desires are represented by the matrix C_2. If C_2, like its predecessor, is not harmonious, then it recommends that it be revised, but surely it should be revised by *itself*, rather than by the old discarded desires. Thus we should move to $C_2 C_2 (= (C_1)^4)$. This procedure can be repeated to obtain $C_3 C_3 (= (C_1)^{16})$. Call this the *fast desire revision method*.

Quite generally, if the slow method converges to an agent-neutral matrix, so too does the fast method, and they yield the same limit C_∞. So it seems we don't have to choose between them. Later we will identify cases in which the slow and fast methods diverge. Then we do have to choose, and the philosophical superiority of the fast method is relevant.

The limiting higher-order desires can be used to refine the base-desire matrix D_1. The result is, of course, the limiting desire matrix: $C_\infty D_1 = C_\infty$. If, as in this case, the ideal first-order desires coincide perfectly, in an agent-neutral manner, then the resulting agent-neutral evaluation D_∞ is naturally identified with real value itself. Value is thus, again, what all would agree on valuing in the limit as desires are perfectly refined by those very desires.

4.6 Instant Refinement

Suppose that you are given all the initial higher-order desires (call them C_I). Suppose, further, that these do undergird a coherent set of ideally refined desires. Any candidate for ideal higher-order desires—dub them C^{Id}—clearly must be internally coherent. That is to say, revising the ideal desires by those very desires will leave them unchanged: $C^{Id}C^{Id} = C^{Id}$. But, further, C^{Id} must cohere with the initial higher-order desires which undergird it. Just as:

ideal second order-desires × initial first-order desires = ideal first-order desires

$$C^{Id}D_I = D_\infty,$$

so too we must have:

ideal higher-order desires × initial higher-order desires = ideal higher-order desires

$$C^{Id}C_I = C^{Id}.$$

That is to say, C^{Id} must also yield *itself* when it is used to refine, in one step, the original desires.

Coherence constraint on ideal higher-order desires

$$C^{Id} = C^{Id}C_I$$

So we know that if there is a coherent set of ideal higher-order desires to be gleaned from the initial higher-order desires, it will satisfy this coherence constraint. A result in the theory of Markov Chains guarantees two things. First, the limiting matrix C_∞, if there is one, satisfies this coherence constraint on the ideal-desire matrix (Kemeny and Snell, 1967: 70 ff.). Second, if the limiting matrix is agent-neutral (all the rows are the same), then there is one and only one matrix that satisfies this coherence constraint. This means that where we get convergence to agent-neutral higher-order desires, those limiting desires uniquely satisfy the coherence constraint on ideal desires. Thus *ideal* desires and *limiting* desires will be one and the same.

Under suitable conditions, then, there is a unique set of ideal higher-order desires, and those coincide with the limiting desires arrived at by both the slow and the fast methods of desire revision. These ideal higher-order desires can be used to refine initial first-order desires to obtain ideal first-order desires in one step.

Four different procedures for revising desires thus yield the same set of ideal, agent-neutral first-order desires—given suitable conditions. But what are 'suitable conditions' for agent-neutral value to emerge from agent-relative desire?

4.7 Connectedness Guarantees Agent-Neutrality

Convergence to agent-neutral values depends on the initial shape of the web of second-order desires. As it turns out, there is a qualitative, logically weak, but intuitively very attractive sufficient condition for convergence to agent-neutrality.

Consider the graph associated with a given higher-order desire matrix (fig. 4.2). Let us say that X is connected to Y if X cares for someone A, who in turn cares for B, who in turn ... cares for C (and so on), who cares for Y. A sufficient condition for convergence to agent-neutral values is that any two individuals are connected in this way through a chain of care, and that at least one individual cares about his own desire satisfaction. We can put this slightly differently: that there is a chain of connectedness which embraces the whole community, and that at least one individual cares about himself. This condition—dub it *connectedness*—is clearly satisfied in the example above. That connectedness is a weak condition is illustrated by the situation shown in table 4.7. The graph for this has fairly simple structure (fig. 4.2). The agent-neutral desire

TABLE 4.7. *Minimal care for others*

	Romeo	Juliet	Nurse	Lady Capulet
Romeo	0.999	0.001	0	0
Juliet	0	0.999	0.001	0
Nurse	0	0	0.999	0.001
Lady Capulet	0.01	0	0	0.999

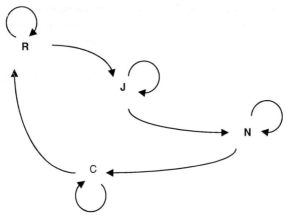

FIG. 4.2   *Minimal care for others*

matrix that this converges to is the same as in the previous case: namely, the one in which equal weight is assigned to all. This matrix is the limit of any connected higher-order desire matrix in which the columns, like the rows, sum to one.

This last fact has an interesting consequence. Let's say that X and Y *reciprocate care* just in case $c_{XY} = c_{YX}$. That is to say, each one invests the same amount of care in another as the other invests in the one. A reciprocating world is one in which all carers reciprocate care. The ith row will thus be identical to the ith column, for every i. Since the rows sum to 1, the columns will also sum to 1. In a connected, reciprocating world, where n is the total number of individuals, the limiting weight for each carer will be the same: $1/n$. Each one will thus count for one in deriving value from desire satisfaction. This limiting desire matrix is an *equalizer.*

More generally, let us say that a connected higher-order desire matrix is *balanced* if the columns as well as the rows sum to one. Reciprocating matrices are obviously balanced, but there are clearly others. For a matrix to be balanced, each person is the object of the same amount of total care as any other. A balanced, connected care matrix will also converge to an equalizer. These observations vindicate an earlier remark about resilience. Provided that in the initial higher-order desire matrix each individual attracts the same overall care from members of the connected community at large, the limiting matrix distributes value evenly over base-desire satisfaction. And the more balanced the original web is, the closer in general the limit matrix will be to the equalizer.

4.8 The Nature of this Ideal

There is a problem for this account which is an instance of a deeper problem with the general merit connection. If the good is what merits desire, then, ideally, all our desires should converge. They should all be proportional to value, so they should all line up together. Ideally, our desires should be as agent-neutral as the agent-neutral values themselves. But this seems not just too demanding, it seems positively undesirable. Should Romeo really care no more for Juliet's desire-satisfaction than for that of the Nurse? Should his peculiar and partial love for Juliet be refined away into a general benevolence? And should this happen *ideally* even if everyone else remains highly partial?

The idealist theory presented here has at least a partial answer to this worry. The limiting desires—both higher-order and first-order—are *ideals*. They are the desires the community would arrive at if *each* were to refine his desires while others simultaneously refine theirs. The ideal is heavily conditionalized. The ideal desires are not desires which each has an *unconditional* obligation, or even an unconditional reason, to adopt unilaterally, but only conditional upon others refining their desires.

What we have here is a familiar phenomenon of group action. Suppose something is the best thing for a group of individuals to do—say, to push a car to the top of the hill—and suppose this can be achieved only if everyone does their bit. Suppose not everyone else is going to push. Even though it is best for the *group* to push, it does not follow that the best thing for any one individual to do is to push. It would be silly for you to fruitlessly push the car, for example, while everyone else stands around chatting. The best thing for you to do is to push *provided* everyone else is pushing similarly; it may be best for all to revise their desires to the ideal limit. So, if all the others are revising their desires, then it would be best for me to revise also. But typically people do not in fact revise their desires. And in case they don't, there is no reason for one or two individuals to unilaterally revise while the rest stick with their original desires.

To see why unilateral revision may in fact be bad, consider the first scenario. Suppose Romeo alone repeatedly refines his desires in the light of his own desires, while the others stick firmly to their initial desires. Romeo's higher-order desires will not be drawn to the agent-neutral equalizing matrix, but to that shown in table 4.8. The self-centred Lady Capulet draws Romeo further into her self-evaluation, while Romeo's value plummets.

If Romeo and Juliet revise, while the others don't, then both are drawn gradually into Lady Capulet's desire structure. The limiting matrix under this partial revision will still be agent-relative, and Romeo and Juliet will have moved *further* from the ideal (under-girded by the original desires) rather than closer. The ideal desires that the new agent-neutral matrix generates are quite different from the equalizer which emerges from the original desires. It is skewed unpleasantly in Lady Capulet's favour. Thus it is not necessarily better for one individual to revise unless the others do likewise, and in fact it may make things (intuitively) worse. If the others don't revise, then if Romeo fails to stick to his original desires, his value will go down. The ideal is thus primarily a *group* ideal, and individuals should move towards it only if other individuals are doing likewise.

This places at least some limitation on the merit connection—the principle that ideally one should desire things just to the extent that they are valuable. If value is undergirded by desire (as the idealist maintains), then changes in desire will often change the distribution of value. So, if the idealist is right, one person cannot normally revise his desires unilaterally to match actual value without that *changing* the actual value of things, making his own desires possibly further from actual value at the end of the process.

TABLE 4.8.   *Romeo alone revises*

	Romeo	Juliet	Nurse	Lady Capulet
Romeo	0.055	0.173	0.239	0.532

Only if all co-ordinate their changes will the values remain intact. So the idealist need not necessarily endorse conforming one's desires to the values.

Still, there is a residual worry here. The peculiar and partial love which Juliet has for Romeo does not seem to be something she should strive to eliminate even if others are bringing their partial desires into line with real value. It seems that there is legitimate agent-relativity even in the desires of the most refined. We will return to this issue, a pressing one for the realist, in the final chapter.

4.9 The Attractions of Refinement Idealism

This version of dispositional idealism has, then, answered Smith's question:

Is it plausible to suppose that there are some desires that all subjects would converge upon if they had desire sets that are maximally informed and coherent and unified? (Smith 2002: 343)

The answer is *yes* subject to the fairly modest constraint of connectedness. Furthermore, the account delivers some pretty interesting consequences.

First, the account delivers an appropriate connection between value and desire. It explains the magnetism not just of the apparent good (that much is explained by the experience conjecture) but also of the actual good. If all were to revise their desires consistently by allowing their own higher-order desires to guide them, then all desires would be gradually conformed to agent-neutral value. Agent-relative desires, under the rational pressure of those very desires, would converge on the agent-neutral good.

The valuable is what all would be led to desire in the limit if our desires were collectively, systematically, and thoroughly refined in the light of our very own desires—rendered completely 'coherent and unified'. Something approximating step-by-step revision, locally and at the early stages, actually happens in our negotiations with each other. I desire something. Then I learn that someone I care deeply about wants something different. I don't want her desires to go unsatisfied, so I desire to desire differently (and so does she). If our second-order desires are effective, we move closer together in our first-order desires, and typically closer to the ideal. Repeated revisions of our desires in the light of our own desires would draw all of our desires closer to real value.

While the account explains the magnetism, it does not exaggerate its strength. The magnetic field generated by the good is still a rather weak one. The account helps to explain why actual desires typically do not line up perfectly with value. The limiting desires constitute an ideal for the community of desirers, something their desires will move towards if all refine their first-order desires in the light of their higher-order desires. But first-order desires are often resistant to second-order desires. (Witness the recidivism rate for nicotine addicts who want to quit smoking.) And when others do not revise, the motive for me to revise is withdrawn. So there is no mystery as to why we don't all desire what is valuable. Desires remain highly agent-relative, and it is at least conditionally justifiable for an agent's desires to remain so—conditional upon others persisting with their agent-relative desires.

The account makes it intelligible how we have some epistemic access to value, while nevertheless allowing knowledge of value to go awry. Each person's first-order desires are highly perspectival, a rather inaccurate take on the overall shape of real agent-neutral value. Cognitive access to value can be gained by calculating what revision of desires would lead to in the limit, and one can have at least some idea of where that process would lead. But to gain perfect knowledge of value, one would need to know the first-order and higher-order desires of all, leaving more than enough room for error.

The account clearly delivers the result that not all of what is valuable is so independently of our desires. Desiring is clearly not always the appropriate response to antecedently given value. Value takes its shape from desire. Different desire sets can create different value distributions. The shape of desire gives shape to value.

One worry about the idealist enterprise is whether it can even get off first base. Suppose that you like swimming and I like skiing. On the basis of this the idealist might claim that the combination of your swimming and my skiing is *better than* the combination of your skiing and my swimming. But in so doing the idealist has apparently posited the relation of *better than* which transcends our desires, something *over and above* individual desirings. Idealism seeks to reach beyond the subjectivist's multitude of agent-relative desirings, to one overarching, agent-neutral distribution of value. But to take that step requires the assumption that individual desires *can* be forged into a single, agent-neutral distribution, and that already seems to give the game away to the realist.

The thesis of the supervenience of value on desire goes some way to answering this worry, for it spells out a precise sense in which value is strongly tied to desire. But the refinement account presented here goes somewhat further than the supervenience claim alone. If it is right, it shows how each and every desirer in the web is, in some sense, *already* committed to the one agent-neutral value distribution by the way in which his own purely agent-relative first-order and second-order desires mesh with everyone else's to give rise to ideal desires.

Finally, it's time to cash in a promissory note. We started with the simplifying assumption that the initial base desires are self-regarding. But that is not only a simplification, it is a kind of category error. Whether, or to what degree, one is self-regarding enters in at the level of *higher-order* desires, not at the level of first-order desires. And whatever shapes the 'initial' distribution of first-order desires, if they are out of harmony with higher-order desires, then coherence demands revision. Through revision one's higher-order desires concerning others inevitably reshape one's first-order desires. This is a reflection of the strongly Aristophanean aspect of the theory. Coherence demands that in caring for another one's desires become inextricably bound up with those of one's beloved.

This last observation raises some interesting possibilities, as well as some troubling questions. It suggests a way of characterizing egoism and altruism, partiality and impartiality, and it raises questions about how those conditions would, according to idealism, impact on the shape of value. These issues are the focus of the next chapter.

Perhaps a less informative theory than [*handwritten annotation*]

5 VALUE BEYOND DESIRE

THE theory of desire refinement presented in Chapter 4 unearthed a sufficient condition for desires to converge, under revision, to an agent-neutral limit: the condition of connectedness. What about patterns of desire which do not satisfy connectedness? Some converge, and the distribution to which they converge may be either agent-relative or agent-neutral. Other patterns of desire do not converge at all, either to an agent-neutral or to an agent-relative distribution. When non-connected patterns of desire do admit of agent-neutral limits, the limiting desires may not have anything like the shape one would expect real value to possess.

In this chapter I investigate what happens when certain patholo-gies of desire are systematically refined. The results aren't pretty. The conclusion to be drawn from these results is not, however, that there is nothing to be said for value idealism. There may still be something in the idea that value depends, in part, on the contingent likes and dislikes of desirers. Rather, the results suggest that there is a desire-independent *value residue*, one to which the pure idealist cannot appeal, but one which it seems necessary to invoke if de-sire-refinement is to converge on the good. That there is a value residue at the level of higher-order desires is pretty well undeniable. At the end of the chapter I raise the question of whether there is a value residue at the first-order level as well.

5.1 Egoism

The pure egoist loves himself alone. That is to say, he cares only about his own desire satisfaction. He invests a maximal degree of care in himself, and cares not one whit for anyone else. The pure egoist is a problem for us all, but he presents a special difficulty for a refinement theorist.

TABLE 5.1.   *Higher-order matrix for psychological egoism*: I

	Romeo	Juliet	Nurse	Lady Capulet
Romeo	1	0	0	0
Juliet	0	1	0	0
Nurse	0	0	1	0
Lady Capulet	0	0	0	1

Suppose that a very strong version of psychological egoism is true, and that everyone is a pure egoist. The initial distribution of higher-order desires, if psychological egoism is true, is simple (see table 5.1). The matrix has already been dubbed, with some poetic justice, the big 'I'. A pure egoist is never moved simply by the fact that others desire differently, since he doesn't care a fig about anybody else. A bunch of pure egoists who refine their base desires by their higher-order desires will thus not have to make any changes at all. There is a perfectly precise sense, then, in which egoists are necessarily *incorrigible*. There is no way they can correct their initial desires from within, even when they know and take into account what others desire. Formally, this is reflected by I's status as the *identity* matrix. Multiplying any matrix by **I** leaves everything unchanged. The process of revision thus leaves the egoists' desires the same.

$$D_2 = I \, D_1 = D_1$$
$$D_3 = I \, D_2 = I \, D_1 = D_1, \text{ etc.}$$

A community of pure egoists has already achieved a stable desire state at the higher order. No matter how often such egoists revise their higher-order desires by what they themselves desire, each ends up caring maximally about himself. This is so whether revision is slow or fast.

Slow method: $I^2 = II = I$,
$\qquad\qquad I^3 = II^2 = I \ldots$ etc.
Fast method: $I^4 = I^2 \, I^2 = I$,
$\qquad\qquad I^{16} = I^4 \, I^4 = I, \ldots$ etc.

The limiting desires are thus identical to those at the outset, and share their relativity. So, according to this account, *psychological egoism is incompatible with the emergence of agent-neutral value.*

Actually, this is not true, but it's *almost* true. In a thoroughly egoistic universe there will be agent-neutral limiting desires only on one special condition: that the original first-order desires are themselves agent-neutral. That is to say: for each state S every egoist desires S to exactly the same degree as do others. That's possible (consider a universe with just one person in it—God, say), but for a bunch of egoists it appears slightly paradoxical. It would be something of a miracle if pure egoists were to happen to agree on their base desires. We can state the result unconditionally this way: psychological egoism prevents the emergence of value from agent-relative desires. If, as some have argued, psychological egoism is a conceptual truth, then the emergence of real value from agent-relative desires is rendered impossible.

From the point of view of realism about value there is something attractive about this result. Unfortunately, even if psychological egoism is false (as it surely is), egoists and approximate egoists generate other, less desirable results. Consider the *egoist infiltrator*: Romeo is an egoist in an otherwise fairly normal caring community. That is, the caring relations are the same as in our original story except for the Romeo row (table 5.2). Every individual is connected to an egoist (namely, Romeo) who cares only about himself. There are limiting agent-neutral desires in this case. All higher-order caring gets concentrated on Romeo (table 5.3). This is a quite general result. If there is a single egoist who is cared for to some degree, no matter how minimally, by one who is otherwise well connected, in the limit that egoist infiltrator hogs all the weight. A single egoist's base desires will thus become the agent-neutral limiting desires for the whole community. (The corresponding state in the theory of Markov Chains is known as an 'absorber', a term which is rather apt in this application of the

TABLE 5.2. *The egoist infiltrator*

	Romeo	Juliet	Nurse	Lady Capulet
Romeo	1	0	0	0
Juliet	0.1	0.5	0.2	0.2
Nurse	0	0.1	0.8	0.1
Lady Capulet	0	0.1	0	0.9

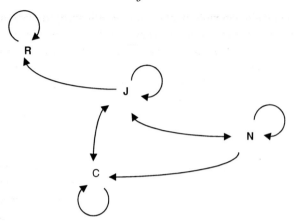

FIG. 5.1   *Romeo, the egoist infiltrator*

theory (Kemeny and Snell 1967: 35). The self-absorbed becomes an absorber of all.)

The idea that everyone's will should conform to some one person's will is unacceptable with the exception of one possible case – God. The refinement model suggests a way of modelling a Divine Command theory of value. If there is One to whom everyone is connected (even though not everyone cares for the One), and the One places maximal weight on himself, then *ipso facto* the One's desires become the ideal agent-neutral desires, and everyone else should adjust their own desires to accord with the One's. Now, there is a rationale for allowing a certain One's desires to prescribe desire generally, a rationale that is missing in the case of others. It is natural to think of God as *objectively* the most important person around. God is, quite simply, the Best, possessing every good-making feature to the max, and so it is entirely appropriate for

TABLE 5.3.   *The limiting distribution for the egoist infiltrator*

	Romeo	Juliet	Nurse	Lady Capulet
Romeo	I	o	o	o
Juliet	I	o	o	o
Nurse	I	o	o	o
Lady Capulet	I	o	o	o

God (being all-benevolent, all-knowing, all-wise) to place maximal weight on his own desire satisfaction. It is also appropriate for others to care, at least to some extent, about God's desire satisfaction. Thereby God's *will* (viz. God's second-order desires) become mandatory for all, and that doesn't seem too bad.

Euthyphro is lurking here, just below the surface. The justification for allowing God's will to legislate for all involves the assumption that God is the Best. That presupposes a previously given Good to which God's second-order desires and first-order desires are appropriately responsive—and that, of course, is incompatible with a Divine Command theory. In God's case it is natural to assume that the weight he places on his own desire satisfaction is acceptable because his first-order desires already embody a totally agent-neutral regard for overall desire satisfaction. That is to say, God's first-order desires would never need refining, because they already reflect what's valuable. So skewing the consensus valuation in favour of God's desires would have no untoward deleterious effects. Clearly this justification for God's pre-eminence, involving as it does an independently given objective Good, is incompatible with the basic thrust of the idealist's programme.

Returning to our story, Romeo is not at all like God. He is just a self-centred brat who has managed to inveigle Juliet into caring for him. And given Juliet's connectedness, that's all it takes for Romeo's self-absorption to absorb all value.

Note that this throws light on a familiar feature of group dynamics. A rampant egoist can sometimes garner a small amount of support from one or two members of a well-connected and otherwise reasonable group. Over time the egoist will often drag consensus desires closer to his own desires, which of course never change in the light of other people's desires. The more time, the closer the consensus will come to the egoist's original base desires. Intuitively, the resulting desires do not necessarily track real value. What we really want to say here is that there are limits on how much people should care for themselves. In particular, no one should give *maximal* weight to himself. Or, if he does, his higher-order desires should be excluded from the limiting desires. In other words, only given an independent constraint on higher-order desire (e.g. the prohibition on relentless self-absorption) will limiting desires approach real value. But this means that the idealist project

cannot quite meet its obligation. Real value cannot quite be
accounted for simply in terms of desires. There is a desire-
independent constraint to which desires must answer.

What happens if there is more than one egoist in an otherwise
reasonably connected community? Since one egoist absorbs all the
care in the limit, does that suggest that some kind of contradiction
follows from the existence of two egoists? Obviously that can't be
right. Consider fig. 5.2. An egoist is like a black hole in desire space.
All the arrows of desire go in, none come out. Recall that in a chain
of connections the arrows of desire all go one way. Thus there is no
chain that embraces two egoists. Consequently the limit theorem
does not apply. Further, it is clear that an egoist's self-concern can
never be ameliorated, even when he is connected through the cares
of others. Nothing impacts on an egoist. Consider a realization of
this graph (table 5.4). In this case the limiting desires are agent-
relative (see table 5.5). In the limit non-egoists become consumed
by concern that the egoists in the community get what they want,
but their concern will be split in ways that reflect their initial
distribution of concern for the egoists. Thus a single egoist in a
connected community would thoroughly skew the distribution of
limiting agent-neutral desires, and several egoists destroy the possibility of agent-neutral ideal desires altogether. Refinement in the
presence of egoists has two unfortunate consequences. First, if
there are a number of egoists, they will block the emergence of
agent-neutral limiting desires. And even when they don't, revision

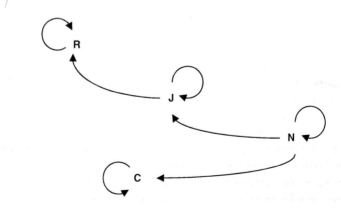

FIG. 5.2   *A pair of egoists*

TABLE 5.4. *A pair of egoists*

	Romeo	Juliet	Nurse	Lady Capulet
Romeo	1	0	0	0
Juliet	0.05	0.9	0.05	0
Nurse	0	0.05	0.9	0.05
Lady Capulet	0	0	0	1

TABLE 5.5. *Limiting desires for a pair of egoists*

	Romeo	Juliet	Nurse	Lady Capulet
Romeo	1	0	0	0
Juliet	0.67	0	0	0.33
Nurse	0.33	0	0	0.67
Lady Capulet	0	0	0	1

leads to limiting desires that are intuitively undesirable. The pure egoist should be marginalized rather than rewarded by hogging the community's concern.

5.2 Altruism

Egoists typically block the emergence of agent-neutral valuing. What about that other extreme of partiality—altruism? We are not concerned here with the moderate altruist—one who cares about others but who also invests in his own base-desire satisfaction. That, I imagine, is the standard case. Rather we are interested in ~~pure altruists~~, those who invest all their care in others, and in particular one kind of pure altruist—*obsessive* altruists, those who invest all their care in just one other (see fig. 5.3). This graph can be realized in only one way (table 5.6).

Let the matrix be **A**. What happens as these pure altruists revise? Consider first the slow method of updating. Romeo cares exclusively about Juliet. But when he sees that she cares exclusively about the Nurse, he will update. He will shift to caring exclusively about the Nurse. Quite generally, multiplication by **A** will move the 1 one

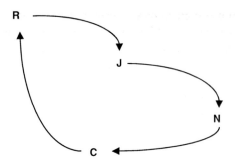

FIG. 5.3 *Pure obsessive altruists*

TABLE 5.6. *Pure obsessive altruists*

	Romeo	Juliet	Nurse	Lady Capulet
Romeo	O	I	O	O
Juliet	O	O	I	O
Nurse	O	O	O	I
Lady Capulet	I	O	O	O

column to the right (or to the extreme left if it is already furthest to the right). So if we keep multiplying by **A** we will cycle through until we reach egoism:

$$\mathbf{A}^4 = \mathbf{AAAA} = \mathbf{I}$$

Consequently, one further multiplication by **A** will return us to our starting-point:

$$\mathbf{A}^5 = \mathbf{AA}^4 = \mathbf{AI} = \mathbf{A}$$

This process cycles indefinitely, and there will be no limiting matrix.

There is something intuitively unsatisfactory about the slow method which this case brings to light. Suppose everyone revises their higher-order desires in the light of their own higher-order desires. Then they exhibit $\mathbf{A}^2$. This is also an unstable pure obsessive altruism. So they should revise again. But why should they use their *original* desires (**A**) rather than their updated desires ($\mathbf{A}^2$)? If they were to use their updated desires, they would revise directly to A^4. As already noted, A^4 is just the pure egoists' matrix **I**. If they revise by their newly embraced egoism, they will of course remain egoists. Fast revision will thus be stable after all, and the limiting matrix is pure egoism! If each one cares maximally about someone else, and for each there is a circle of care leading back to its starting-point, then eventually each will find she should care maximally about herself, and once she takes that on board, she can't be budged from it.

Either way, whether we use the fast or the slow method, we have the same result as far as agent-neutral limiting desires go: none emerge. Pure altruism can thus be just as inimical to the emergence of real value as pure egoism.

Unlike pure egoism, however, pure altruism need not block the emergence of value, because there are ways of being purely altruistic which are not obsessive. The pure egoist is necessarily obsessed with just one individual—he has no choice as regards whom to direct his egoism towards—but there is more scope for the pure altruist, because there are so many more others. Consider a very small change to the pure altruism matrix, one in which each person invests most of their concern in one other, but branches out into caring a little for some third person (table 5.7). Note that this matrix closely resembles *minimal concern for others*. The entries are all shifted one place to the right. While the matrix is minimally different from that of both pure altruism and minimal concern for others, the graph is rather more interesting than either (fig. 5.4). Interestingly, this matrix, like that of *minimal concern for others*, converges to the equalizing matrix. If everyone were to revise their desires systematically in the light of their higher-order desires, then all would end up according each other equal weight.

TABLE 5.7.   *Pure altruists branch*

	Romeo	Juliet	Nurse	Lady Capulet
Romeo	0	0.999	0.001	0
Juliet	0	0	0.999	0.001
Nurse	0.001	0	0	0.999
Lady Capulet	0.999	0.001	0	0

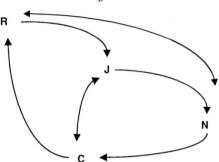

F IG. 5.4 *Pure altruists branch*

What this shows is that it is not so much caring about oneself or about others that generates endemic agent-relativity. Rather, it is focusing one's initial cares too narrowly, to the point of obsession, either on oneself or another. A small amount of diversity in the portfolio of desire goes a long way to ensuring agent-neutrality in the limit.

5.3   Infatuation

It is a notorious fact that those in the early throes of passionate love live in a world all of their own. The infatuated exist only for each other. Suppose Romeo and Juliet are infatuated with each other. Romeo and Juliet care only about Juliet and Romeo, but they are cared for by members of an otherwise connected community (fig. 5.5). What are the limiting desires of this set? Think of Romeo and Juliet as a *joint identity, a single unit* (Solomon 1981). Then they function just like the egoist who is otherwise connected. The whirlpool of their mutual obsession will inexorably suck in all the surrounding desirers, concentrating all care and concern in the community on the two of them. It will be distributed over them exactly in proportion to the weight that they put on each other.

Egoism is an extreme form of partiality, one which an obsessive altruist (an altruist obsessed with exactly one other person) shares. But an infatuation with another may be just as destructive of

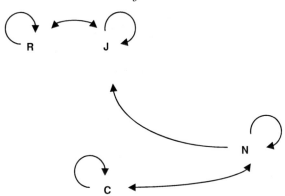

FIG. 5.5 *Romeo and Juliet are infatuated*

limiting desires as egoism and obsessive altruism. By contrast, our branching altruists are not exactly *good* impartialists, but at least they have moved a step in that direction.

5.4 Partiality

What exactly is partiality? One might characterize the impartialist as the one who cares equally for everyone. But that builds in the strongly egalitarian assumption that everyone merits equal concern—hardly something the value idealist can begin with.

Let's say that an *impartialist* is someone who cares to *some* degree about each being who possesses a non-zero weighting in the ideal limiting desire matrix. *Impartialism* holds if everyone is an impartialist. A *strict* impartialist is one who accords to each *exactly* the degree of concern that is mandated by *ideal* higher-order desires. A strict impartialist cares about each person *precisely* to the same degree as the ideal limiting desires mandate. *Thoroughgoing impartialism* obtains if *everyone* is a strict impartialist. That is, everyone cares about everyone exactly to the degree mandated by the limiting higher-order desires.

Thoroughgoing impartialism is stable. Since everyone's cares coincide with the limiting cares, everyone cares exactly to the same degree about everyone else, the degree which each ideally merits. So they already all agree, and any matrix representing thoroughgoing impartialism is its own limit.

Could there be strict impartialists in an otherwise partial community? You might be sceptical about that. For this implies that some but not all rows are identical to the limiting desires. To see that this really is possible consider table 5.8 in which Romeo starts off as an egalitarian, although no one else is. This is a balanced matrix (the columns as well as the rows sum to one), and it satisfies connectedness. Consequently, it converges to an equalizer matrix, and as it happens, in the limit everyone ideally revises to Romeo's initial egalitarian distribution.

So far, so good. Suppose, however, that Romeo cares for everyone, but this time he is ostracized by the others, who care nothing at all for him, while they all care for each other (fig. 5.6).

This graph can be realized in a number of ways, but let's suppose that Romeo, an apparent *paragon* of impartiality, cares equally for all, while the others care mostly for themselves, nothing for poor Romeo, and otherwise divide their affections equally (table 5.9). Note that Romeo is now a shining star rather than a black hole. All the arrows of care flow out, none flow in. Still, the graph satisfies connectedness, and so the matrix converges. But what it converges to is most unsatisfactory (table 5.10). Romeo's limiting weight is thus zero. In the limit, no one would care about him, even Romeo himself. All the others have non-zero limits. By completely discounting Romeo from the start, the others end up hogging all the limiting care. What is intuitively worse, because the others hog the limiting care, it is *they*, rather than Romeo, who are judged impartial *at the outset*, for each accords some care to each of those who ideally should attract care. By contrast, at the outset Romeo

TABLE 5.8. *One egalitarian*

	Romeo	Juliet	Nurse	Lady Capulet
Romeo	0.25	0.25	0.25	0.25
Juliet	0.4	0.5	0	0.1
Nurse	0.25	0.1	0.5	0.15
Lady Capulet	0.1	0.15	0.25	0.5

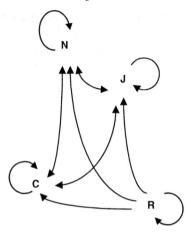

FIG. 5.6   *Ostracized egalitarian*

TABLE 5.9.   *The ostracized egalitarian*

	Romeo	Juliet	Nurse	Lady Capulet
Romeo	0.25	0.25	0.25	0.25
Juliet	0	0.8	0.1	0.1
Nurse	0	0.1	0.8	0.1
Lady Capulet	0	0.1	0.1	0.8

TABLE 5.10.   *Limiting desires: ostracized egalitarian*

	Romeo	Juliet	Nurse	Lady Capulet
Romeo	0	0.33	0.33	0.33
Juliet	0	0.33	0.33	0.33
Nurse	0	0.33	0.33	0.33
Lady Capulet	0	0.33	0.33	0.33

lacks impartiality. Agent-neutral ideal desires emerge, but Romeo's desire satisfaction turns out to be worthless.

In order to avoid this kind of unpalatable result, what we require is a constraint on higher-order desires, one which does not itself arise out of those very desires. Something like the following would do the job: anyone who cares about some members of an otherwise mutually caring community merits some reciprocal care. This would ensure that no one, apart from a ruthless egoist, could be legitimately discounted. But it need hardly be added that such a constraint doesn't sit happily with the pure idealist's enterprise, in so far as the idealist takes *every* aspect of value to be reducible to desire.

5.5 Hatred

People care for some and are indifferent to others. Some entries in the initial higher-order desire matrix are positive, and some are zero. But these are not the only two possibilities. Lady Capulet, a regular Capulet, neither cares for Montagues, nor is indifferent to them. She *hates* the Montagues. For her, Romeo's happiness *detracts* from the overall desirability of a state of affairs, and his unhappiness is a positive boon. The more she hates Romeo, the more Romeo's happiness will detract from, and his unhappiness enhance, her evaluation of a state of affairs. There is no room in the present model for hatred, for desiring that another's desires not be satisfied.

This is partly a consequence of the account's origins. The Lehrer–Wagner theory of consensus by aggregation draws its inspiration from the theorems of Markov Chain theory. In a Markov Chain the matrix entries are transition probabilities between kinds. The transition probability (the matrix entry in the ith row and jth column is the conditional probability that the system will go into state i from state j. Probabilities, including conditional probabilities, are always positive. So in the original mathematical apparatus negative weights do not appear. The initial application of the apparatus to philosophical problems was to *epistemic respect*. Lehrer and Wagner were interested in the trust people invest in others as sources of information. Zero respect is accorded those whose opinion is worthless—an opinion that is no better than some randomizing device. But why couldn't someone be regarded as *worse* than useless? This is Lehrer and Wagner's response:

It may have occurred to a reader to wonder why a negative weight could not be assigned to a person. One answer is that a person cannot be worse than worthless as a guide to truth. Suppose that a person is a perfectly reliable counter-inductive guide to the truth, however, in the sense that when a person assigns a probability of p to some hypothesis, the opposite probability 1 − p is the correct probability to be assigned.... we allow treating the person as his... mirror opposite and assigning a positive weight. To avoid problems arising with negative values the person may be treated as though he assigned the value 1 − p and be assigned a positive weight. (Lehrer and Wagner 1981: 21)

Negative values are definitely a problem when dealing with probabilities. So the suggestion is that those whose opinions merit less than no respect can be regarded as *reverse* indicators, and the 'reverse' probabilities are given positive respect. But even if this works in the epistemic case, nothing comparable applies in the case of utilities. For a start, there is no problem with negative utilities, and indeed it seems necessary to incorporate them to represent the effects of hate. That Romeo gets what he desires is a source of desire satisfaction for Juliet, but of dissatisfaction for Lady Capulet. If Lady Capulet puts a negative weight on Romeo, her desire satisfaction in any state in which Romeo gets what he wants is reduced, even while that enhances Juliet's satisfaction. Conversely, should Romeo be miserable, that would enhance the overall desirability of the state for Lady Capulet, and detract from it for Juliet. So it should be clear that an accurate representation of hatred would involve negative weights. And then we must also countenance negative values for first-order desires as well. For when we revise a first-order desire matrix by a higher-order matrix involving negative values, we can clearly end up with a new set of first-order desires that will also involve negative values.

Once we allow negative weights, we have to reconsider normalization. What does it mean to say that the entries in the matrix represent proportions of one's care? Suppose Lady Capulet loathes Romeo. Is it possible, for example, for her hatred to take a negative value, like −1? If so, and if weights have to sum to one, does she have to compensate by, say, assigning + 2 to herself? For if she does, then she will more than skew the weights in her own favour. Could Romeo retaliate by hating her to a negative degree, say − 2, and then compensate for this negative quantity by loving himself to degree + 3? But why should they have to compensate for their hatred? Some people are full of hate without any counterbalancing love to make up for it. They may hate everyone, including themselves.

Recall the motivation for requiring that the weights sum to one. Each person divides up her total caring resources amongst the members of the group. The weighted measure gives the proportion of caring she invests in each individual. But negative and positive desires both take up a *proportion* of a person's total space of desire. For each person, proportions of that total space must sum to one. A natural idea, then, is that each chunk of caring is a proportion of total caring, and that it may be either negative caring or positive caring. You can invest all your care in love, or all of it in hatred, or you can have a mixture of the two. To normalize an arbitrary numerical distribution involving negative weights, we can use what I'll call *absolute normalization*. For each row, sum the absolute values of the entries, and then divide each entry in that row by the total. The absolute values of the entries of a row will then sum to 1.

For example, suppose Romeo and Juliet love each other as before, and each cares somewhat for one of the others. Further, we have what might be called *positive connectedness*: this holds just in case, when you delete all negative desires and replace them with indifference, you have a web which is connected in the old sense. Both Lady Capulet and the Nurse hate Romeo, and in fig. 5.7 hatred is depicted by a shaded arrow.

Consider the realization of this web shown in table 5.11, noting that it is absolutely normalized. We can generalize revision to accommodate hatred. To revise matrix **B** by care-matrix **A**, multiply **B** by **A** and then carry out absolute normalization. This yields

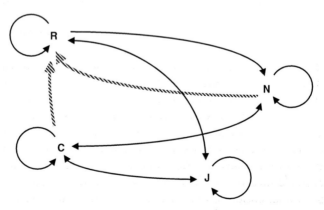

FIG. 5.7   *Two hate Romeo*

TABLE 5.11. *Two hate Romeo*

	Romeo	Juliet	Nurse	Lady Capulet
Romeo	0.5	0.4	0.1	0
Juliet	0.4	0.5	0	0.1
Nurse	−0.2	0.2	0.5	0.1
Lady Capulet	−0.1	0.1	0.1	0.7

TABLE 5.12. *Limiting higher-order desires: two hate Romeo*

	Romeo	Juliet	Nurse	Lady Capulet
Romeo	− 0.17	0.12	0.19	0.52
Juliet	− 0.17	0.12	0.19	0.52
Nurse	− 0.17	0.12	0.19	0.52
Lady Capulet	− 0.17	0.12	0.19	0.52

TABLE 5.13. *Base desires for two hate Romeo*

	S_1	S_2	S_3	S_4	S_5	S_6	S_7	S_8
Romeo	− 1	0	1	1	1	− 1	1	1
Juliet	1	1	1	1	0	− 1	1	− 1
Nurse	1	1	1	1	0	− 1	− 1	− 1
Lady Capulet	1	1	1	0	0	− 1	− 1	− 1

the original revision procedure (simply multiplying by **A**) as a limiting case, for in the absence of hatred **AB** is automatically normalized. What is the impact of hatred on the emergence of real value?

Hatred introduces some rather unpleasant outcomes. For example, in the case where two hate Romeo, he ends up, unsurprisingly, with a negative weight overall (table 5.12). Suppose we have the following sample of states: 1 represents strong base-desire satisfaction (happiness, say) and −1 strong base-desire dissatisfaction (misery, say). As before, the rows can also be taken to give the strength of the relevant agent's first-order desire for the relevant state (table 5.13). You might wonder why I have arranged the states in this rather curious order. To see this, multiply the vector by the columns, thus obtaining the agent-neutral values of the states (table 5.14). The ordering is thus from best to worst. The best state is the one in which Romeo is miserable and the others are happy. The worst is the one in which Romeo is happy and the others are miserable. The state in which everyone has their base desires satisfied is only moderately good, and the state in which the two lovers are happy and the two haters are miserable is nearly as bad as it gets.

Consider a situation in which there is a fair amount of mutual caring, but in which Romeo and Lady Capulet hate each other (table 5.15). One might have thought that Lady Capulet's greater hatred for Romeo would skew limiting higher-order desires against Romeo. Very surprisingly, this is not the case. The limiting higher-order desires are as shown in table 5.16. Despite being the object of the most hate, Romeo emerges with the greatest agent-neutral weight, more even than Juliet, who initially is the object of universal love. The reason is that Juliet, by virtue of her love for Romeo, redirects much of the bulk of the community's care in Romeo's direction.

One person's *reductio* is another's interesting consequence. As such, these either unpalatable or else interesting consequences of the refinement model of value may or may not be taken to defeat the theory. On the one hand, these cases show that desires, refined

TABLE 5.14. *Limiting desires: two hate Romeo*

	S_1	S_2	S_3	S_4	S_5	S_6	S_7	S_8
Romeo	1	0.82	0.65	0.13	− 0.17	− 0.65	− 0.76	− 1
Juliet	1	0.82	0.65	0.13	− 0.17	− 0.65	− 0.76	− 1
Nurse	1	0.82	0.65	0.13	− 0.17	− 0.65	− 0.76	− 1
Lady Capulet	1	0.82	0.65	0.13	− 0.17	− 0.65	− 0.76	− 1

TABLE 5.15. *Two hate each other*

	Romeo	Juliet	Nurse	Lady Capulet
Romeo	0.5	0.4	0	− 0.1
Juliet	0.4	0.5	0.1	0
Nurse	0	0.2	0.5	0.3
Lady Capulet	− 0.2	0.3	0	0.5

TABLE 5.16. *Limiting higher-order desires: two hate each other*

	Romeo	Juliet	Nurse	Lady Capulet
Romeo	0.43	0.42	0.10	− 0.05
Juliet	0.43	0.42	0.10	− 0.05
Nurse	0.43	0.42	0.10	− 0.05
Lady Capulet	0.43	0.42	0.10	− 0.05

to eliminate incoherences, do not always yield what one would expect of real value. On the other, they might be taken to illustrate the real effects of hatred on value—but such effects can be taken to be pernicious only if something other than desire undergirds value.

These results, whether they are interpreted as favouring or undermining the desire refinement theory of value, are somewhat atypical. The more typical effect of hatred is that connectedness is no longer sufficient for convergence to agent-neutral values. In fact it does not even guarantee convergence to limiting agent-*relative* desires. This is so whether we define connectedness narrowly (counting only the darts of love) or broadly (including the poison-tipped arrows of hatred). Typically, negative weights cycle through the community endlessly, preventing the stabilization of desire. Hatred thus not only typically blocks the refinement of desires into agent-neutral values, it even blocks the emergence of stable, agent-*relative* valuing. In this respect hateful desires are even worse than egoistic desires.

Viewing the account sympathetically, one could regard this consequence as an accurate reflection of the destructiveness of hatred. Less sympathetically, however, one could regard it as further evidence that for a desire refinement account to work, there must be certain constraints on desiring, constraints which cannot be extracted from desire alone. In particular, hatred must be purged if base desires are to be refined into the pure gold of value.

5.6 Perversity

Pathological higher-order desires typically produce disastrous limiting desires under refinement. If higher-order desires alone

can be pathological, then any pattern of initial first-order desires
would be legitimate, and would lead, by refinement under acceptable higher-order desires, to genuine values. That would leave the
possibilities for value rather wide open. But are first-order desires
immune from pathology?

Here is a fairly disturbing report that cropped up in The *Atlantic
Monthly* in the year 2000:

> In January of this year British newspapers began running articles about
> Robert Smith, a surgeon at Falkirk and District Royal Infirmary, in
> Scotland. Smith had amputated the legs of two patients at their request,
> and he was planning to carry out a third amputation when the trust that
> runs his hospital stopped him. These patients were not physically sick.
> Their legs did not need to be amputated for any medical reason. Nor
> were they incompetent, according to the psychiatrists who examined
> them. They simply wanted to have their legs cut off. In fact, both the
> men whose limbs Smith amputated have declared in public interviews
> how much happier they are, now that they have finally had their legs
> removed. (Elliot 2000)

Apotemnophilia, or the desire to be an amputee, is a strange and
disturbing phenomenon. An apotemnophiliac desires, sometimes
desperately, to have one or more of his own healthy limbs amputated, and some have evidently persuaded others to help them
fulfil this desire. Cases are not as uncommon as you might have
hoped. Elliot reports several, including that of a 79-year-old New
Yorker who travelled to Mexico in May of 1998, paid $10,000 for a
leg amputation on the black market, and subsequently died of
gangrene in a motel.

Those of us who do not suffer from such desires probably judge
them to be perverse. That someone desires the amputation of a
healthy, functioning limb does not seem to us to make the amputation good in the least. We feel very uncomfortable about Dr
Smith's helping his patients to satisfy such desires. If apotemnophiliac desires are first-order, as they seem to be, then the standard
reaction to them (*my* reaction) is fitting only if value places antecedent constraints not just on second-order desires, but also on
first-order desires.

There is another apparent problem with apotemnophiliac desires which can be briefly dismissed. If such desires really are
perverse, then their existence might be taken to undermine the

thesis that desires constitute anything like value data. I am neither very interested in, nor very troubled by, this problem. That people have desires for what is in fact very bad is not in itself a problem for the thesis that desires are value data. That a thing can appear very different from the way it is in fact is something which a realist will happily acknowledge, as we have seen. The existence of even extreme illusions does not threaten realism, and it doesn't in itself threaten the general accessibility of truth about the real. That apotemnophiliacs suffer from extreme illusions about the goodness of lopping off a healthy limb seems exactly right, and so their having such desires in no way impugns our appreciation of the goodness of possessing healthy limbs.

Robust realists will welcome the suggestion that there are perverse first-order desires. Since the robust realist holds that value does not reduce to desire or desire satisfaction, she will relish cases of desire satisfaction that are evidently quite horrible. And cases of first-order desire satisfaction that apparently have *nothing* at all going for them—like those of the apotemnophiliac—would be the best sort. On the other hand, realism does not *require* that any first-order desires be ruled out. It will be useful to see if we can accommodate the thought that apotemnophiliac desires are defective without conceding that there are any value constraints on first-order desires.

One strategy for accommodating the badness of apotemnophiliac desires would be to invoke majority desires. Most people not only don't want to have their own healthy limbs amputated, they don't want the healthy limbs of anyone to be amputated. Since the rest of us have strong first-order desires for the apotemnophiliac to keep his healthy limbs, and we vastly outnumber the apotemnophiliacs, our first-order desires will far outweigh the desires of the apotemnophiliacs. So in the limit the limb lopping will be a bad thing, all desires considered. Hence the apotemnophiliacs' initial base desires will be well out of kilter with the good, and that's what the perversity of his desires consists in.

Even if the apotemnophiliac is in the minority, still his first-order desire satisfaction will contribute *something* to goodness. Because he wanted his limb lopped off, that will make the lopping a little bit better than it would otherwise have been. A realist might rest content with this. He might be happy to note that the limb lopping may be bad, all desires considered, while conceding that in itself, independently of everyone else's desires, satisfying the desire for limb lopping would contribute to goodness. If nobody else cared about the limb lopping, for example, it would constitute an unqualified good. If you reject that conclusion, however, then there must be more to say about the badness of apotemnophiliac desires.

The desire to have a limb amputated is clearly not *always* bad in itself. Suppose you notice that your foot is going gangrenous. Other things being equal, you would prefer not to have it amputated, but its continued attachment to your leg threatens the satisfaction of other more important desires that you have—like the desire to go on living. You care about yourself (you place considerable weight on your own overall desire satisfaction) and so you call Dr Smith and set up an appointment to have him lop off your foot—admittedly without any enthusiasm for the project.

Something like this may be what is going on inside apotemnophiliacs, or at least some of them. For it turns out that some apotemnophiliacs apparently want to be seen as heroes—heroically overcoming a major loss, like the loss of a limb. The desire to be a hero who is admired for courageously overcoming an obvious disability can be thwarted by the fact that one does not have any obvious disabilities. So producing an obvious disability might seem like a good first step. Is this perverse? Maybe not as perverse as the desire to simply lop off the limb willy-nilly, or precisely *because* it is healthy. If pursuing admiration through limb lopping strikes one as weird, that might be because the underlying *beliefs* are crazy, rather than the underlying first-order desire. While we do admire people who overcome adversity—we might have a great respect for someone who overcomes the loss of a limb in an accident—we would not be inclined to admire a person who overcomes an adversity which he inflicted on himself with a view to being admired for overcoming that very adversity. So, that kind of apotemnophiliac has a bunch of borderline beliefs, and the fact that he acts on them is not something we would be inclined to admire. What's wrong with the apotemnophiliac is that he is just plain *crazy.*

Craziness, however, is not necessarily a *perversion.* Perversity, then, must be located elsewhere. (As it happens, this kind of instrumental valuing of limb lopping, accompanied by crazy beliefs, although it occurs, is not actually typical of apotemnophilia, as Elliot notes.)

Recall that through the refinement process, higher-order desires can mould and shape one's first-order desires. One's first-order desires can thus become shaped, in particular, by pathological higher-order desires. Capulet hates the Montagues, and because of his hatred he does not want Romeo to be happily married to Juliet. He wants the marriage ceremony not to take place at all. One consequence of this is that he does not want a gold band placed on Juliet's ring finger today. Desiring that there be no gold band placed on Juliet's ring finger today is a first-order desire, and the liberal realist might say there is nothing bad about that in itself. But we do think there is *something* wrong with Capulet's desire. This is because it is constitutive of another, deeper desire—that Juliet not marry Romeo—and that desire is one which involves his hatred of the Montagues. Capulet's first-order desire not to have a gold band placed on Juliet's finger is thus embedded in his *intrinsically* bad, higher-order desires—hatred. So the first-order desire inherits something of the pathology of the higher-order pathology with which it is connected. Let's see if something similar might hold for apotemnophiliac desires.

Apparently the apotemnophiliac is not happy with himself—at least not as he is, with a full complement of healthy functioning limbs. He does not identify with the individual (himself) who enjoys rude bodily health. There does seem to be something perverse about that. In what does the perversity reside? Suppose that the apotemnophiliac has the normal kind of first-order desires to walk and leap and run and utilize his own healthy limbs in the usual manner. Unlike a normal person, however, he does not desire to satisfy these healthy first-order desires. He does not desire that his own normal first-order desires for these things be satisfied. He thus has another set of desires—desires that those normal first-order desires not be satisfied. We are already familiar with these second-order desires. They are a peculiar species of hatred: *self*-hatred, or *self*-loathing. And the satisfaction of hateful desires, whether directed at another or oneself, does not enhance value. Rather, those desires and their satisfaction detract from value.

The apotemnophiliac's first-order desires for limb lopping may thus be informed by, and constitutive of, a species of second-order desire which we can happily classify as pathological, and those desires detract from, rather than enhance, overall goodness.

I am not at all confident that this explanation of the perversity of apotemnophiliac desires—or any other explanation that locates the problem at the higher order—will stand up. We can certainly *imagine* an apotemnophiliac who is *not* plagued by self-hatred. Suppose he just doesn't have any of the usual first-order desires to walk and leap and run on healthy legs. His desire to rid himself of his healthy limbs is not motivated by self-hatred, the desire to thwart his own desire satisfaction. He would simply be happier tooling about in a wheelchair, rather than utilizing a natural endowment of healthy, functioning limbs. My reaction to this apotemnophiliac is roughly the same—his desires are perverse. They are bad. If apotemnophiliac desires are perverse, and we have no plausible higher-order explanation for their perversity, then first-order desires must also be constrained by desire-independent values.

A popular teleological view (of the sort often incorrectly attributed to Aristotle) has a ready explanation for the badness of apotemnophiliac desires—they are desires the satisfaction of which would thwart the natural function, or the *telos*, of one's body or parts of one's body. But there seem to be other desires that also aim to thwart the natural function of parts of one's body which we do not think perverse—the desire for contraception, for example, or the desire to avoid the natural processes of ageing.[1]

 A more promising, and not unrelated, explanation of the perversity of apotemnophilia can, however, be derived from the idea that *organic unity* has a distinctive value. An object exhibits organic unity to the extent that it is a highly unified complexity. There is strong evidence that we do value organic unity in a wide variety of different contexts—art, music, literary works, architecture, scientific theories, ecosystems, persons, and organisms, to name just a few. Christopher Kelly (2003) has argued, rather convincingly in my view, for the monistic thesis that organic unity—or what he calls *richness*—is the *only* intrinsic good.[2] But even if that monistic

---

[1] For the correct Aristotelian view, see Shields 2003: 123–32, 136–41.

[2] The idea is not completely original with Kelly—both Leibniz (1961) and Nozick (1981), e.g., have espoused versions of it. What is novel in Kelly's dissertation is the thoroughness of his defence and his defusion of apparent counter-examples (like pleasure and pain).

thesis is false, organic unity is something we do value, and if we are right about that, it is valuable. The organic unity of a biological organism is, of course, the paradigm of organic unity. And so the desire to lop off one's healthy limbs is a desire to diminish the organic unity of one's own body. It is thus a desire to destroy something valuable. But it is not just that. It is a desire to destroy *manifest* goodness—goodness that should be completely obvious, because it is not a thing far removed, but something so close to one's own being. There is something pathological about that.

5.7   What Desire Can Do for Value

If we grant just one case of an unacceptable first-order desire—a desire which is bad independently of any higher-order desires, or the desires of others, or inconsistency with one's other desires— then that makes for one small hole in the dike of idealism. And if organic unity, for example, is valuable independently of desire, then the hole is rather large.

Suppose P has a value independently of anyone's desiring P. What does the desire for P do to the value of P? We have already noted (in section 3.7) that the desire for something good will itself be good, and necessarily so, inasmuch as it inclines one to pursue or preserve that good. And a desire for the bad will itself be bad, inasmuch as it inclines one to pursue or preserve the bad. But this is to concentrate on the motivational aspect of desire. As experiences of the good, they also have a representational aspect. It is natural to think that appropriate or accurate experiences are good in themselves, and this would be an additional value possessed by a desire for the good or an aversion to the bad. Likewise, a desire for the bad or an aversion to the good would have an additional disvalue. Either way, the goodness of desire fulfilment looks to hang on the antecedent value of what is desired. A desire for some bad state P does not render P any better if P happens to come about. Rather, if P is realized, the overall situation (P + desire that P) is, if anything, worse than the situation in which such a desire is absent. Having a healthy limb lopped off is bad. Things seem worse if that is accompanied by the apotemnophiliac's desire for the lopping. So desire satisfaction can add to, or subtract from, the value of states that are good or bad where the value is possessed independently of the desires in question. This is a clear sense in which desires make a contribution to the shape of value, but their contribution is dependent on previously existing value.

Let us turn now to the case of a desire for something which, independently of that desire, is neither good nor bad. Does the desire for a valueless state do anything to alter the value of the realization of that state? Does it, for example, bump P's value up from zero (or, for that matter, down from zero)? That might seem to be at least one small concession to the idealist programme which it would be reasonable for a realist to concede. Consider again an example I have used several times: the desires to go skiing or swimming. I want to go skiing more than I want to go swimming. On the face of it, there is nothing either good or bad in itself in my skiing or swimming. But given that desire, surely it is better for me to go skiing than to swimming! And what other explanation could there be of that other than the idealist's—that desire creates value where none existed before?

On further reflection, however, it isn't clear that the idealist explanation is the best explanation of the data. Here is an alternative explanation which sits happily with robust realism. People's desires are, typically, a reasonably good guide to what's good for them. That is to say, what seems good *to* them is often what is good *for* them. Why do I like skiing more than I like swimming? It's probably because I am actually better at skiing than I am at swimming. On the slopes I get to exercise a range of rather complex skills which far exceed anything I achieve in the swimming pool. Further, while I ski, I can also take in the beauty of the mountain scenery. So, all told, the experience is a better one for me. It is richer and thus more satisfying, but not simply in virtue of my desiring it—rather, it is because of the richer features it possesses. And the pleasure I take in those is itself an appropriate response to their richness. (Here I am again drawing on the insights of Chris Kelly's work on the value of richness in his (2003).) It *is* better for me if I go skiing, and hence *seems* better to me (I desire it more). Now, since you are a better swimmer than you are a skier, you like swimming more than you like skiing, because it is actually better for you if you swim than if you ski. I can well imagine that

I might go on desiring to ski even after my skiing skills decline to the point where it is not really a rich activity after all, or after the local ski resort becomes crowded and polluted. When I act on such outdated desires, the activity will not be nearly so good for me. My desires at that point will have become somewhat unreliable guides to the good, although I dare say they would quickly be rendered accurate once again by a few bad experiences on the slopes.

The desire for P enhances value not by making P *itself* better, but rather by adding value to the whole situation when P is realized. We might put it crudely like this: when P is good, then the state (P *and* P is desired) is better than the state of affairs (P *and* P is not desired). So it follows that (P *and* P is desired) is better than the state of affairs P itself.[3] So, given that P is good, the state (P is desired) adds to the value of P when P is realized. But likewise, desire can detract from value in the same way. Suppose P is a bad state of affairs. Then the state of affairs (P *and* P is desired) is worse than the state of affairs (P *and* P is not desired), and is consequently worse than the state P itself.

This is crude, because both value and desire come in degrees, and the appropriateness of a desire will depend on the degree of the good and the strength of the desire. A very great good merits a strong desire, a small good, a weak desire. There is a further factor which I will examine more closely in the last chapter—the relation of the valuer to the good, or the 'distance' of the valuer from the good. For simplicity I will ignore that factor here. In other words, I will assume something like the merit connection—that one should desire things *precisely to the extent that they are good* (or *in direct proportion to value*).

The merit connection must be supplemented by an accuracy principle: that *a miss is not as bad as a mile*. In other words, it is better to be closer to the ideally appropriate. Being very close is almost as good as getting it absolutely right. Because there are three magnitudes at issue—the value of the state P, the strength of the desire

---

[3] I assume that if P and Q are mutually exclusive, the value of their disjunction (P *or* Q) lies between the values of P and Q. Clearly this will hold if value is expected value of realization. I also assume that necessarily equivalent states have the same value. Since P is equivalent to the disjunction of (P *and* P is desired) and (P *and* P is not desired), the inequality follows.

for P, and the appropriateness of the response—we would need three dimensions to graph their relationships perspicuously. To simplify, we can fix one of these three magnitudes—the value of P—and show how the appropriateness of a desire for P varies with the strength of the desire for P. So let the horizontal axis measure strength of desire for P, and the vertical axis measure the appropriateness of a desire for P of a given strength. Let $V(D)$ be the value of a desiderative response of strength D to P, and let D^P be the most appropriate desiderative response to P. The appropriateness of a desiderative response to P will fall off the further it is from D^P—in either direction. And there doesn't seem any reason to think that it should fall off more quickly in one direction or the other. A smoothness assumption also seems reasonable—namely, that around the optimal response the value should fall off rather gradually, and that it should diminish more quickly the further it is from the optimal response. So we have a symmetrical curve of some sort with a maximum value at D^P (fig. 5.8). The *shape* of this curve presumably does not change with different states. The x-co-ordinate of the highest point on the curve will be greater, the greater the value of P, since greater goods merit stronger desires. It may also be that the y-co-ordinate of the highest point on the curve will also increase with increasing value, since the more valuable a state, the more valuable it is to have one's response be appropriate. Also, an aversion to a bad state will be good. So we can supplement the curve for P with a curve for state Q, which is good, but somewhat less good than P. The most appropriate desire for Q will have a strength D^Q, which is somewhat less than D^P. Similarly, for states R and S which are as bad respectively as Q and P are good, aversion will be the appropriate response, and both the strength and the value of the appropriate aversion will be greater, the worse the state is (fig. 5.9).

Finally let us consider the curve of appropriateness for neutral state N which is neither good nor bad. Indifference will be the appropriate response, and so indifference will be the most valuable reponse. Desire for N and aversion to N will both be less valuable than indifference, but the value will fall off smoothly from $V(0)$.

Now we can see that the smoothness and accuracy principles yield some interesting consequences about desire's contribution to value. The best response to a value-neutral state N is total indifference, but a very small desire for N, while not as good as

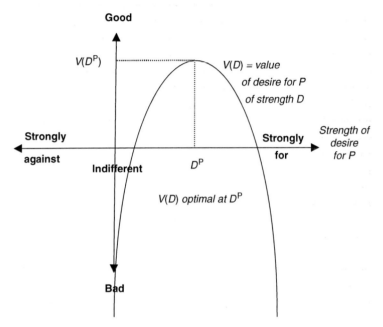

FIG. 5.8 *Appropriateness of strength of desire*

indifference, will still have some positive value, as will a small degree of aversion to N. So it isn't necessarily *bad* to desire something that is of neutral value. Desire that is close to indifference will still add some value. And if we look back at fig. 5.9, it is also clear that indifference to something good (or to something bad) may be of positive value, so long as the good (or the bad) is a small one. And even a (very small) desire for a bad state like R, may be better than strong aversion. These reflections on the value of desire entail that the answer to the question 'Does desire add value?' is not entirely straightforward. The simplest general principle is this: that the more appropriate a desire, the greater its contribution to value. So the contribution of desire to value is entirely dependent upon, and a function of, the antecedently

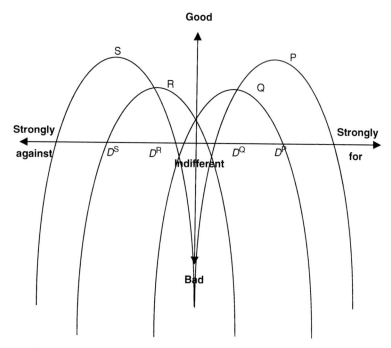

FIG. 5.9   *Appropriateness of strength of desire: the general case*

given values of states. Even in the case of a small desire enhancing
the value of a neutral state of affairs, it is only because the
desiderative response is close to the ideal response—which
would be total indifference—that it makes a positive difference
to the good. The value-neutral state, which happens to be desired,
is no better for being desired. It remains valueless.

5.8   The Value of Refinement

The idea that the valuable is what we would desire were we to
refine our actual contingent desires into a completely coherent set
is a very appealing one, for two reasons. First, it would apparently

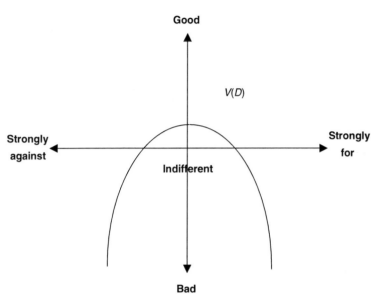

FIG. 5.10 *Appropriateness of desire for valueless N*

naturalize value, and by so taming it make it entirely intelligible. But secondly, it would explain why, even though it is desire that undergirds value, not all desires are necessarily generators of value—only those that survive the fires of refinement.

The refinement model which I have used to articulate this basic idea embodies additional powerful and attractive features. The model comes very close to delivering core realist platitudes about value, platitudes on which realists typically draw to contrast their position with idealist theories. Given the rather weak condition of connectedness, for example, we are guaranteed the agent-neutrality of the limiting ideal desires, something dear to every realist's heart. Given further constraints on the nature of the connectedness, the agent-neutral desires that emerge from desire will have a number of attractive features. The refinement model clearly accords actual contingent desires a fair amount of jurisdiction over the ultimate shape of the good, and under favourable conditions the shape that the good possesses will be intuitively attractive even to realists.

The model also exposes some severe limitations of the idea. Unfortunately for the idealist, there appears to be a *value residue*, one which is desire independent, one to which higher-order desires have to answer before they qualify as suitable for refinement. For example, the egoist's desires cannot be counted amongst those being refined into coherence. A single egoist can wreak havoc with the limiting desires, and a pair of egoists can prevent the emergence of agent-neutral limits altogether. Other partial higher-order desires, like those of the obsessed altruist, also produce somewhat disastrous results. Even worse are the destructive desires characteristic of hatred. Finally, not just higher-order desires, but also first-order desires, appear to be subject to desire-independent constraints. For example, the desire to wilfully destroy organic unity for no apparent gain in any other good seems, on the face of it, seems perverse.

The realist has an immediate and quite plausible explanation of the disastrous outcomes of desire refinement in these cases—namely, that the desires in question are *bad*. If the basket of initial desires contains even one rotten apple, then there is no guarantee that juggling the apples so that they fit together neatly won't simply spread the rottenness around. Refining bad desires in the light of those very desires produces limiting desires which may well be far from ideal—desires which do not track value in any sense. The realist will insist both that connections in the web of higher-order desires and distributions of first-order desire must be purged of bad elements before embarking upon refinement.

The robust value realist holds that there are facts about value which hold independently of, and prior to, desire. Not all of what is valuable is so in virtue of desire. But there are two ways in which robust realism can go at this point, one more radical than the other. The less radical assumes that there is a kernel of truth in the rejection of idealism—namely, some (albeit not all) of what is valuable is so in virtue of desire, and that the shape of value is at least partially determined by distribution of desire. Let's say that an initial distribution of desire is *acceptable* if none of the desires lie outside the limits of appropriateness, given the desire-independent values.[4] The two assumptions entail that not any old *initial* distribution will be acceptable, but also that more than one initial distribution will count as acceptable. Consider the following modification of the refinement theory: the good is what we would desire if all were to collectively, systematically, and perfectly refine acceptable agent-relative desires, in the light of those very desires, into perfectly coherent, agent-neutral limiting desires.

This modified refinement account allows initial desires, both first-order and higher-order, an important role in the distribution of value. But by incorporating a desire-independent value residue, the theory can block the unpalatable consequences of refining pathological desires into their perfectly coherent, but still pathological, ideal limits. It simply rules out initial pathological desires as illegitimate starting-points. If the constraints on initial desires are not reducible to desire, then there will, of course, be a gap between what is good and what would be desired in the ideal limit.

It is not particularly the size of this gap that matters. What matters is that there is any possibility of a gap at all. So the cost of placing desire-independent constraints on desire is the abandonment of the idealist programme. In that case the robust realist may embrace the conclusion of the previous section and discount completely the role of desire in *generating* value. Desire may enhance or detract from antecedently given value, by virtue of the appropriateness of the desire to the value of its object, but desire cannot create value *ex nihilo.*

These two versions of the desire-independence of value can both account for the role that desire plays in shaping value. Both can accommodate the idea that desire enhances the value of good states. The more radical version is not at all troubled by the fact that desire does not enhance the value of the bad, whereas the less radical version will have to come up with some story to account for this. On the other hand, the less radical version has a good explanation of the value of simple pleasures and the disvalue of simple pains. A good explanation of the value of simple sensory pleasures is that they are sensory states which are greatly desired. A good

[4] We don't need to say exactly what inappropriateness amounts to here. The merit connection is one very demanding articulation of what appropriateness amounts to, but as we have already seen in Ch. 3, it needs to be revised. We will investigate possible revisions in the final chapter.

explanation of the disvalue of simple pains is that they are sensory states to which one has a strong aversion. If the quality of the experience were to remain the same while the desire (or the aversion) were removed, the value of the pleasure (or the disvalue of the pain) would apparently evaporate. Indeed, this is how some people describe the palliative effect of morphine—that the pain remains qualitatively untouched, but that one no longer cares about it. It would be strange, however, to say that the pain treated with morphine has the same *disvalue* as before, and that it differs only in its disvalue now going *unnoticed* by its bearer.[5]

Both these versions of realism—the more radical and the less radical—seem to be live options awaiting the development of some decisive argument in favour of one or the other.

What of a positive nature can the realist learn from this exploration and ultimate rejection of refinement idealism? The idealist may be wrong that refined desire *constitutes* value; but even if that's right, the process of desire-refinement may nevertheless provide the realist with an additional *epistemic* handle on the good. Desires are experiences of the good, but any one individual's desires are also a highly agent-relative representation of the good. The process of collective refinement can be viewed as a way of synthesizing different and apparently conflicting viewpoints into a coherent, agent-neutral representation on the good. I will take up this idea again in the last chapter. In the meantime, the next task on the realist agenda is to show that the valuable is not only something over and above desire, but something over and above all the natural, non-evaluative states.

---

[5] In the final chapter of his dissertation, Kelly (2003) goes a considerable way to defusing the pain/pleasure objection to radical realism.

6 IRREDUCIBLE VALUE

THE robust realist holds that value isn't reducible to desire, but goes further than this, holding that value isn't reducible to anything else either. In other words, value isn't reducible to the non-evaluative, to what we might call the *purely natural*. Value is something 'over and above' the natural. The robust realist is a non-naturalist.

Non-naturalism about value faces a problem. Almost no one denies the *universalizability* of value with respect to nature, and universalizability amounts to this: any two objects with the very same natural features must have the very same value features. This in turn entails the thesis of the *determination* of value by nature: that there can be no difference at the level of value without some difference at the natural level. So the non-naturalist who embraces universalizability needs determination without reducibility. A handy term has been coined in the philosophical literature—*supervenience*—for this notion of non-reductive determination. (Like most terms of art, the term is used in many ways. Some authors use it in the way I stipulate here. Others use it simply to mean the weaker notion of *determination*, leaving open the question of whether supervenience entails reducibility or not.) One domain (like the domain of value) supervenes on another (the natural domain, say), provided the former is fully determined by the latter without being reducible to it. The main focus of attention has in fact been on the possibility of the supervenience of the physical on the mental, but the supervenience of value on nature was the original model on which mental–physical supervenience was based.

Like others (following the rich debate precipitated by Jaegwon Kim's (1978) seminal article) I have been rather sceptical about the possibility of supervenience—understood as a relation of determination which does not entail reducibility (Oddie 1991). There are a number of plausible proofs that any concept of determination

strong enough to secure the desired dependence of the supervenient on the subvenient entails the reduction of the supervenient
properties to their subvenient base.

Robust realists about the *mental* need not be perturbed by such
proofs, because they can simply reject that kind of determination of
the mental by the physical. It isn't terribly difficult to deny that the
physical determines the mental if the determination is supposed to
hold by necessity. If Berkeleian worlds are possible, then the
distribution of mental states is not determined of necessity by
physical states. Two Berkeleian worlds can share the same physical
states while differing in their mental states. So the proofs that
determination entails reduction will not trouble a robust realist
about the mental. Of course, the debate at this stage will typically
focus on the relevant notion of necessity and possibility. Berkeleian
worlds are logically possible, but are they possible in the sense
which correlates with the necessity required by determination?

The robust realist about value, however, cannot be so sanguine.
One cannot comfortably deny the universalizability of value with
respect to the natural. It is hard to imagine how identical distributions of natural properties could result in distinct distributions of
value. Consider a radical position about value analogous to Berkeleian idealism about the mental—that the world could be in any
one of a wide range of distinct value states even if there were *no*
underlying natural facts *at all*. This position has not even been
formulated (as far as I am aware), let alone defended. Even G. E.
Moore, whose position on value is usually characterized as an
extreme version of value realism, combined his anti-reductionism
with determination. The point is that in the case of the mind–body
problem we can usefully debate whether or not the undisputed
logical possibility of Berkeleian worlds undermines physical–mental determination, or whether a stronger notion of possibility (say,
nomological possibility) would be required. But in the case of the
valuable and the natural, that debate cannot really get started, since
no one appears to want to defend even the bare logical possibility
of the value correlate of Berkeleian worlds.[1]

---

[1] Well, *almost* no one. I come dangerously close to entertaining such possibilities in
my (1991) and (1992).

So the non-naturalist about value has a deep problem. An apparently essential feature of moral properties (universalizability with respect to the natural) entails supervenience. If supervenience in turn entails reduction, then an essential feature of value entails naturalism. So it seems that anyone who wants to eschew naturalism, like G. E. Moore, will have also to eschew universalizability.[2] *Hmm* That's a tall order.

In this chapter I elaborate a promising way of defending the determination of value by nature, while resisting reduction. Recent developments in both property theory and value theory help clarify a thesis about the relation between irreducibility and multiple realizability which has not, I think, been as clearly articulated as it can be. And this in turn will help to establish and illustrate the possibility of supervenience without reduction.

6.1   Three Stories

An elegantly dressed woman, sipping a martini at an up-market party in her friend's well-appointed apartment, overhears a conversation not intended for her ears. Apparently her ex-husband, whom she left some years before and has come to hate, has suffered a bad accident, the details of which she cannot quite decipher. As she picks up these few snippets drifting over the background noise, she tries to suppress an unbidden, but not entirely unwelcome, surge of satisfaction.

Earlier that day a bunch of disaffected young hooligans from a less salubrious neighbourhood, cruising around in a beat-up vehicle, looking for a bit of fun, spot a well-dressed man walking along the motorway in the rain, some distance from his broken-down car. With jeers and hoots of laughter, they swerve in his direction, knock him down, and tear off. Injured and unconscious, the man is found a couple of hours later by a road-worker, and is taken by ambulance to a nearby hospital.

The hospital is often overloaded with urgent cases. Many such cases are financially problematic for the hospital, since few in that

---

[2] This is essentially Dreier's argument in his (1992).

area have adequate medical insurance. (Note: this story takes place in the USA, where 40 million do not have medical insurance.) The staff are overworked, conditions are poor, the pay is low compared with the hospital in the up-scale neighbourhood. The sister in charge of the Emergency Ward is tired and short-tempered. She is just about to go off duty when a well-dressed, middle-class guy is brought in with some injuries. She makes a cursory assessment. She can see that his injuries may well be more serious than those of some others waiting for treatment, but she thinks, rather callously, that he has probably already had enough privileges in life. The man loses a leg which more timely treatment might have saved.

These three episodes are very different at the purely natural level, as evidenced by the fact that evaluatively neutral descriptions of them would be radically dissimilar. Although from the point of view of value there are important differences, there is nevertheless an important commonality as well. The wife's *Schadenfreude*—her reacting with pleasure to the news of the unnecessary suffering of her ex—certainly detracts from value. The hooligans' cruelty, their pleasure in their infliction of unnecessary suffering, is worse. The nurse's callousness is located somewhere between. The three incidents can be located, as it were, along a dimension of a *value space*—a dimension involving our causal and psychological relationship to unnecessary suffering—with the third incident resting somewhere between the first and the second.

This rather innocuous-seeming observation turns out to have important ramifications for the ontological independence of value. It holds the key to reconciling an essential feature of the evaluative—its universalizability with respect to the natural—with its irreducibility.

6.2 Reducibility

'Reduction' is, somewhat paradoxically, both a term of art and a hotly contested notion. Many of these contests have focused on one or other *linguistic* notion of reducibility—usually involving the definability of the predicates, or other terms, of one language within some reducing language. Clearly a concept of linguistic reduction will make reduction relative to the expressive power of the reducing language. The issue in which I am fundamentally interested here, however, is not linguistic reducibility, but *ontological* reducibility—whether the entities in one domain, or ontological category, constitute something 'over and above' the entities of the some other domain or ontological category.

Take two ontological domains, A and B, like the mental and the physical, or the evaluative and the natural. Here is an undeniably *sufficient* condition for the reducibility of the A-domain to the B-domain in the ontological sense: every entity in the A-domain is *identical* to some entity in the B-domain. This is the paradigm exemplified by the Frege–Russell reduction of numbers to sets. Every number-theoretic entity ends up being identified with (i.e. taken to be identical to) some set-theoretic entity. Natural numbers are identical to sets of sets. Properties of natural numbers are identical to properties of sets of sets; functions on natural numbers are functions from sets of sets to other sets of sets; and so on. It is also what the identity theorists wanted for the reduction of the mental to the physical. Mental properties are identical to physical properties, mental events to physical events, and so on. Finally, it is also what intensionalists wanted from their identification of intensions with various functions from worlds to extensions (Oddie 2001*d*).

I will assume, for the sake of simplicity, that value would reduce to nature if the domain of value properties reduced to the domain of natural properties. Thus, for the reduction of all value properties to natural properties, the following is an undeniably *sufficient* condition: every value property is identical to some natural property.

This might seem a rather strong sufficient condition. But consider the following. Let us say that an entity is type-T if either it is one of the 'basic' type-T entities, or else it can be 'constructed' out of type-T entities by any of the full array of type-preserving operations. 'Construction' here simply means applying operations that take us from type-T entities to other type-T entities. So, for example, set-theoretic union and intersection are set-preserving operations by means of which we can construct sets out of given sets, and successor, multiplication, and addition are number-preserving operations by means of which—given some natural numbers—we can construct (specify) new natural numbers. Every natural number, for example, can be constructed (in this sense) from the number 0, and the successor function.

Now suppose there is a type-A entity, X, that is not identical to *any* type-B entity. That is, X is neither a basic entity of type B, nor can it be constructed out of basic entities of type B. It cannot be arrived at by applying any type-preserving operations to basic entities of type B. Then the A-domain *does* seem to be something 'over and above' the B-domain. If this is right, then we can happily dub the sufficient condition for reducibility necessary as well: that is to say, the A-domain is reducible to the B-domain if and only if every A-type entity is identical to some B-type entity. The real work will come in specifying which constructions are legitimate—that is to say, which operations are type-preserving.

6.3   Supervenience

The core which every concept of supervenience respects is the following principle: there can be no difference in the distribution of the supervening properties without some difference in the distribution of the base properties. Different concepts of supervenience articulate this principle in different ways, but here I will concentrate on the strongest notion in the literature: strong, logical, local supervenience. Let us say that two individuals are *A-twins* if, for each A-property, either both have it or both lack it.

> *Strong, logical, local supervenience.* A strongly supervenes on B $=_{\mathrm{df}}$ for any possible worlds U and V, and individuals X and Y: if X in U is a B-twin of Y in V, then X in U is an A-twin of Y in V.

What makes this *strong*, rather than weak, are the *inter*-world comparisons. Weak supervenience stays with intra-world comparisons. We can state weak supervenience as follows:

> *Weak, logical, local supervenience*: A weakly supervenes on B $=_{df}$ for any possible world U, and individuals X and Y: if X is a B-twin of Y in U, then X is an A-twin of Y in U.

Clearly the strong principle entails the weak.

What makes these two principles logical, rather than nomological, is that the quantifiers range over all possible worlds. Nomological supervenience restricts the quantifiers to nomologically possible worlds.

What makes them *local* rather than *global* are the comparisons between individual A-twins and B-twins. Global supervenience could be stated thus:

> *Global logical supervenience*: A globally supervenes on B $=_{df}$ for any possible worlds U and V, if U is a B-twin of V, then U is also an A-twin of V.

The strong principle also entails the global. The weak does not, however, entail the global, and the global principle does not entail either the weak or the strong principle. Thus, if any version of supervenience is going to guarantee reduction, it is the strong principle. What might be called the *main result* is the following: that strong, local, logical supervenience (strong) guarantees the necessary coextension of each A-property with a certain condition specifiable by means of Boolean operations (conjunction, negation, disjunction) on B-properties. Specifically, let a *B-conjunction* be any conjunction which entails, for each member of B, either that property or its negation. Then, given strong supervenience, every A-property is necessarily coextensive with a unique disjunction of B-conjunctions.

This result doesn't yet yield reduction. So far we have nothing that tells us that any old condition or concept specifiable by a disjunction of B-conjunctions is a genuine B-*property*. On a liberal view of properties, every condition definable in terms of B-properties is a B-property, but we can certainly entertain sparse property theories that deny this.[3] While most hold that the Boolean operation of conjunction is property preserving, disjunction and negation are more controversial. Suppose, for the moment, that the Boolean operations are all accepted as property preserving:

> *Boolean closure*: The Boolean operations are all property preserving.

Now we have that every A-property is necessarily coextensive with some B-property. But nothing we have said so far guarantees that

---

[3] Armstrong (1978), (1989). See Swoyer (2001) for an excellent survey.

the A-properties are *identical* to those B-properties with which they are necessarily coextensive. So to obtain reduction we need:

> *Necessary coextension*: Necessary coextension is sufficient for property identity.

Combine the principles of Boolean closure and necessary coextension with the main result, and we have that strong supervenience entails reducibility. Now the non-naturalist has a problem.

Anti-reductionists who embrace supervenience have three options: retreating to a weaker notion of supervenience or jettisoning one of the two principles (Boolean closure or necessary coextension). Probably the most popular response has been to retreat to a weaker version of supervenience—like weak local supervenience (where all the comparisons are intra-world) or global supervenience (B-twin worlds are A-twins). I don't wish to pursue these, since their advantages and disadvantages are well documented in the literature on supervenience (Oddie and Tichý 1990; Oddie 1991). And in any case, neither weak nor global supervenience yields a notion of determination strong enough for the appropriate connection between the natural and the evaluative, one which guarantees the right kind of universalizability. What would be interesting would be a *non ad hoc* way of retaining strong, logical, local supervenience without conceding reducibility. Consequently we need to look closely at the two auxiliary principles.

6.4   Avoiding Reduction by Going 'Fine-Grained'

One response available to a non-reductionist is to deny that necessary coextension is sufficient for identity. Here a theory of 'structured' or 'fine-grained' properties might be invoked (see Swoyer 2001). According to such a view, *equiangular* and *equilateral* may be distinct properties of polygons, even though necessarily coextensive. The two properties can be set apart by Leibniz's principle. For example, one may infer something from the *equiangularity* of a figure, but not from its *equilaterality.* Or one could be attempting to give an analysis of *equiangularity* but not of *equilaterality.* These applications of Leibniz's principle may be suspect to some, because they involve features constructed from intentional contexts (*attempting, inferring*). Suppose, however, there is such a thing as the *proper analysis* of a *property*—not of an expression, nor of a property concept. Then maybe the proper analysis of *equiangularity* involves, in some sense, the property of *angularity*, whereas the proper analysis of *equilaterality* does not. It would then be natural to think of *equiangularity* as possessing a structure, involving the property of *angularity* as part of that structure, and *equilaterality* as having a different structure, involving the property of *sidedness* as a part. So, in addition to what we might call *coarse-grained properties*, individuated by necessary coextension, there are *fine-grained properties*, and there can be many fine-grained properties, perhaps infinitely many, for every coarse-grained property associated with them.

Clearly the problems of hyperintensionality demand more than intensions (objects individuated by necessary coextension) for their solution.[4] The above line of argument for fine-grained *properties* is, however, misguided. For while there are many distinct fine-grained entities associated with each property, those fine-grained entities are not necessarily distinct *properties*.

Consider another domain where something very similar appears to be going on—the domain of numbers. Take *the cube root of 729* and *the square of 3*. It seems that one can be focusing on the former without focusing on the latter, and one can focus on both without focusing on *the number 9*. Moreover, in some sense one can give a different analysis of the former than of the latter. The proper analysis of *the cube root of 729* certainly involves the cube-root function, whereas the proper analysis of *the square of 3* does not. But should these facts incline one to say that corresponding to every 'coarse-grained' number (like *the number 9*) there are a plethora of distinct fine-grained *numbers* (like *the cube root of 729* and *the square of 3*). Hardly. Yet the reasoning is exactly parallel to the property case. It is sound in the one case if and only if it is sound in the other.

What we have here, in addition to the number 9, are not mysterious fine-grained *numbers*, but two ways of *arriving* at the

---

[4] See Lewis (1972); Bealer (1982); Cresswell (1985); Tichý (1986) and (1988).

number 9, two different intellectual *procedures* which yield that number. One procedure involves applying the cube-root function to the number 729. This procedure clearly involves two entities: a function (cube root) and a number (729) and the procedure of *application*—applying the function to that argument. The other procedure involves applying a quite distinct function, the square function, to a quite different number, the number 3. These procedures thus have different components. The numbers 729 and 3 are components of the respective procedures, but (*pace* Frege) they are not parts of the number 9. If they were parts of the number 9 by virtue of being parts of those two procedures, then we would get the absurd result that every number is a part of every other number—since any number at all is a part of some procedure for arriving at a given number. Procedures have been given different labels, but so as not to import doctrines from any well-known semantic theories, I will go with the term *construction*.[5]

Pretty much the same considerations apply to conditions which objects may or may not satisfy. *Divisible by the cube root of 729* and *divisible by the square of 3* present us with two procedures for arriving at a condition which a number may or may not satisfy, but it is the same condition in each case. For a simpler example, consider four different specifications which involve property *P* and the Boolean operation of negation: P, $\sim \sim P$, $\sim \sim \sim \sim P$, $\sim \sim \sim \sim \sim \sim P$. These do not present four different conditions for an object to satisfy. Rather, what we have four of here are *ways of specifying a condition*, the very same condition in this case. Similarly, one can arrive at a certain condition of polygons (viz. *regularity*) by citing the equality of its sides, or by citing the equality of its angles. *Equiangular* and *equilateral* yield the same condition of polygons, but present us with two different ways of specifying the condition. Two procedures zero in on the same condition. Different journeys arrive at the same destination.

This account also clarifies *analysis*. Analysis is properly directed at *procedures*, and those procedures do involve parts and do have a structure. The analysis of *equiangular* involves dissecting a certain way of specifying a condition into its component parts, one part of which is the property of *being an angle*. This account of constructions

---

[5] Tichý (1986) and (1988); Materna (1998).

or procedures explains the data, however, without jettisoning the idea that *properties* are individuated by necessary coextension.

6.5 Avoiding Reduction by Denying Boolean Closure

A third response is to take issue with Boolean closure, to deny that the Boolean operations are (in my terminology) property preserving. It is quite common to deny this for both disjunction and negation. *Being a raven* and *being black* may both be properties, along with *being a black raven*. But *being a non-raven, being either black or a non-raven,* and *being a raven if and only if black* are not typically taken to be properties. This is the import of such claims as 'there are no negative properties' or 'there are no disjunctive properties' or that some condition or other is too 'horribly disjunctive' to be a genuine property (Armstrong 1978, 1989). There is a deep problem with such denials which mostly goes unnoticed. Once we have made the appropriate distinction between properties, on the one hand, and procedures for arriving at properties, on the other, it is no longer clear what a *negative* or *disjunctive* property could be. Since negation and disjunction are not *parts* of any property, it is no longer clear what it takes for a *property* to be 'negative' or 'disjunctive'. The negation operation is no *part* of the property *P*, although it is part of many distinct procedures for *specifying* the condition *P*: for example, $\sim \sim P$, $\sim \sim \sim \sim P$, and so on. A negative property is clearly not just a condition that can be *specified* by means of negation, because any property can be so specified. Likewise with disjunctions. So it seems as though talk of 'negative' and 'disjunctive' properties is the result of a failure to make the appropriate distinction between properties and procedures for determining properties.

Consider numbers again. Talk of negative numbers is entirely appropriate. But a negative number is not just any number that results from applying the function *Neg* (where $Neg(n) = -n$) to a number *n*. For then every number would be negative. Rather, we assume a privileged class of numbers, the *positive* numbers, and a negative number is any number *n* such that for some positive number *p*, $n = Neg(p)$. And of course it follows, from the nature of numbers, that no negative number so defined is also a positive number. Suppose that we start with a privileged class of conditions, the *positive conditions*. Then couldn't we say that a *negative condition* is a condition which results from negating a positive condition? Thus if P is a positive condition, the condition $Q = {\sim}P$ is a negative condition. The negation of Q, ${\sim}Q$, however, does not yield a negative condition at all—despite the presence of negation in this procedure for specifying it—but rather yields the positive condition P. Now suppose that properties just are the positive conditions. Do we then have the desired result: that there are no negative properties—that is to say, no negative condition is identical to a property? If so then we would have something much stronger than the denial that negation is property preserving.

If this is on the right lines, then maybe we can have a sparse or restrictive account of properties which enables us to deny Boolean closure without conflating properties with procedures for determining properties. This is the kind of theory I will outline in the next section.

6.6 Properties as Convex Conditions

While we may have here the beginnings of a promising approach, it suffers from one considerable defect. In order for us to obtain the result that the Boolean operations are not property preserving, we would need to constrain the class of positive conditions in such a way that no negative condition can also be a positive condition: that is to say, no condition that can be specified by negating a positive condition is itself a positive condition. Nothing in what we have said so far guarantees this, and just to stipulate it seems *ad hoc*. (In the case of numbers this is, of course, guaranteed by their structure.) Further, sometimes the negation of a property of a certain type *does* seem to be a perfectly good property of that type. Similarly, the disjunction of two distinct B-properties can be a perfectly good B-property. Without some more detailed account of what kind of a condition a property is, all this seems a bit puzzling.

To see that negation and disjunction don't always destroy propertyhood, consider a simple temperature domain, and let three temperature conditions carve out nice regions of that domain. Suppose, for the sake of the argument that *hot*, *warm*, and *cold* are chosen so that they are mutually exclusive and jointly exhaustive. All, we may suppose, are genuine positive properties. Each carves out a region of a space of temperature conditions—but not just any region. Each is a rather nicely behaved region, as fig. 6.1 suggests.

Now consider the three derived conditions shown in fig. 6.2. The three conditions have all been disjunctively *specified*, but there is a difference between (cold or hot), on the one hand, and (cold or warm), and (warm or hot), on the other. The difference is that there is a clear sense in which (cold or warm) and (warm or hot), just like their underived disjuncts, pick out nicely behaved regions of the space of conditions, whereas (hot or cold) does not. The condition (hot or cold) is *disjointed*, in a way that (warm or hot) and (warm or cold) are not. The disjuncts of (hot or cold) are not 'adjacent' but 'separated'.

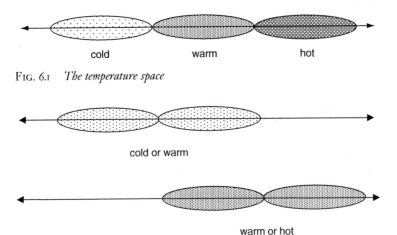

FIG. 6.1 *The temperature space*

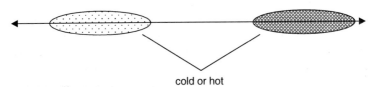

FIG. 6.2 *Three temperature conditions*

The same three conditions can be specified by means of negation as well:

(cold or warm) = not hot
(warm or hot) = not cold
(cold or hot) = not warm.

Of course, whatever is true of the conditions *specified disjunctively* is also true of them *specified negatively.* Whether or not a condition is disjointed depends not on how it is *specified,* but on the *geometry* of an underlying space of properties of which it is a constituent (Gärdenfors 2000).

Disjointedness can be captured in a number of ways, depending on the geometry of the relevant space, but the notion which turns out to be the most fruitful here is that of *convexity.* This notion presupposes a concept of *betweenness.* Degrees of warmth clearly exhibit such a relation. For example, in our simple space of three degrees, warm is between hot and cold. Or if we think of the members of this simple three-property domain as determinables of more determinate degrees of warmth, then every degree w that is a determinate of warm is between c and h, where c is a determinate of cold and h of hot. A collection of determinates is *convex* if it is closed under the betweenness relation: that is to say, any item between two members of the collection is also a member of the collection. Now it is easy to see why (hot or cold) counts as disjointed and (warm or hot) does not. The former carves out a convex region of the temperature space, whereas (hot or cold) does not. Convexity captures what we want in a 'nicely behaved' condition. It is the polar opposite of disjointedness. A condition arrived at by disjunction *may or may not be disjointed,* since a particular application of disjunction may or may not take us from a collection of convex regions to one that is also convex.

Peter Gärdenfors (2000)—building on a truly impressive array of logical and empirical data from linguistics, psychology, and the cognitive sciences generally—has argued thoroughly (and in my view rather convincingly) that in general the conditions that we think of as *properties* (or *natural* properties as opposed to *gerrymandered* properties) are well-behaved regions of a certain sort of space: a domain of a *conceptual space.* (I have a mild preference for the term *quality space* to distance it from the possibly idealistic connotations of the term *conceptual*.) I will use a version of this convexity hypothesis as the basis of a sparse theory of properties.

This sparse theory of properties—that properties are *convex* conditions—immediately explains how and why Boolean closure fails, even in the very simple one-dimensional temperature space considered above. The conditions hot, cold, and warm are all convex regions, as are (cold or warm) and (warm or hot). The condition (hot or cold) is not. Typically, of course, a conceptual space will be a multi-dimensional affair. For example, let's add a *raininess* dimension to the temperature space. Let's suppose that each of these comes in three degrees. For simplicity call these *dry, drizzly, pouring*. Again we have an intuitive betweenness relation for this dimension: *drizzly* is between *dry* and *pouring*. We can combine both dimensions into a single two-dimensional quality space with nine elements. The large space also exhibits betweenness relations. For example:

> (warm & *dry*) is between (hot & *dry*) and (cold & *dry*).
> (warm & *drizzly*) is between (cold & *dry*) and (hot & *pouring*).
> (cold & *pouring*) is not between (warm & *dry*) and (hot & *drizzly*).

We can see what underlies these judgements if we map out the possible positions on a two-dimensional grid (see fig. 6.3). Already the diagram suggests that the various discrete qualities could be replaced by much more finely discriminated magnitudes. Let's stick with the discrete space for illustrative purposes. A point is *between* two points if it lies on some shortest path between the two. (*Some*, rather than *the*, since in a discrete space such as this one, there may be more than one shortest path between points.) The basic idea here can be captured by the so-called *city block metric*. A path of length n from p to q can be identified with a sequence of $n + 1$ adjacent positions starting with p and ending with q. Between any two points there is a set of *minimal* paths. For example, between (cold & *dry*) and (warm & *drizzly*) there are two minimal paths of length 2: one which goes via (cold & *drizzly*), and the other which goes via (warm & *dry*). So, both (cold & *drizzly*) and (warm & *dry*) lie between (cold & *dry*) and (warm & *drizzly*).

The following regions of this little space are all convex:

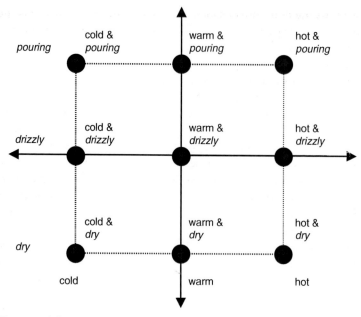

FIG. 6.3 *The weather space*

Vertical straight lines:	cold, warm, etc.
Horizontal straight lines:	*dry, drizzly,* etc.
Singletons:	(cold & *dry*), (cold & *drizzly*), etc.
Vertical rectangles:	(cold or warm), (warm or hot)
Horizontal rectangles:	(*dry* or *drizzly*), (*drizzly* or *pouring*)
Small squares:	(cold or warm) & (*dry* or *drizzly*), etc.
Parts of straight lines:	((cold or warm) & *dry*), etc.

If we think of each dimension as a discrete magnitude, then the basic convex regions assign an interval to a magnitude, and all the other convex regions conjoin two such basic interval assignments.[6] Interval assignments are the analogues, in this domain, of *primitive properties* where the dimensions are bivalent—they admit of only

---

[6] This is proved quite generally in Oddie (1987), itself a response to a proposal in Goldstick and O'Neill (1987) which utilizes the convexity of propositions in the context of truth-likeness. There are crude intimations of the role of convexity in carving out a class of 'privileged' propositions in Popper's (1963), introduced to save his account of truth and falsity content. See Oddie (1987).

two possible determinates. So one way of putting this result is the following: every convex condition is either a primitive property or a conjunction of primitive properties.

Conjunction is a property-preserving operation regardless of the dimensionality or complexity of the space. For suppose that *P* and *Q* both pick out convex regions of the space. Suppose *p* and *r* are within the region picked out by *P & Q* and that *q* is between *p* and *r*. Since *P* is convex, *q* is in *P*'s region, and likewise for *Q*. Since *q* is in both *P* and *Q*, it is also in their conjunction. Hence *P & Q* is also convex. Disjunction is clearly not property preserving: (hot or cold) is not convex, for example. Nevertheless, some conditions that can be specified by disjunction are convex—like (warm or hot) and (warm or cold). The same goes for negation. The negation of hot (not-hot) is necessarily coextensive with (warm or cold), which is also convex.

Non-convex, or disjointed ('unnatural') regions include *inter alia* the conditions shown in figs. 6.4 and 6.5. Other non-convex conditions are (if *dry* then cold), not-(warm & *dry*). All four of the regions associated with these conditions contain both (cold & *dry*) and

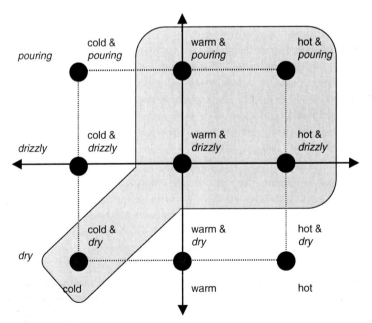

F<small>IG</small>. 6.4   *Region corresponding to cold if and only if dry*

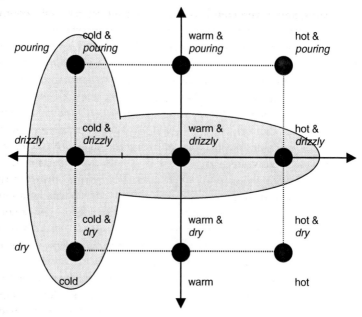

FIG. 6.5 *Region corresponding to cold or drizzly*

(warm & *drizzly*) but exclude (warm & *dry*), which lies between the other two. We can have a rough measure of how disjointed a condition is by comparing it to its *convex closure*: the smallest convex superset of the condition. A convex condition is its own convex closure. The larger the difference between a condition and its convex closure, the more disjointed it is.

Given this sketch of a sparse theory of properties, we have clear and principled counter-examples to the theses that disjunction, negation, the conditional, and the biconditional are property-preserving operations. This sparse theory of properties thus delivers the judgements which many property theorists have intuitively endorsed.

6.7 Value Properties

So much for properties in general. Now we must turn our attention to the value properties, if there are any. There are, of course, value

predicates, and, given cognitivism, those predicates specify conditions. But are those value conditions genuine *properties?*

The quality space in which we live and move and have our being
embraces a multitude of natural dimensions. These include the basic
qualities embraced by the natural sciences, but also natural features
embraced by the folk (like *hot, water, storm, desire*). The natural
dimensions jointly constitute a natural space, a subspace of the entire
logical space. A point in the natural subspace is determined by an
assignment of values to each of the natural dimensions. Each such
point is a maximally specific natural property. A complete, moment-
ary, natural *state* is an assignment of a point in the natural subspace to
each individual. And a complete *history* is an assignment of a mo-
mentary state to each moment of time.[7] Naturalism is clearly connected to the issue of whether or not this natural subspace is a proper
subspace of our quality space, or whether we need to traffic in
dimensions 'over and above' the natural ones.

Almost everyone, including those with non-naturalist inclin-
ations, accepts that value supervenes on the natural. Strong local
supervenience tells us that two distinct points in the quality space
cannot agree on every natural dimension. In other words, every
point in the natural subspace has a unique value profile. Alternatively, given the natural dimensions of a point, you are thereby
given all the other dimensions, if there are any. It follows that no
two distinct states (and no two distinct histories) agree on all their
natural dimensions and differ only in value. (That's global supervenience.) This might appear to give the game away to naturalism,
because it suggests that the natural space is all we need to fully
characterize the world. And, as we have seen, the supervenience of
value on the natural guarantees that each value property is necessarily coextensive with a condition definable by Boolean operations on natural conditions. Call the natural condition which is
necessarily coextensive with a value property the *natural basis* of
the value property. The reducibility of value to the natural, however, turns on whether each value property is identical to a natural
property. Since candidates for identity will have to be necessarily
coextensive, the only condition which is a candidate for identity

---

[7] Gärdenfors (2000) takes a state to be a collection of points, effectively endorsing
the Leibnizian principle that no two things can differ purely qualitatively.

with a value property will be its natural basis. The issue of reducibility of value thus turns on whether the natural basis of each value property is itself a *natural property*.

There is a simple point here which, as far as I know, has been overlooked in the large literature on naturalism. Obviously the naturalist must hold that *all* value properties are reducible to (viz. identical to) natural properties. He cannot allow the odd exception. The non-naturalist holds that *not* all value properties are reducible. She need not, however, hold that *all* value properties are irreducible. The non-naturalist can allow exceptions to the irreducibility of value to nature. According to the non-naturalist, there might well be some value properties which are identical to natural properties. Indeed, it might even be the case that *most* are. The partial irreducibility of value to nature is a version of non-naturalism, albeit one which, as far as I know, has not been advocated explicitly. I think that the partial irreducibility thesis is correct. Some value properties are indeed natural properties—that much of the naturalist thesis is true—but not all are. Value partially reduces to the natural, but does not totally reduce to the natural.

To establish the (possibly partial) irreducibility thesis, we must first show that there are indeed some candidate *properties* in the value domain. This is tantamount to showing that value conditions, like natural conditions, admit of intuitive judgements of betweenness, and that when they do, what we think of as value *properties* are conditions which satisfy convexity. Call this the *value–convexity hypothesis*.

So far we have trafficked mostly in the so-called thin value concepts (like *good*, *bad*, and *better than*) rather than the thick value concepts (like *cruelty* and *callousness*). What exactly is the relation between the thin and thick concepts? One can realize the bad without being cruel—one can be *callous*, for example—but one cannot be cruel or callous without, to some extent, realizing the bad. *Being cruel* and *being callous* are thus two different concrete ways of realizing the bad. And there are a multitude of different ways of realizing the bad. This suggests that the thick concepts stand to the thin as determinates to determinables.

The thesis that cruelty is a determinate of the bad might be thought to rule out varieties of antirealism, like nihilism, by conceptual fiat. For if the determinate–determinable relation is a conceptual affair, then it would apparently make it a purely conceptual fact that cruelty is bad, and that seems to stack the deck too heavily against the antirealist. Surely we can't make realism about value true just by adopting a bunch of concepts, and we cannot discover that it is true by analysing *cruel* and discovering that it entails *bad*.

Compare this with the case of phlogiston. Suppose that, according to phlogiston theory, the stuff comes in various determinate kinds, say of varying weights. Recall that when it was discovered that burning resulted in a net weight gain, phlogiston theorists maintained that the stuff had a negative weight, so that with phlogiston loss there was an overall weight gain. Inflammability was explained by quantity of phlogiston. Highly inflammable things had a lot of phlogiston in them. Note, however, that quantity of phlogiston and kind of phlogiston might well be separate features. Suppose that degree of flammability and amount of weight gained in burning came apart, as they conceivably could. Then a phlogiston theorist might well be tempted to distinguish the quantity of phlogiston that a certain sort of matter had in it and the kind of phlogiston it contained. So *light phlogiston* has a lot of negative weight, while *heavy phlogiston* is very close to zero weight. Thus something with a lot of light phlogiston would be both highly flammable and gain a lot of weight in burning. Something with a lot of heavy phlogiston might be just as flammable, but gain much less weight in burning. In this scheme *light phlogiston* and *heavy phlogiston* are determinates of *phlogiston*. This, despite the fact that neither the determinate nor the determinable applies to anything in fact. We can have a determinable embracing a range of determinates, the application of all of which involves some unfulfilled presupposition. Analogously, even if the nihilist is right, *bad* can still be a determinable embracing various determinates like *cruelty* and *callousness* even if nothing can correctly be characterized as being either bad or cruel. The purely conceptual thesis that the thin concepts are determinables and the thick are the corresponding determinates in no way begs the question against nihilism.

Consider the stories with which we began. The first was a case of *Schadenfreude*—of responding with pleasure to the unnecessary suffering of another. The second was a case of *cruelty*—of intentionally bringing about unnecessary suffering of another for fun.

These cases are both instances of the bad, if anything is. The third case is, as noted, plausibly located somewhere between the other two in value, and as the value–convexity hypothesis would lead one to expect, given that the other two realize the bad, it is also a realization of the bad. In fact, it is a case of *callousness*, which we know independently to be a determinate of the bad.

Crimson is a determinate of the determinable *red*, and crimson in turn is a determinable of which *deep crimson* is determinate, and so on. A determinate may itself be a determinable, and this is no less so in the domain of values. *Cruelty* is itself a determinable, of which *mildly cruel* and *very cruel* are two determinates. *Frustrating cats for fun* is a determinate way of being *mildly cruel*, while *torturing cats for fun* is a determinate of a rather more serious kind of cruelty. *Tormenting cats for fun* lies somewhere between these two, and, as one would expect according to the value–convexity hypothesis, it too is a determinate of cruelty.

So far, then, we have some confirmation that, at the intuitive level, value conditions of both the thick and the thin varieties satisfy convexity, and thus that they qualify as properties.

6.8   Convexity and the Natural Basis of a Value Property

Consider, then, the natural bases of these value properties. Take the natural basis of *bad*, for example. This is a condition which picks out, in a natural space, a Boolean combination of natural features. Is it plausible to suppose that, *at the natural level*, every determinate realization between two determinate realizations of the *bad* is itself a realization of the *bad*? This certainly isn't obvious. The three stories we started with would have extraordinarily different natural realizations, very far apart as characterized by their natural dimensions. There is nothing to guarantee that small differences at the neuronal level, say, might not engender enormous differences at the level of value, while a vast distance between the physical dimensions of two points might make no difference at all in their value profile. It thus seems reasonable to conjecture that convex conditions at the level of value will be highly disjointed at the level of the natural.

These kinds of considerations, while certainly suggestive, place too much reliance on a rather amorphous hunch. (In this respect, they are like the analogous and oft-repeated claim that mental states would be 'very messy' at the physical level.) If we want to *establish* that value conditions are not convex conditions of a natural space, we will have to do so by means of definite cases. And those cases will have to be much simpler than the rather complex cases we began with. They will have to be of roughly the same kind of complexity as the simple weather examples. The simple case I construct makes use of a couple of substantive value assumptions, but a similar argument would go through with almost any non-trivial assumptions.

Suppose one person—call him *X*—is in a state of pain or pleasure, and a second—*Y*—is in a state of desire, taking as object *X*'s state. The various possibilities can be mapped on a two-dimensional graph, both dimensions (*X*'s pleasure state, *Y*'s desire state) of which are natural if anything is natural (see fig. 6.6). For simplicity, let the horizontal axis embrace just three possible states of *X*, *pain* and *pleasure* together with a *neutral* (pain-free/pleasure-free) state which lies between them. The vertical axis details *Y*'s desires concerning *X*'s condition. Either

> *Y* desires that *X* be in the state he is in (abbreviated to: *desires X's state*); or
> *Y* desires that *X* not be in the state he is in (abbreviated to: *averse to X's* state); or
> *Y* neither desires *X*'s state nor is he averse to it (abbreviated to: *indifferent to X's state*).

As in the simple weather space, the betweenness relations of this natural space are parasitic on the betweenness relations of its two dimensions taken separately. So, for example, if we hold one dimension fixed (say *Y*'s desiring *X*'s state) and vary *X*'s state, the middle point on the line still lies between the two extremities.

Now let's introduce the value aspect. Suppose that *X*'s pleasure is a good thing, his pain is a bad thing, and his being in the neutral (pleasure-free, pain-free) state is neither good nor bad. So the region corresponding to *X* being in a neutral state lies between the regions corresponding to his being in pain and his being in pleasure, from the purely natural point of view. If we switch to the value of *X*'s state, we get the same result. *X*'s state is good if *X*

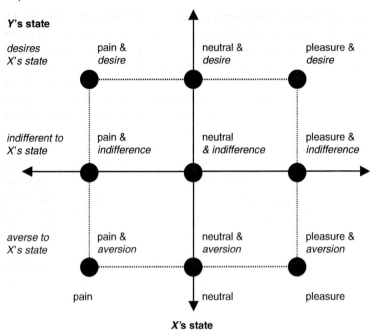

FIG. 6.6 *Two-dimensional natural space involving pleasure/pain and desire/ aversion*

experiences pleasure, bad if he experiences pain, and so on. The evaluative states here are not only coextensive with the underlying natural states, but share their convexity in the natural space. So these value conditions are also convex.

Now consider the value of *Y*'s states. Given the experience thesis, *Y*'s three different desires are simply experiences of value:

> *Y* desires *X*'s state = *X*'s state seems good to *Y*;
> *Y* is indifferent to *X*'s state = *X*'s state seems neither good nor bad to *Y*;
> *Y* is averse to *X*'s state = *X*'s state seems bad to *Y*.

How good is it that *X's state seems good to Y*? The answer here is rather obvious—it is good just in case *X*'s state is good. It is not good just in case *X*'s state is not good, and it is bad just in case *X*'s state is bad. So, *Y*'s desire concerning *X*'s state enhances value just to the degree that *Y*'s desire is *appropriate* to its object—the more appropriate it is, the better. (In section 5.7, 'What Desire Can Do for Value', I argued for this in the more fine-grained setting where both value and desire are continuous magnitudes. For illustrative purposes here, a discrete space is adequate.) The region carved out by *Y*'s desire being completely accurate, or completely appropriate, is given in fig. 6.7. This region is non-convex. The point <neutral, *desire*>, for example, is outside the condition, but it is between two points <neutral, *indifference*> and <pleasure, *desire*> which are within the condition.

Let's turn to another value condition: the badness of *Y*'s experience (fig. 6.8). *Y*'s experience is *very* bad if it is way off course—he either experiences a *bad* thing as good or he experiences a *good* thing as bad. So *Y*'s state is totally inappropriate (very bad) if he either desires *X*'s state when *X* is experiencing pain, or he has an aversion to *X*'s state when *X* is experiencing pleasure.

Finally, *Y*'s experience of value might be neither good nor very bad (see fig. 6.9). It might lie somewhere between the two

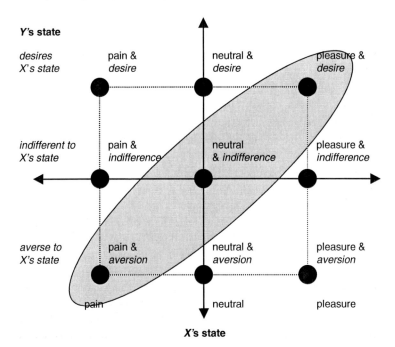

FIG. 6.7   *Region corresponding to: Y's response is appropriate*

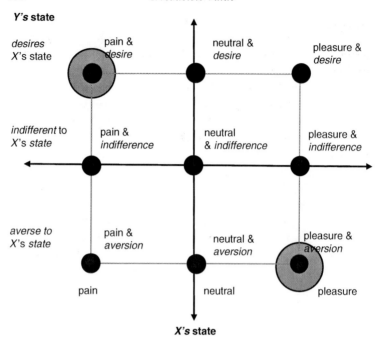

Y's state

desires *X's state*	pain & desire	neutral & desire	pleasure & desire
indifferent to *X's state*	pain & *indifference*	neutral & *indifference*	pleasure & *indifference*
averse to *X's state*	pain & aversion	neutral & aversion	pleasure & aversion

pain   neutral   pleasure

X's state

FIG. 6.8   *Region corresponding to: Y's response is totally inappropriate*

extremes: that is to say, *X* either desires or is averse to a neutral state, or he is indifferent about either a good or a bad state. This is not good, but it is not very bad either. Let's say it is *somewhat bad*. What we have, then, is that the three value states (*Y*'s state is good, somewhat bad, or very bad) are not convex. Rather, they are highly disjointed states.

So far, then, it looks as though these particular value conditions are not convex natural conditions. It thus seems that these value conditions are not themselves natural properties.

6.9   The Evaluative Transformation of the Natural

The non-convexity of these value conditions is closely related to the non-additivity, or organic unity, of value (Oddie 2001*a*, 2001*c*).

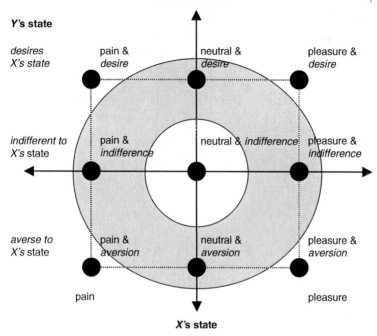

Y's state

desires X's state · pain & desire · neutral & desire · pleasure & desire

indifferent to X's state · pain & indifference · neutral & indifference · pleasure & indifference

averse to X's state · pain & aversion · neutral & aversion · pleasure & aversion

pain · pleasure

X's state

FIG. 6.9   *Region corresponding to: Y's state is somewhat bad*

Take the four corners of fig. 6.9. The best state amongst our small set of possibilities is surely the one in the top right-hand corner, which embodies both good states (X's pleasure together with Y's appropriate response to it).

S_1 X experiences pleasure, and Y desires X's state.

The worst state of all, since it involves two bad states—X's pain and Y's inappropriate response to it—lies in the top left-hand corner:

S_4 X experiences pain, and Y desires X's state.

Worse than S_1 but better than S_4 are two states located at the bottom two corners, each realizing a good and an evil.

S_2 X experiences pleasure, and Y is averse to X's state.

S_3 X experiences pain and Y is averse to X's state.

S_2 involves something good (X's pleasure) and something bad (Y's aversion to it). Likewise, S_3 involves something bad (X's pain) and something good (Y's aversion to it). So, from the evaluative point of view, S_2 and S_3 lie between S_1 and S_4. But from the natural point of view, nothing could be further from the truth. S_2 and S_3 are certainly not in the convex closure of S_1 and S_4.

It is not hard to see that this evaluative ordering of S_1, S_2, S_3, and S_4 cannot be represented as an additive function of the two factors taken separately: *X's state* and *Y's response*. For suppose we assign p to pleasure and q to pain, d to desire and e to aversion. Both of the following inequalities would have to be satisfied to preserve the intuitive value ordering of the states:

S_1 is better than S_2: p + d > p + e.
S_3 is better than S_4: q + e > q + d.

The first implies that d > e, while the second implies that e > d. So we cannot preserve the ordering by any assignment of numerical values to X's experience and Y's desires and have the value of the whole equal to the sum of the values of these component factors. The non-convexity of value conditions is thus closely linked to the organic unity of value.

Although this fact is not widely appreciated, additivity and organic unity are, in a precise sense, *relative* affairs (Oddie 2001*a*). An evaluative ordering of states which fails to be additive relative to one way of cutting up the space of possibilities may turn out to be additive relative to another. We can demonstrate this rather easily with our simple natural space. Consider a numerical evaluation of the points of the space. To each point attach an ordered couple, <*u, v*>, where *u* measures the value or disvalue of X's state, and *v* measures the value or disvalue of Y's response in the circumstances (i.e. given X's state). Table 6.1 shows one such numerical evaluation. We need not suppose that the overall value of a point in the natural space is given by the simple sum of the values of its two component factors. One of the two factors might deserve more weight than the other, for example. Let's attach their values to the points (fig. 6.10). This assignment of numerical values induces a mapping from this natural space on to another space, an evaluative space, with a different co-ordinate system (fig. 6.11). The axes of the new co-ordinate system detail, respectively, X's experience (horizontal) and the *appropriateness* of Y's desire (vertical).

Within this new space the intuitive evaluative ordering of points *can* be represented additively. That is to say, we can assign numerical values to the positions on each axis, treat the overall value of a

TABLE 6.1.   *A numerical assignment to the natural states*

State	Numerical value assignment
Pleasure	1
Neutral	0
Pain	− 1
Appropriate desire	1
Somewhat inappropriate desire	0
Very inappropriate desire	−1

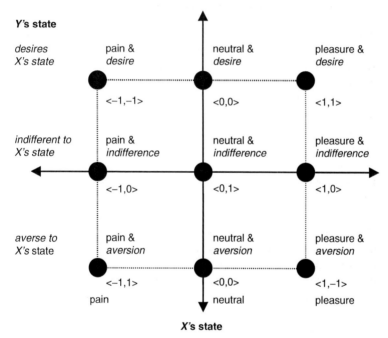

FIG. 6.10   *Points assigned values*

state as the sum of the values of its two co-ordinates, and thereby realize the qualitative evaluative ordering of states. Indeed, the one given above will do the job. The basic qualitative data put S_1 at the top of the evaluative ordering, S_4 at the bottom, with S_2 and S_3 between. Other additive realizations of the basic set of qualitative judgements are, of course, possible.

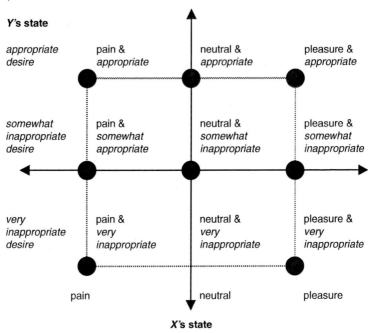

Y's state

appropriate desire — pain & appropriate — neutral & appropriate — pleasure & appropriate

somewhat inappropriate desire — pain & somewhat appropriate — neutral & somewhat inappropriate — pleasure & somewhat inappropriate

very inappropriate desire — pain & very inappropriate — neutral & very inappropriate — pleasure & very inappropriate

pain — neutral — pleasure

X's state

FIG. 6.11 *A transformation of the natural space*

Now in this space, the value conditions—like *Y's state is good*, and so on—are clearly convex. The natural bases of these conditions, in the natural space, were horribly disjointed, but those natural conditions correspond to convex conditions in the value space. For example, that *Y's response is good* is coextensive with *Y's response is appropriate*, and that carves out a beautifully convex condition in the new space (fig. 6.12). So, if we start with a space generated by *X's* pain/pleasure factor along one dimension, and *Y's* desire factor along another, then the regions corresponding to some value conditions will not be convex, because value is not additive in those factors. Despite this, we may be able to map the points of the space into a quite different space, one in which the dimensions correspond to different factors. In the new space *both* dimensions correspond to what we might call *values*—that is, simple evaluative factors which contribute systematically to the overall value of the points in the space. The transformed space is a *value space*.

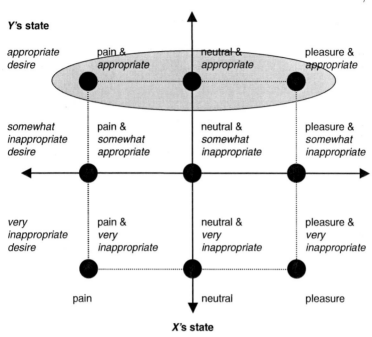

FIG. 6.12 *Region corresponding to: Y's response appropriate (good)*

We can make a first stab at the argument for our target conclusion—that the supervenience of value on nature is compatible with the irreducibility of value to nature. Clearly we have the requisite determination: no difference in value without some difference in the natural basis. But a value condition—like *Y's desire being good*—is a genuine convex condition, and so it is a value property. On the other hand, its *natural basis* is *not* convex. By Leibniz's principle, the convex conditions of the value space cannot be *identical* to their non-convex natural bases. A condition which is convex cannot be identical to *any* condition which is non-convex. Because there are value *properties* (convex conditions of the value space) which are not identical to any natural *property* (convex conditions of the natural space), value is not reducible to the natural. The evaluative transformation of the natural thus adds value properties where there were none before. Value is something over and above the natural.

6.10   Conceptual Expansion

This first stab at the argument is subject to three connected, and troubling, objections. First, the value space seems inadequate for making all the distinctions we want to make. The two spaces are not equivalent ways of carving up the possibilities. Second, as a matter of fact, we clearly operate with both sets of properties— evaluative and natural—at once. It is not as though we are constantly switching between two distinct quality spaces. Rather, we combine all the qualities in one space. Third, there does seem to be just *one* condition underlying both the value property (like the *appropriateness of desire*) and its natural basis. That *one* underlying condition may be convex *relative to* the value space, and non-convex *relative to* the natural space, but then we do not really have a straightforward application of Leibniz's principle securing the distinctness of two properties. The apparent contradiction (and the distinctness derived from that) is really an illusion.

Consider the natural space again. Two of the points in that space – namely, <neutral, *desire*> and <neutral, *aversion*>—have the same *value* structure. Consequently, these distinct points are mapped to the same point of the value space (namely <neutral, *somewhat inappropriate*>). Further, there is no point in the natural space in which X is in a neutral state and Y's experience of that is very inaccurate. Thus there is no condition corresponding to the point at the intersection of X being in a neutral state and Y's response to that being very inappropriate. (This lack of occupancy is indicated in fig. 6.11 by lack of a black circle.) Since there are only eight occupied positions in the value space, and nine in the natural space, this means that two positions in the natural space are not distinguishable within the value space. What this reflects is that while the feature of the *appropriateness* of Y's response supervenes on X's experience together with Y's response, the natural feature, *Y's response*, does not supervene on evaluative features. Since Y's desires can be construed as natural features, what this illustrates is the pervasive fact that while value supervenes on the natural, the natural does not supervene on value. There can be differences at the natural level without any differences at the level of value. The two states <neutral, *desire*> and <neutral, *aversion*> are evaluatively indistinguishable, but naturalistically distinguishable. Thus it is that the natural space is more fine-grained than the value space.

This observation brings the second objection more clearly into focus. We traffic in both natural and evaluative attributes, in one all-encompassing conceptual space, as we negotiate the world. But the judgements of convexity and propertyhood have been based on different spaces. This suggests that we have to choose the space within which we are going to conceptualize the world, and hence which conditions (the evaluative or the natural) are to count as *genuine* properties. We cannot, however, jettison the natural features, because, as we have just shown, we would then not be able to make all the discriminations that we clearly want to make. And we cannot jettison features like *appropriateness* without jettisoning intuitive judgements of betweenness. To make all the discriminations that we want to make, we have to have all the natural properties in the generating base. But to make all the judgements of betweenness that we want to make, we have to have the value features in the generating base. So it seems that we need both evaluative and natural dimensions as fundamental.

Consider the three-dimensional graph which I have labelled *the combined natural-value* space (fig. 6.13). The points on the furthest surface of the cube—all those that involve *Y*'s desiring *X*'s state— have been labelled with the values in each dimension, but in order that the diagram not be too cluttered, the others have been left to the imagination.

Note that several points on the grid are not occupied by a black circle. Only those positions on the grid that are occupied by genuinely instantiable conditions have been so marked. For example, there is no circle at the origin because it is not possible for *X* to be in a neutral state, for *Y* to respond indifferently, and for that response to be inappropriate.

Note also that each determinate of a generating quality corresponds, of course, to a plane orthogonal to the relevant axis. Clearly we would want our definition of betweenness to capture these as convex. Further, the complete set of occupied points on that plane should also count as convex. The fact that some of the unoccupied points are not in that collection should not count against their convexity. We can achieve this quite naturally. We define *paths* and

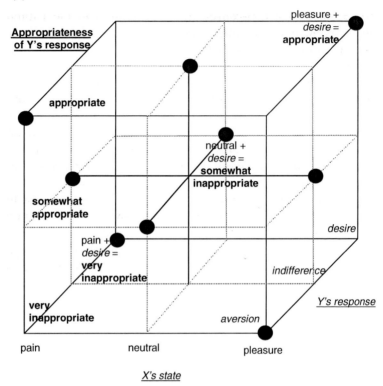

FIG. 6.13   *The combined natural-value space*

lengths of paths by treating all the intersections, occupied and unoccupied, alike, and then simply taking over the former definition of *betweenness* and *convexity*, restricting variables to occupied points. So (occupied) point *q* is between (occupied) points *p* and *r* just in case *q* lies on a shortest path between *p* and *r*. And a set of (occupied) points is convex just in case it contains all the (occupied) points between any two points in the set.

Now we have all the properties, evaluative and natural, captured within the one three-dimensional conceptual space. Recall that our first stab at reconciling supervenience and non-reduction required the distinctness of necessarily coextensive properties. The value property was shown to be distinct from its natural basis. The evaluative condition is convex within the evaluative space, but it corresponds to a non-convex natural condition in the natural space. Now, if all conditions, both evaluative and natural, are captured in the one expanded space, this line of argument is not obviously available. In the expanded space, the property *somewhat inappropriate* and its natural basis carve out *exactly the same region.* Since these pick out the very same region of our expanded space, either *both* are convex or *neither* is. (They are one and the same region!) In fact both are convex, and since they are both convex, there are no grounds for denying that *somewhat inappropriate* is identical to its natural basis. We are thus deprived of the master argument against reduction.

Essentially the same symmetry objection is made by Kim in the following criticism of non-reductive materialism, albeit in a different way:

If pain is nomically equivalent to N, the property claimed to be wildly disjunctive ... *why isn't pain itself equally heterogeneous ... as a kind?* (Kim 1993: 323; my emphasis)

6.11 Nature and Value

What the objection shows is this. If we work with the expanded conceptual space—and we must do this if we are to satisfy the desideratum that both the natural and the evaluative properties be present in the one encompassing space—then we have to be able to say of one and the same condition *both* that it is value property *and* that it is *not* a natural property. It is not that one and the same *condition* is both convex and non-convex. Rather, one and the same condition might be a property *in virtue of* the purely natural, or it might not be a property *in virtue of* the evaluative. That is to say, the convexity of a condition might derive from one or other of two different sources. So what we need to do is to spell out what this amounts to in terms of the framework of conceptual spaces. In fact, there is a straightforward way of accommodating this idea, one which builds directly on the space-relative argument already developed.

Our expanded space has both natural dimensions as well as value dimensions, and as a consequence it embraces a natural subspace and a value subspace. Each region of the expanded space can thus be <u>projected on to the different subspaces</u>. And the projection of a region on to a subspace may or may not be convex. The question arises as to whether a condition might project on to a convex region of one subspace, but on to a disjointed region of the other. If it projects on to a convex region of the value subspace, for example, but on to a non-convex region of the natural subspace, then it would clearly count as a value property, but not as a natural property.

Indeed, this is precisely the situation that we have with the condition of being *somewhat inappropriate*. The natural subspace is the space consisting of the two dimensions *X's state* and *Y's response*. And the region of that natural space which *somewhat inappropriate* carves out is a highly disjointed doughnut-shaped region, as we have seen. Project that condition on to the value subspace—the space consisting of the two dimensions *X's state* and *appropriateness of Y's response*—and the region it carves out is nicely convex. So a convex condition of the combined space—a property—may turn out to be a value property, but not a natural property. It is convex in virtue of the geometry of value, not in virtue of the geometry of nature.

Are there properties—convex conditions of the combined space—which are *natural* properties but not *value* properties? Take the condition of *Y's desiring X's state*. This projects on to a convex region of the natural subspace—it thus counts as a natural property. But it projects on to a disjointed region of the value subspace. It is not a value property. In other words, it is a property in virtue of the geometry of nature, not the geometry of value.

Nothing in what we have said so far rules out the possibility that a convex condition of the combined space may project on to convex regions of *both* subspaces. So immediately this account opens up the possibility that the evaluative and the natural are not exclusive categories. Are there any such conditions? It is clear that any singleton in the extended space—a maximally specific condition—picks out a singleton in both the value and the natural subspaces. And a singleton is always convex. So every maximally specific condition is both a natural property and a value property. This result is quite general. A maximal condition in any space at all will be maximal when projected on to any of its subspaces, so all of its projections on to all of its subspaces will be convex. Hence, for any kind of subspace, the maximal conditions will count as properties of that kind.

Now that we have established, on the basis of this analysis of property kinds, that the categories of evaluative and natural are compatible, the question arises as to whether there are any *non-maximal* conditions that count as both natural and evaluative.

Consider a conjunction of a value property and a natural property. Take the convex value condition (*appropriate or somewhat appropriate*) and the convex natural condition (*desires Y's state or is indifferent to Y's state*). Conjoin these two convex conditions, and we have a further convex condition C in the combined space. This convex condition projects on to convex regions of both the value space and the natural space. In the value space it projects on to the region corresponding to the condition (*appropriate or somewhat appropriate*), and in the natural space it projects on to the region corresponding to the condition (*desires Y's state or is indifferent to Y's state*).

There are also basic conditions in this space which are both natural and value conditions. One of the dimensions of the expanded space is that of X's state—that is to say, his degree of pain or pleasure. This is typically classified as natural, whatever one's views about the nature of value. Now suppose, as we have done, that the more pain there is—other things being equal—the worse things are. That is to say, pain is an intrinsically bad thing. The degree of pain and pleasure is a dimension of the value subspace, and as a consequence determinates of pain and pleasure pick out convex regions of the value subspace. So we have good reason to classify pain as belonging to the value realm as well as to the natural realm.

What if pleasure is not intrinsically valuable, or pain disvaluable? What if it is better that the wicked experience pain rather than pleasure? Then, I submit, we would be justified in not treating pain/pleasure as a generating dimension of the value subspace, and treating some other dimension—like *just deserts*—as basic.[8] That condition would be a generating dimension of the value space.

Are there conditions of the expanded space which are *neither* natural *nor* value properties? Take the following gerrymandered

---

[8] See Oddie (2001a) for an extensive discussion.

condition D: *Y* satisfies D if either *Y* desires *X*'s pain, or he desires *X*'s pleasure, or he is neutral about *X*'s being in a neutral experiential state.

D = Either (*X* experiences pain and *Y* desires *X*'s state)
    or (*X* is in a neutral state and *Y* is neutral about *X*'s state)
    or (*X* experiences pleasure and *Y* desires *X*'s state).

The projections of D on to both natural (fig. 6.14) and evaluative (fig. 6.15) subspaces are not just disjunctive, but badly disjointed.

We now have a clear account of what it takes for a condition to be a natural property and what it takes for a condition to be a value property, and I have shown that these are logically independent traits. This suggests a convenient typology of conditions. A condition is a *purely natural property* if it is a property in virtue of the geometry of nature, but not in virtue of the geometry of value, like (*Y*'s desiring *X*'s state*). That is to say, its projection on to the natural space is convex, but its projection on to the value space is not

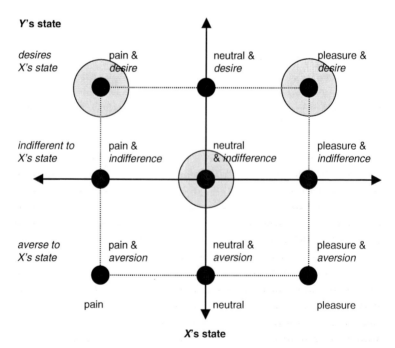

FIG. 6.14   *Projection of D on to natural subspace*

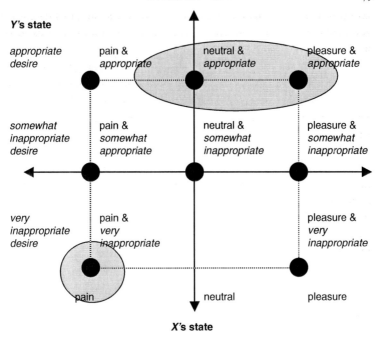

FIG. 6.15   *Projection of D on to value subspace*

convex. A condition is a *purely value property* if it is a condition which is convex in virtue of the geometry of value, but not in virtue of the geometry of nature, like (*X's response being somewhat inappropriate*). Its projection on to the value space is convex, but its projection on to the natural space is not. A condition is a *fusion* of nature and value, if it is both a value property and a natural property—like *pain*. Its projection on to both subspaces yields a convex region of the subspace. And finally a condition is *heterogeneous* if it is neither a natural property nor a value property—like the gerrymandered condition D. It is neither a natural property nor a value property.

Given that value is determined by the natural, there must be a purely natural space with a geometry which underwrites the natural properties. Given that there is also a value dimension, there are also value properties, and a value space the geometry of which underwrites the value properties. The existence of value dimensions does not it itself entail that value is irreducible. The irreducibility of value can be formulated in a number of different but essentially equivalent ways. Is every value property identical to a natural property? Is every value property such that its natural basis is a natural property? Is every value property a fusion? We have good reason for answering these questions negatively. First, there do seem to be good reasons for holding that value predicates carve out convex regions at the evaluative level. Both the intuitive examples we started with, and the toy example we constructed, support this. So, there are value properties. Further, intuitively there seems no good reason to suppose that value properties will project on to convex regions of a purely natural space. This hunch, which seems quite strong at the intuitive level, is born out in the toy model we constructed. So some value properties are not natural properties. Some value properties are pure. It is the existence of these pure value properties which guarantees that value is not reducible to nature.

6.12   The Problem of Causal Networking

A summary of how far we have come, and of how far we still have to travel, may be useful at this stage. I began by defusing the queerness argument against value facts, by making extensive use of the experience conjecture—that there are experiences of value. I argued that value data would have to be analogous to perceptual experiences in salient respects, and that desires are the most plausible candidates for the role of experiences of the value of states of affairs. This conjecture provides a ready answer to an otherwise troubling question for any kind of realism—namely, where are the value data which give us a purchase on the value facts? I then argued that even though we have experiences of value (viz. desires), value is not reducible to such experiences. In this chapter, I have argued additionally that value is not reducible to anything else purely natural. This is because there are value properties which are not identical to any natural properties. The last step in the argument for robust realism is that of establishing the somewhat controversial idea that irreducible values are active members of the causal network.

7 VALUE AS CAUSE

THAT values be causally efficacious is desirable for two related reasons. First, only if values are causally efficacious, do they satisfy the Eleatic Stranger's criterion of the fully real. Supervenient values, even though not reducible to the natural, would be a little disappointing if they turned out to be mere epiphenomena, if all the real work in the world were carried out at the natural level. Second, if value isn't reducible to experiences of value, then in order for our experiences of value to constitute a source of knowledge, we need to have some reason to think that our desires are *responsive* to value—that they can track value in the right way. And this requires that values be causally networked.

There is an argument against the claim that *moral* experiences, assuming we have them, constitute reasonable grounds for moral belief. The idea is that we don't need moral facts to *explain* moral experiences, and consequently moral experiences do not provide evidence of such facts. While I have not treated of *moral* facts, or *moral* knowledge here, it is fairly obvious that a parallel argument could be run against value experience as a source of value knowledge. Maybe we do have experiences of value (so the parallel argument would run), but even if we do, those experiences would not provide any evidence for value, because we don't need to postulate value facts to explain them.

There are also related arguments against the causal efficacy of the *mental*—I am thinking here of the recent flurry of causal exclusion arguments. These start with some kind of causal exclusion principle—that one fact cannot have two different, complete causal explanations, or two distinct causes. If the physical realm is a causally closed system, then any given physical event cannot have both a physical cause and a *distinct* mental cause. Consequently, a mental cause of some physical event, if there is such a thing, would have to be identical to the physical cause of that event. If this mental–physical exclusion argument is valid, then a parallel exclusion argument, one which substitutes the valuable for the mental and the natural for the physical, would also be valid.

It behoves the robust realist to address both kinds of argument.

7.1   The Argument from Explanatory Idleness

A physicist, observing a vapour trail in a cloud chamber, thinks *there goes a proton*. The physicist's experience gives her evidence for her belief that a proton goes there, and maybe that belief in turn coheres with, and helps to confirm, her microphysical theory.

You turn the corner of a street and come upon some young larrikins dousing Cuddles with gasoline and setting him alight, apparently for the fun of it. This cat-bating episode *seems* very bad to you, and without much reflection you think *something very bad is going on here*, and maybe that judgement in turn coheres with and helps confirm your overall theory of good and evil.

Grant, for the moment, that your initial reaction to the cat-bating episode is an experience of its badness—something like an observation. Whatever the nature of your experience—whether it is constituted by desire (as I have argued) or by something more complex with a desiderative component (like an emotion), or by something mysterious (like a 'value intuition')—does it give you any *evidence* for your subsequent judgement that *something very bad is going on here?* And can that judgement in turn be used to support your overall theory of the good and the bad?

No, says Gilbert Harman (1977). Harman claims that the physicist's observation of a vapour trail gives her reason to believe that *there goes a proton*, because the best explanation of her observation involves postulating the existence of a proton in the cloud chamber. But the best explanation of your experience or observation of the badness of the cat-bating episode does not involve postulating badness. All we need to explain your experience is your evaluative mind-set—perhaps the fact that you believe Cuddles's pain to be a bad thing, or the fact that you believe that inflicting pain on a sentient creature for the sheer hell of it is cruel, and that cruelty is bad. So your reaction to the cat-bating episode is not evidence of the value properties of the episode, but merely evidence that you endorse certain evaluative beliefs.

If the physicist is asked why she thinks *there goes a proton*, she may well reply (rather tersely), 'Observation of that vapour trail!' The term *observation*—like the terms *belief, desire, thought,* and so on—is ambiguous, between the content of the observation and the mental episode which has that content. Suppose we asked the physicist: 'Tell us about your observation.' She might reply: 'It was a vapour trail, a textbook example of the kind you would expect a proton to make.' She has interpreted you as asking for the content of her observation, not about her mental state. She won't talk about the fact that her observing the vapour trail was a visual experience, or about the quality of that visual experience.

In conjunction with a substantial body of theory and various auxiliary assumptions about the apparatus, the existence of a proton clearly explains the content of the physicist's observation, the vapour trail itself.

existence of proton at such-and-such a position in the cloud chamber
+ physical theory
+ auxiliary hypotheses (viz. cloud chamber is working properly, etc.)

|

explains

↓

content of experience: that there exists just such a vapour trail.

We might extend this to an explanation of the mental state itself. First, in conjunction with an auxiliary assumption—that the physicist's perceptual apparatus is in a good working condition—the existence of just such a vapour trail explains the physicist's having just such an experience of a vapour trail. We can diagram this explanatory chain thus:

existence of just such a vapour trail
+ auxiliary hypotheses (viz. visual apparatus in working order, etc.)

|

explains

↓

experiential state: the having of an experience of just such a vapour trail.

Second, given that her perceptual apparatus is in good working order, and given that her physical theory in conjunction with the existence of a proton explains the vapour trail, the existence of the proton also explains her *having* a certain visual experience. We can thus put the two explanatory chains together to obtain an explanation of the physicist's experiential state in terms of the existence of the proton. If A explains B, and A is the best explanation of B, and you accept B, then that gives you a reason to accept that A is the case. So the physicist's experience of the vapour trail gives her a reason to accept that there is a vapour trail, and that in turn gives her a reason to accept the existence of the proton and the physical theory that goes along with it.

Back to the boys and Cuddles. As you turn the corner and see the boys burning Cuddles, and Cuddles writhing in pain, you experience a strong aversion to the event. It seems to you that something very bad is going on here, and straightaway you think: *here is something really bad going on.* What is the best explanation of the observation here? Do we need to invoke the badness of what's going on here in the explanation?

First, let's make the same distinction as above: between the content of your experience and the having of that experience. If the experience conjecture is right, then your experiential state is a desire (or aversion), while the content of your experience is: *something very bad is going on here.* What is the best explanation of the propositional content of your experience? Here is one explanation:

> What's going on here is that the boys are wantonly causing Cuddles unnecessary excruciating pain for the sheer fun of it. Cuddles's excruciating pain is itself a bad thing, and causing excruciating pain for the fun of it is also a bad thing. So all told, what's going on here is very bad indeed.

In one clear sense this is an explanation of the fact that *something very bad is going on here* by showing that what's going on here is an instance of two things which, quite generally, are very bad. And that explanation does, of course, make an ineliminable reference to badness. We can diagram the explanation thus:

The boys are causing Cuddles unnecessary pain for fun
+ Pain is intrinsically bad
+ Inflicting unnecessary pain for fun is intrinsically bad

|

explains

↓

Content of experience: what's going on here is very bad.

[handwritten annotation: True only from experience]

Is this the best explanation of the proposition at issue? Maybe not. Maybe there is a better and deeper explanation, one that explains *why* sensations of pain are bad, if and when they are bad. For example, it may be that what makes certain sensations bad is just the very strong desire not to experience those sensations, and it is this intense aversion on the part of the bearer of pain that undergirds pain's disvalue. Or it may be that pain is not intrinsically bad. Maybe it wouldn't be a bad thing for the boys, after having maliciously tormented the cat, to experience the very kind of pain that they inflicted. Maybe that's something they deserve. So the best explanation may be more complicated. Perhaps it is the property of *undeserved* unnecessary pain which is intrinsically bad. But any such explanation, if it is to explain the badness of Cuddles's pain, is going to have to invoke, explicitly or implicitly, badness itself.

Harman also draws the content–state distinction, and maintains that his argument concerns the explanation of the observation *state*, not the observation *content*. He concedes that we may very well need to invoke badness to explain the content of your experience (that something very bad is going on here), but that we do not need to invoke badness in the best, most economical explanation of the experiential state. All we need to explain that state is your mind-set—in particular, your beliefs about value.

As we have seen in the case of the proton, one general strategy for explaining why things *appear* to you a certain way is this: things really *are* that way, and your perceptual apparatus is functioning correctly. So we can extend the explanatory chain as above:

What's going on here is very bad
+ Auxiliary hypotheses (viz. you are responding appropriately to
value)

|

explains
↓

Experiential state: its seeming to you that what's going on here is very
bad.

That, of course, is not the kind of explanation that Harman thinks does the best job here. In the case of the proton, he has in mind a detailed explanation of the causal chain leading from the proton, *via* the vapour trail, the reflected light which forms a pattern on your retina, the triggering of a pattern of neuronal firings in your visual cortex, which somehow either is, or gives rise to, the visual experience that you have. The proton features in this more detailed explanation of your visual experience in a way that badness does not feature in a detailed explanation of your evaluative experience. Micro-physical theory, of which the postulation of protons is a part, is needed to explain what goes on in visual experience. But (Harman would argue) value theory, of which the postulation of goodness and badness is a part, is not needed to explain what goes on when you experience a strong aversion to the cat-bating episode. All we need to explain your aversion is that you *endorse* a value theory according to which cat bating is very bad, and you then presumably project that belief on to the episode through an experience—of extreme aversion, say.

There are particular features of the proton case which may be responsible for driving a false wedge between it and the cat-bating case. In general, when we want some data explained, we don't seek a detailed explanation of how it is that you end up having an experience. For example, when a geologist observes striations on the side of a fiord, and seeks an explanation of that, he is not seeking an explanation of how it is he gets to have visual experiences of striations. The explanation he seeks will appeal to objects and events at the macro level—the movements of glaciers during the last ice age, the resistance of the rock to erosion in the intervening period, and so on. A micro-physical explanation in terms of photons bouncing off the side of the fiord, hitting his retina, and the subsequent effects of that on his brain are not components of a salient explanation of the data in question. In other words, the geologist takes it for granted that his perceptual apparatus is veridically revealing to him some very large scratches on rocks, and it is *that* fact that he wants to explain. What explains his having an *experience* of those large scratches is the existence of those large scratches, together with the fact that his visual apparatus is in good working order—whatever that amounts to. Doubtless, there is a more detailed story to tell here of what makes his visual apparatus tick, and that explanation probably also involves protons and photons and neurons. But that micro-story doesn't seem relevant to explaining (the content of) the geologist's observation of the large striations on the side of the fiord.

Analogously, if we want to explain your observation that the cat episode is very bad, we first appeal to the badness of pain in general, together with the badness of the wanton infliction of unnecessary pain. Conjoined with a couple of auxiliary assumptions, this entails that the episode is bad, and it does so by subsuming the features of the episode under more general principles of value. If we want an explanation of why the episode *seems* very bad to you, then the badness of the episode can also provide the ingredients of that explanation, given a further auxiliary assumption that you are in fact responding appropriately here—that your desires in such cases are reliable indicators of value.

7.2 The Argument from Causal Exclusion

But (a Harman-sympathizer might retort) even if one granted that there are facts about value, we just don't have a causal story to tell about how desires *could* track values, because that would require that values be active constituents of the causal network. And the reason we don't have such a story is that there couldn't be one, given something we have already conceded: the supervenience of value on the natural. Given supervenience—determination without reducibility—we can prove the impotence of values, a proof which parallels familiar exclusion arguments in the philosophy of mind.

How would the proof go? Let's do a quick and dirty version first, and then try to make it a bit more rigorous. What we want to show is that value facts, if there are any, are not the causes of any natural facts. Suppose, then, that value is determined by nature, as required by supervenience. A complete specification of the natural facts would thus be a complete specification of the world *simpliciter.* Suppose in addition that the natural world is causally closed—that for any natural fact E^N there is a true and complete causal explanation of that natural fact in terms of other natural facts. Call the conjunction of those the *cause* of E^N. This does not, by itself, rule out the possibility that there is a complete causal explanation of E^N in terms of some value event or fact, C, or that a value fact causes E^N. To rule that out, we need a causal exclusion principle: that there cannot be two complete and distinct causal explanations, or causes, of any given fact. So, if there is a natural fact and a *distinct* value fact both of which are causes of E^N, then causal exclusion is violated. So, for the value fact C to be the cause of E, it would have to be identical to some natural fact C^N. Hence value facts can be causally active only at the cost of being identical to natural facts. This presumably presupposes the reducibility of value to nature, because the reducibility of value facts would have to piggyback on the reducibility of the respective causally efficacious properties. So, given the exclusion principle, we cannot combine supervenience (determination without reducibility), the causal closure of the natural, and the causal efficacy of value.

I warned that this would be a quick and rather dirty argument. I certainly don't wish to imply that it is valid. The worst feature of it is this: it is not at all clear why a robust realist about value should concede the causal closure of the natural at the outset. That seems to be at least part of what is at stake here, and to assume it at the outset is to beg the question against the causal role which the robust realist wants to assign to value. But perhaps the argument can be tightened up. Perhaps we can derive the conclusion without assuming the causal closure of the natural at the outset. To do so, we would need to have a proof of the causal closure of nature from the determination of value by nature alone (something that all parties to the debate typically concede).

Here is a rough sketch of such proof. If value is determined by nature, then a specification of the natural facts yields all the facts. Suppose that some natural fact E is caused. Then, given determination, there is some event C, specifiable by means of natural properties, which yields a complete causal explanation of natural fact E. Since C is specifiable by means of purely natural features, C itself is a natural event. So for any natural event for which there is a causal explanation, there is a causal explanation that is natural. Hence, barring some kind of overdetermination, every natural event that has a causal explanation has a natural causal explanation. So if value properties play any kind of causal role, those value properties will have to be identical to natural properties. The only causally efficacious value properties would be those that are reducible to natural properties.

How does the exclusion argument apply to the Cuddles episode? You have an experience E—it seems to you that something very bad is going on here. Even though this experience has as its content a proposition about value, this does not mean your experience of value is something over and above the natural. That there are mental states which have contents which involve value should not, by itself, stack the deck in favour of non-naturalism, giving us irreducible value facts for free. So if these experiences *are* value facts, then they must be the kind of value facts which are identical to natural facts. Furthermore, however, the existence of such experiences shouldn't stack the deck against nihilism. The nihilist does not have to deny that people have illusory experiences of value. For experiences of value to be compatible with nihilism, they must not only be illusory, but those experiences themselves must be purely natural facts. So E is a natural event or state.

Suppose there is a causal explanation of your experience E (that it seems to you that something very bad is going on here). One possibility is that the cause of E, C, is a natural event or a complex of such events (involving *inter alia*, the fact that the boys are causing Cuddles extreme pain, by dousing him with gasoline and setting fire to him, for the sheer fun of it). Alternatively, C involves additionally some value facts—for example, that pain is bad, and causing unnecessary pain for fun is bad. If the cause is itself a natural event, then it is not a putative counter-example to the conclusion of the exclusion argument. If the cause involves some value fact, but that value fact is itself a natural fact, then there is still no putative counter-example here. Suppose, however, that the value component of C is not identical to any natural fact. Still, given determination, there will be some natural event or complex of such, C^N, which realizes C. Since C^N is the natural realizer of C, C^N necessitates C, and since C^N causes your experience E, C^N is also causally sufficient for E. So there is a natural event C^N which is causally sufficient for your experience E. Consequently, we do not need to involve the supervenient value fact C in our causal explanation of E. Briefly, if the exclusion argument is sound, C^N does the causal work by itself, without the aid of the value fact. Since the argument is quite general, the best explanation of experiences of value will not invoke the values themselves. Harman's strictures thus fall naturally out of the exclusion argument.

Again, I do not want to imply that this argument is sound. In fact, given the account of why the reducibility of value fails, we will be able to locate rather precisely where it goes wrong. But the argument does seem reasonable, and it, or something like it, clearly motivates the general antagonism to causation by values.

This kind of exclusion argument, applied to the value–natural case, is actually more vexing for the value realist than its mental–physical counterpart is for the realist about minds. A dualist, for example, can comfortably deny the supervenience of the mental on the physical. It is not absurd for a dualist to suppose that the mental has a robust existence which is not dependent on the physical. It would be absurd for the value realist to suppose that value could have a comparably robust existence completely independently of the natural (the non-evaluative). To see this, note that Berkeleian idealism is an extreme version of this detachability of the mental, and Berkeleian idealism is not incoherent. We can understand the claim that Berkeley is making. By contrast, there is no comparably intelligible niche in the value debate corresponding to Berkeleian idealism. There is, of course, *idealism* about value. That is to say, value may stand to the *mental* as Berkeley maintains that the physical stands to the mental. But value cannot stand to the *natural* in the way that Berkeley maintains that the mental stands to the physical. Value cannot float completely freely of any realizing natural basis. The supervenience of value entails that two worlds cannot differ in value without differing at the natural level. An extremely weak consequence of this is that there cannot be two different distributions of value without any underlying distributions of natural traits.

Exclusion arguments in the philosophy of mind are typically taken to present a dilemma for the mental realist: either embrace the identity theory or be forced to adopt some version of epiphe-nomenalism. The parallel exclusion argument, if sound, presents an analogous dilemma to the value theorist: embrace the reduci-bility of value to nature or adopt some kind of epiphenomenalism.

What follows? If value is both irreducible and epiphenomenal, then this appears to have an immediate implication for the know-ability of value. Harman would seem to be right that value wouldn't feature in the best explanations of value experiences, so that particular avenue to knowledge of them would be blocked. Would this have any bearing on the ontological status of value? Not if we take our cue from the Eleatic Stranger. In one respect the Eleatic Stranger is more generous than some of his niggardly current-day counterparts. Recall the Stranger's statement of his principle):

My notion would be, that anything which possesses any sort of power to affect another, *or to be affected by another,* if only for a single moment, however trifling the cause *and however slight the effect,* has real existence; and I hold that the definition of being is simply power. (Plato 1953: 246–7, my emphasis)

The Stranger deems effects, as well as causes, real. So if the role which value plays in the causal network is simply that of causal by-product of natural states, then the Stranger gives them a pass into the realm of being. If the strong Eleatic Principle is our criterion of causal networking, then irreducible epiphenomenal values might still satisfy the ontological demands of robust realism. But it has to be admitted that epiphenomenal values would be profoundly disappointing for the value realist, for they appear to threaten us with value scepticism. So, whatever the Stranger might have thought he was getting at, what *we* want are causally effica-cious values.

7.3 Determinables, Determinates, and Causation

The defects of the kind of exclusion argument which I have sketched here have been exposed by Stephen Yablo (1992). His analysis involves the key notion of the *commensurateness* of the cause with its effect. Commensurateness has two parts: the contingency of the effect on the cause, and the adequacy of the cause to its effect. These correspond to the traditional idea that the cause is, in some sense, both necessary and sufficient for its effect.

First, adequacy. Yablo's important insight here is that determinables may not be competitors with their determinates for causal adequacy. As a consequence, they may not be competitors for explanation either. Romeo gives Juliet a rose. The redness of the rose may be adequate, in the circumstances, to arouse Juliet's interest. Perhaps Romeo is exploiting a certain standing background condition, that red roses are a conventional sign of romantic intentions and that Juliet knows this. But, as it happens, the rose is an Uncle Walter, deep crimson. The crimsonness of the rose is also causally sufficient to arouse her interest. *Being crimson* is a determinate of *being red*, but in the circumstances both are causally sufficient for Juliet's interest being aroused. We can explain the arousal by citing the redness of the rose (perhaps together with various standing background conditions), but we could also explain it by citing its crimsonness.

Second, contingency. While determinates and determinables may not be rivals for *causal sufficiency*, they can be rivals for the role of *the cause*, and in many cases a better candidate for the cause of a certain effect, one which better satisfies commensurateness, is a determinable rather than one of its determinates. Causes must be commensurate with their effects in the sense that they should not contain too much. Commensurateness involves the contingency of the effect on the cause, and a causally adequate determinate might be too determinate for the effect to be contingent on it.

What was the cause of the arousal of Juliet's interest? Was it the redness of the rose (the determinable) or its crimsonness (a determinate of that determinable)? A rose of any other shade of red would have aroused her interest just as well, so it seems that the arousal is contingent on the rose's being red, but not on the rose's being crimson. 'The contingency condition', Yablo says, 'exposes an overly determinate pretender' to the role of cause (1992: 275). It rules out those contenders for the role of cause which contain more than is necessary to secure the effect in question.

One way of explicating the contingency condition involves the following counterfactual:

C_1 *Had the rose not been red, the arousal would not have occurred.*

C_1, we may suppose, is true. Maybe that's what underlies the fact that the arousal is contingent on the redness. Had the rose not been red, it would have been some other colour (yellow or white or whatever), and that (we may suppose) would have done nothing to arouse Juliet's interest. Consider the corresponding conditional about its crimsonness:

C_2 *Had the rose not been crimson, the arousal would not have occurred.*

Had it not been crimson, it might still have been red, perhaps a rose of a different variety. So had the rose not been crimson, it might still have been red, and so had it not been crimson, it might still have effected the arousal. That's incompatible with C_2. So the counterfactual condition 'exposes the overly determinate pretender', and thus seems like a reasonable way to articulate contingency.

Whatever theory of counterfactuals we espouse, we countenance situations in which C_1 is true and C_2 false, and in such situations that may be what is involved in the arousal's being contingent on the redness of the rose, not on its crimsonness. Unfortunately, however, the trouble with the counterfactual condition is that it doesn't really capture contingency. Suppose Romeo picks up the rose at the market on the way to Capulets. The only varieties available are red (including, amongst others, the Uncle Walter) and yellow. Romeo chooses an Uncle Walter, wisely as it happens, because Juliet loathes yellow roses. Indeed, yellow is a colour that quite generally repulses her. But, as it turns out, a rose of any colour *other* than yellow would have done the trick, arousing her interest just as effectively as any red rose. In that case C_1 would still be true (in the circumstances) and C_2 false, but is her arousal contingent on the rose's being red? Is the rose's being red really a better candidate for the causal role than its being crimson? What does the causal work in this situation seems to be the rose's being some colour *other than yellow.* The test conditional C_1 is still true, but only because of an irrelevant contingent fact, that there were no colours other than red and yellow available at the market. To see that it is not the redness which does the causal work in the circumstances, suppose that the only alternatives to the yellow roses had been Uncle Walters. Then C_2 would have been true in the circumstances. But something even more determinate would also have been true:

C_3 *Had the rose not been an instance of the variety called "Uncle Walter" the arousal would not have occurred.*

Isn't the antecedent condition here overly determinate to be a candidate for the cause of Juliet's arousal? We can imagine circumstances in which even more determinate conditions satisfy the test. Suppose there had been just one red rose left—C_4 would also have been true:

C_4 *Had the rose not been that <u>particular</u> instance of the variety called 'Uncle Walter', the arousal would not have occurred.*

But surely the rose's being called 'Uncle Walter' is no part of the cause of the arousal—a rose by any other name would have done the trick, provided only that it wasn't a ghastly yellow. And (*pace* Gerard Manley Hopkins) it is somewhat absurd to suggest that the rose's *haecceity* could play a role in Juliet's arousal. There is thus something deeper to the contingency condition than these counterfactuals. I propose to leave it unanalysed here.

Of course, contingency alone is not enough to identify the cause. We need the adequacy, or sufficiency, condition: that what does the causing is adequate or sufficient for the effect. A parallel counterfactual condition would seem to be this:

D_1 *Had the rose been red, the arousal would have occurred.*

Although this is true, it seems idle in the circumstances, given that the rose was red and that the arousal occurred. (On a similarity analysis, which Yablo utilizes, all counterfactuals with true antecedents and consequents come out true automatically.) In seeking a counterfactual analysis of adequacy, Yablo substitutes for D_1 a very odd-sounding counterfactual to capture adequacy:

D_2 *If the rose hadn't been red, then if it had been red the arousal would have occurred.*

Suppose the rose hadn't been red—in the circumstances mentioned. Then it would have to have been yellow. So, suppose it had been yellow. In that case, *had it been red*, the arousal would have been effected. The same goes for crimsonness if the only roses available were Uncle Walters. Both crimsonness and redness are thus adequate to the effect, as seems right.

I suppose that, given enough time and ingenuity, one could think of situations in which D_2 turns out to be false (intuitively) even though the redness of the presented rose is adequate to bring about the arousal. The story would doubtless be convoluted, an inevitable consequence of searching for counter-examples to analyses couched in terms of counterfactual conditionals, especially nested counterfactuals. Indeed, the whole programme of analysing causation in terms of counterfactuals has been shown, by Michael Tooley (forthcoming), to be fatally flawed. Again, however, we can adopt the adequacy condition itself, because we do seem to have an intuitive grasp of it, while leaving for another day the job of analysing it.[1]

7.4 Mental Causation

With this intuitive notion of commensurateness (adequacy plus contingency) under our belts, let us turn to the problem of mental causation. To apply these considerations, involving determinates and determinables, to the mental–physical case, Yablo makes his most controversial, indeed rather startling claim: that the determinates of mental determinables are nothing other than their physical realizers. Quite generally, he claims that if we have a supervenience relation, then we have all we need for the determinate–determinable relation. Supervenient properties are determinables of the properties in the supervenience base. Yablo notes that the base properties necessitate the supervening properties without being necessitated by them, and that, he claims, is the essence of the relation between the determinates and their determinables. A determinate necessitates its determinables without being necessitated by them. So if the mental supervenes on the physical, then we can regard physical realizers as determinates of the mental determinables they realize. If this is right, then it opens up the

---

[1] In section 7.7 below I suggest that a more plausible account will appeal to second-order relations of necessitation and probabilification holding between first-order properties.

possibility that a mental event, along with its physical realizer, might not just be causally sufficient for some effect, but might be better a candidate for the title of *cause* than its physical realizer. For some particular effect the mental (determinable) will not carry the strictly redundant baggage that accompanies its physical realizer.

For example, suppose Romeo's love for Juliet arouses her interest. If physicalism is right, his love is realized in his physical state in some particular way. Maybe it is realized in a determinate pattern of neuronal firings, or dispositions to have certain neuronal firings, and that physical state is causally sufficient for his offering Juliet the rose. Of course, his love might have been realized in many other ways. That's just what the thesis of multiple realizability tells us. The *actual* physical realization of his love is doubtless causally sufficient to bring about an arousal of Juliet's interest, but it is not *the cause* of that arousal. Rather, it is the *determinable*, Romeo's *love* for Juliet, which arouses her interest.

Conversely, suppose Juliet is not just aroused, she is overwhelmed by the evident ardency of Romeo's love. Her being overwhelmed is, we might suppose, a determinate of her being aroused. What causes her to be overwhelmed? Romeo's love *per se* is not up to the task. That Romeo loves her causes her arousal, to be sure, but it does not overwhelm her. It is not Romeo's love, but rather his *ardent* love, a determinate of love, which causes her to be overwhelmed. In this case Romeo's love is insufficiently determinate, and hence insufficient. Again, however, the physical realizer of his ardent love is too determinate, since his ardent love could have been realized in many different ways to the same effect. Being too determinate, it is unnecessary to the effect.

Underlying these judgements is the principle of commensurateness of cause and effect. A candidate for the cause must be sufficient for the effect in question. If it is not determinate enough to be sufficient, it is not the cause. But it must not be too determinate, or else it is unnecessary. A candidate can contain too much extraneous, causally irrelevant material. So Romeo's love, rather than his ardent love, is the best candidate for the cause of Juliet's being aroused, and his ardent love, rather than its physical realizer, is the best candidate for the cause of Juliet's being overwhelmed.

Traditionally, of course, paradigm cases of determinates and determinables are drawn from the same conceptual categories.

Red is a determinate of *colour*, *crimson* is a determinate of *red* as well as of *colour*, *deep crimson*, a determinate of *crimson*, of *red*, and of *colour*. *Ardent love* is a determinate of the determinable *love*, *love* is a determinate of the determinable of *caring*. These determinables are clearly cut from the same conceptual cloth as their determinates. Call this the *conceptual condition*. The conceptual condition looks as though it undercuts Yablo's argument, since, although caring, love, and ardent love might all be categorially of a piece, love and patterns of neuronal firings are clearly not.

Yablo suggests that objections to his thesis based on a conceptual or categorial condition like this are a relic of pre-Kripkean thinking. We are reminded that the good Kripke taught us that conceptual relations are not reliable guides to metaphysical relations. So, for example, H_2O is a determinate of the determinable *compound of hydrogen and oxygen*. But water is identical to H_2O and necessarily so. Hence, by Leibniz's law, water is also a determinate of the determinable *chemical compound of hydrogen and oxygen*. This is so despite the fact that this particular determinate–determinable relation was an empirical discovery and could not have been established on conceptual grounds. Now suppose that water is realized not just in H_2O, but in various other determinate compounds of hydrogen and oxygen. Suppose, further, that W is a chemical determinable embracing all and only the chemical compounds which are realizers of water. Then presumably water is *identical* to W, and the chemical determinates of W are thereby also determinates of *water*. If this is right, then maybe the various patterns of neuronal firings that realize love are also determinates of love.

Consider another case. Consider a particular determinate shade of red—*fire-engine red*, say—one with a completely determinate hue, saturation, and brightness. Any two instances of fire-engine red are thus colour-indistinguishable. Suppose that fire-engine red is realized in a small range of physical properties—small, but a range nevertheless. Bert's fire-engine is fire-engine red in virtue of physical realizer P_1, while Ed's is so in virtue of physical realizer P_2, where P_1 and P_2 are distinct. But the two fire-engines look exactly alike to all normal observers in all normal conditions. Isn't it then strange to deem P_1 and P_2 *distinct* determinates of the colour *fire-engine red* given that, under normal conditions, Bert's fire-engine is colour-indistinguishable from Ed's fire-engine? Two items which are indistinguishable as to their colour do not instantiate distinct *determinates* of colour. Thus, whether or not one grants the Krip-kean premisses, Yablo's thesis is entirely resistible. And, to the extent that his argument for the compatibility of mental causation with supervenience turns on that thesis, it's flawed. That's bad news for us, however, because it looked like a promising model for causation by values.

7.5   Causation by Values

Yablo's insight that determinates and their determinables are not necessarily causal rivals, that both may be causally sufficient for a certain effect, still stands. So too do the common-sense intuitions about the commensurateness of the cause to its effect. It turns out, happily, that these ideas are enough by themselves to render causation by values intelligible. A defence of causation by value is not dependent on the adequacy of either Yablo's counterfactual analyses of commensurateness or his defence of mental causation.

The cat-bating episode is bad. Why? Well, for one thing, *pain* is bad, and Cuddles is suffering excruciating pain. For another, tor-menting a cat for the fun of it is cruel, and *cruelty* is also bad. Cruelty is bad not just because it causes pain. This episode is worse than one in which a cat suffers exactly the same degree of excru-ciating pain fleeing, say, an accidental house fire. That's evidence that cruelty, like pain, is bad in itself. It is hard to think of a pair of situations which differ only in that in one of them there is cruelty and in the other not, but which are value-equivalent. Callousness is also bad. The fact that various bystanders don't care about Cudd-les's pain adds to the episode's overall badness. Cruelty is one way of realizing the bad, callousness is another. It is thus natural to think of the property of *badness* as a determinable of which *pain*, *cruelty*, and *callousness* are determinates.

There are a thousand natural shocks that flesh is heir to, differ-ent shocks being constituted by different determinate ways of being in pain. As a corollary, deliberate inflictions of different shocks, for pleasure, are different determinates of cruelty. Causing a cat unnecessary pain for fun is one determinate realization of cruelty, quite a severe one. But there are, of course, myriad others, arranged in a space rich with structure endowed by betweenness.[2]

Determinates of cruelty are themselves determinables. You can cause a cat unnecessary pain for fun in sundry ways. Causing a cat unnecessary pain by depriving it of food or water is one. Tormenting it by dousing it in gasoline and setting fire to it is another. The Cuddles-bating episode is a determinate realization of this latter kind, but it is, of course, realized in a specific way. Maybe the boys are using leaded gasoline, rather than unleaded. These would be two different possible realizations of the episode, but are they two distinct determinates of *cruelty*? Not unless the leaded fuel makes some kind of difference to the badness of the episode, by making a difference either to the cat's pain or to the boy's maliciousness. Cuddles is probably indifferent between being burnt with leaded fuel and being burnt with unleaded fuel. The lead could conceivably make a difference to the boys' maliciousness. Maybe Cuddles's owner owns a lead mine, and the boys choose leaded fuel out of spite. Finally, there is a specific natural event, call it N, which encompasses the whole Cuddles-bating episode. N is the conjunction of a vast number of natural events, and because conjunction preserves naturalness, N will itself be a natural event.

Which of this range of increasingly determinate events is the cause of your experience? That depends. There are more or less determinate aspects of your experience as well: your experience of the badness, your experience of the boys' cruelty, your experience of the awfulness of the cat's pain, your experience of the cruelty of the tormenting of *your* cat *Cuddles*. The best candidate for the cause of your experience depends on the particular aspect of your experience that we are interested in.

Take your experience of the boys' cruelty. Here are some candidate causes: the very determinate natural event N, the fact that the boys are causing unnecessary pain to your cat Cuddles by

---

[2] Here, for example, is a determinate of cruelty very far in value space from the Cuddles-bating episode, from Valerie Steiker's memoir of her mother. 'When my mother, age eighteen, came home one day and told her mother about a beautiful coat she had seen in a boutique—*Will you look at it for me?* she asked—my grandmother returned the next day with the coat in a shopping bag, having bought it for herself. *It's too old for you*, she said as she hung it up in her closet. My mother reacted to this minor cruelty by going too far in the other direction' (Steiker 2001: 64).

dousing him in unleaded gasoline and setting him alight, the fact that the boys are being cruel to a cat, the fact that the boys are being cruel, the fact that something bad is going on here. Simplifying somewhat, all but the last of these may be causally sufficient for your experiencing the cruelty. They are not rivals for causal sufficiency or for causal relevance. That much is covered by Yablo's insight. But they cannot all be *the* cause. Which is the cause depends on which is most commensurate with the effect.

The very determinate purely natural event N contains the particular neuronal firings that the boys and the cat undergo at the exact moments at which they undergo them. But the boys and the cat could clearly have undergone any of a vast array of different neuronal firings, and there would still have been the same cruelty exhibited, cruelty of exactly the same variety and degree, and you would still have experienced it as cruel in exactly the same way. N is thus overly determinate to be the cause of your experience of cruelty *per se*.

At the other extreme, consider the fact that something very bad is going on here. Badness is a determinable of which cruelty is one determinate. Had the boys been doing any number of other bad things at that particular spot—had they been callously indifferent to the suffering of a burning cat fleeing an accidental house fire, for example—you might well not have had an experience of *cruelty*. Rather, you would have had an experience of callousness. So the badness of the episode is not determinate enough to cause your experience of cruelty.

Clearly a better candidate, one more commensurate with the effect in question, must be chosen from among determinates between these two extremes. Which one is best may depend on particular features of the situation, but on the face of it the most obvious candidate looks to be the fact that the boys are being *cruel*. Suppose it would not have made any difference to your experience of cruelty if the boys had been setting alight any comparably sentient creature, like a dog or a squirrel. Then the fact that it is a *cat* to which they are being cruel is not commensurate with the effect. That it is a cat to which they are being cruel is too determinate. It is the cruelty of the episode which is both adequate to your experience, and on which your experience is contingent.

Now if the argument of Chapter 6 is right, cruelty is a value property which is determined by natural properties, but is not identical to any natural property. Cruelty is a convex condition within a rich and highly structured value space. Cruelty is, of course, necessarily coextensive with its natural basis—a condition which can be defined in terms of some very complicated Boolean combination of natural attributes—but the natural basis of cruelty is not a *natural property*. The projection of *cruelty* on to the natural subspace is not convex. So although there are various natural events of increasing determinateness which realize the boys' cruelty, all of which are causally sufficient for your experience of cruelty, none of those purely natural events is the cause of your experience, because your experience is not appropriately contingent on them.

Could we *arrange* it that the cause of your experience of cruelty is the fact that it is a *cat* that the boys are tormenting? Suppose that you don't care about the suffering of any animals other than cats. So far as you are concerned, cruelty is something that occurs only through the deliberate and wanton infliction of suffering on cats. When you see Cuddles the cat being wantonly tormented, you observe the boys' cruelty, but their cruelty alone is not sufficient to cause your observation. Cruelty to a dog would not have done the trick. It has to be cruelty to a cat to trigger your experience. This might be a case in which the more determinate state, cruelty to a cat rather than cruelty *per se*, is the cause of your experience.

There is an alternative, however. It is possible that in this circumstance it is not cruelty as such that you are *experiencing*. Suppose you are a cat-lover of a rather extreme variety. You are obsessed with the welfare of cats to the exclusion of all other sentient creatures. Given your psychological make-up, you aren't appropriately equipped to experience cruelty *per se*, because you do not possess a reliable *cruelty* indicator. Rather, what you register, and experience, in the Cuddles case is cruelty-to-cats. And what is causing *that* is not cruelty, but cruelty to a cat.

Whichever is the correct view of the obsessive cat-lover case, what is clear is that in the normal case you are the kind of person for whom the cause of an experience of cruelty is cruelty itself.

It is not hard to see that what goes for cruelty also goes for badness. You have an experience of the badness of the episode. What is the cause of that? The cruelty, we may suppose, is causally sufficient for your experience, but suppose that an equally bad episode had been taking place that did not involve cruelty—say widespread callousness at the pain of a burning man fleeing a house fire? Suppose that that callousness would have been sufficient for you to have an experience of badness of exactly the same intensity as your current experience of the badness of the boys' cruelty to the cat. Then the boys' cruelty is sufficient but not necessary for your experience of badness. In this case the more commensurate candidate cause is adequate for your experience of badness, but your experience of badness is not contingent on the boys' cruelty *per se*.

If this is on the right track, then not only can individual values and disvalues—like kindness and cruelty—play a role in causing and explaining our experiences of those values, but the determinables under which these particular values fall—goodness and badness themselves—can be the causes, and hence explanations, of our experiences of goodness and badness.

There is, of course, nothing inevitable about this. The hooligans who are dousing the cat are also having experiences of value. They clearly want to do whatever it is that they consider themselves to be up to, and so it seems to them that it is good. But their experiences are wildly distorted and misleading presentations of value. Their desires are thoroughly unreliable indicators of the good, at least in this domain. As with ordinary perception, you have to have suitable receptors in reasonable working order before your experiences are a reliable guide to what's out there. But there is nothing incoherent, or even particularly mysterious, about the possibility of one's experiences of the good—desires—reliably tracking the good.

Looking back to the exclusion argument in the light of this, we can see where it fails. Take the following derivation of the causal closure of the natural from the determination component of supervenience:

> Suppose that some natural fact E is caused. Then there is some event C specifiable by means of natural properties, which gives a complete causal explanation of natural fact E. Since C is specifiable by means of natural properties, C itself is natural. So for any natural event for which there is a

causal explanation, there is a causal explanation that is itself natural.

The fallacy here comes in the following inference:

C is specifiable by means of natural properties, *therefore* C itself is natural.

In light of the discussion on convexity, this is a clear *non sequitur*. A value fact C is the instantiation of a value property V. For each value property V, there is a collection of mutually exclusive natural properties—N_1, N_2,...N_k—which are jointly exhaustive of V. N_1, N_2,...N_k are the *natural realizers* of V, each of which necessitates V, and the disjunction of which is necessitated by V. The disjunction of the natural realizers of V—(N_1 *or* N_2 *or*... *or* N_k)—is the *natural basis* of V. Even though V is necessarily coextensive with a naturalistically specified condition (N_1 *or* N_2 *or*... *or* N_k), it does not follow that V is a *natural property*—because V's projection on to the natural dimensions may not be convex. The disjunction (N_1 *or* N_2 *or*... *or* N_k) may be disjointed or 'messy' in the sense made precise in the previous chapter. That is to say, at the natural level the region it carves out is not convex. There may be a natural property N^* which falls between N_1 and N_2 (say) but falls outside V. So, from the mere fact that C can be specified naturalistically—as an instance of the disjunction (N_1 *or* N_2 *or*... *or* N_k)—it does not follow that C is a natural fact, any more than it follows that V is a natural property.

To summarize, even though all facts are determined by the totality of natural facts, it does not follow that all the causally efficacious facts are themselves natural facts.

7.6 Causation and Convexity

So far this is a relatively straightforward application of the idea of commensurateness to the case of causation by value. In fact, it is rather more straightforward than Yablo's original application to the case of mental causation, because it doesn't turn on a dubious derivation of the determinable–determinate relation from supervenience. The case for value causation can be strengthened by two considerations. One, which we will explore in this section, involves consideration of a feature which has been overlooked, not just in Yablo's treatment but in many treatments of this problem: the *convexity* of a set of determinates. The other, which we will explore in the next section, meshes what I will call the *convexity constraint* with a familiar point about the relations between causation and properties.

It is perhaps not surprising that Yablo overlooked the role which convexity plays in causation, because convexity is closely tied to the conceptual condition, something which Yablo explicitly rejects in order to carry out his derivation of the determinable–determinate relation from supervenience. Think of the traditional paradigms of the determinate–determinable relation. Colours, for example. What is striking about determinates of, say, *blue*, is that any quality which—like Hume's famous missing shade—is between two determinates of blue is itself a determinate of blue. Or consider size. *Large*, a determinate of size, is a determinable of which *somewhat large* and *very large* are determinates. A determinate which falls between these two, say *moderately large*, is also a determinate of *large*. *Cruelty* is a determinate of *bad*, and is itself a determinable of which *frustrating cats for fun* and *torturing cats for fun* are determinates. *Tormenting cats for fun* lies somewhere between these two determinates, and as such it too is a determinate of cruelty. And so on. This suggests a quite general hypothesis: the class of all determinates (of a certain degree of specificity) of a determinable is closed under the relation of betweenness. This hypothesis would go a long way to explaining intuitions driving the conceptual condition. Only those qualities that can be compared for similarity can cluster together as determinates of a determinable.

Convexity is heavily involved in measurement. Consider a measuring device, like a mercury thermometer. Suppose it displays 92 degrees Fahrenheit on a standard Colorado summer day, and suppose that in fact it is 92° F. Does this make the thermometer a good indicator of the temperature in these circumstances? No. It might just be stuck on 92° F. In that case the reading isn't appropriately contingent on the temperature. But suppose the reading does vary with the temperature. We might try to cash this out in some kind of counterfactual: *had it not been 92°F, the thermometer would not have displayed 92°F.* But that counterfactual might be false. It will certainly be false on any similarity theory of counterfactuals which takes the notion of similarity seriously. The world closest to the actual world in which the antecedent is true would be one in which the temperature is only barely different from 92°F, a difference below the threshold which the thermometer registers, and so in which the thermometer, being insufficiently sensitive, still registers 92°F. On any account, similarity or otherwise, the existence of that possible situation will be enough to ensure that had the temperature not been 92°F, the reading *might still* have been 92°F. A thermometer doesn't have to output the *exact* temperature for it to be a reliable guide. Indeed, if that were the case, thermometers would be rendered, for all practical purposes, impossible. No measuring device that we could construct and read could output any one of a continuum of real numbers.

For a thermometer to be a reliable guide to temperature, it has to track the temperature in the following sense: it has to vary appropriately with the temperature within some margin of sensitivity. Suppose R_1, R_2, and R_3 are three different readings that the thermometer might output, and suppose further that, as *readings*, R_2 is between R_1 and R_3. (If it is a mercury thermometer, say, then there is an obvious sense to betweenness. Let $T(R_i)$ be the actual temperature range when the thermometer outputs reading R_i. Then, for the thermometer to be responding appropriately, $T(R_2)$ should be between $T(R_1)$ and $T(R_3)$. Generalize this and call it the *convexity constraint.*

What has to be the case for your experiences to be a guide to value is that under felicitous circumstances they obey a similar convexity constraint. They vary appropriately with different values, in the way in which the output of a good thermometer varies with temperature. But this does not mean that your experiences have to be an absolutely accurate guide to value, or to absolute differences between various values. Your experiences might be a fairly reliable guide to cruelty, say, within a certain margin of sensitivity. Suppose that the Cuddles-bating episode seems moderately bad to you, Steiker's daughter-bating episode (f.n.2) seems mildly bad, and the destruction of the World Trade Center monstrously bad. If experiences of the good are desires, we can cash the convexity constraint out in a straightforward way. The strength of your aversion to the cat-bating episode lies between that of your aversion to the daughter-bating episode and your aversion to the destruction of the World Trade Center.[3]

Once the reliability of experiences of value is cashed out in terms of this convexity constraint, it is clear what must be the causes of your experiences. The natural states which realize, say, *cruelty* do not form a convex set of conditions within the natural space. A very small change at the natural level might make an enormous difference at the level of cruelty, perhaps a rather significant change at the level of value. Your experiences of value, to be reliable, cannot be sensitive to such irrelevant changes at the natural level. For your experiences to be tracking *cruelty*, two very different natural realizations of cat bating (very different at the natural level) which involve the same degree of malice and the same degree of suffering have to elicit the same cruelty aversion. But this means that it cannot be a natural state or property that is the cause of your experiences of cruelty, since the causally relevant conditions are not convex in the natural dimensions. Rather, it is the value states and properties which do the relevant causal work. Experiences of value are not sensitive to the details of natural realization. Rather, they follow the contours of value.

7.7 Causation and Properties

The convexity constraint is a condition on a representational device, whether it be a thermometer or an experiencer of value. Interestingly, the convexity constraint, together with a familiar thesis about the relation between causation and properties, enables us to go one step further in the argument for causation by values.

That there is a connection between causation and laws, or law-likeness of some kind, is a familiar enough point. The exact nature of the connection is disputed, but that there is some kind of connection is widely accepted. One class of very similar accounts of the connection between causation and laws is the DTA

---

[3] The convexity constraint is there in the neurobiological accounts of standard perception. See Gärdenfors (2000) and Churchland (2001) for discussions of the links between conceptual space theory and perception.

account—where 'DTA' is short for 'Dretske–Tooley–Armstrong', the three philosophers who independently arrived at these very similar accounts in the late 1970s (Dretske 1977; Tooley 1977; Armstrong 1978).

The basic idea behind DTA-style accounts is this. Causation is subject to a kind of universalizability, rather like the universalizability of value. Suppose a brick's hitting the window *causes* the window to break. This connection between the brick and the window 'transfers' to any other brick and window that are just the same apart from this causal connection. *Any* object that is just like the brick would cause *any* object just like the window to break, provided the brick replica hits the window replica in the same way. Take a simple schematic example of this: if X's being P causes X to be Q, then *anything's* being P will cause that thing to be Q. This transfer of causal connection might be just some kind of inexplicable brute fact—that certain pairs of events are logically connected to other pairs of events in a mysterious way. Alternatively, there might be some kind of explanation for this otherwise mysterious necessary transfer from one pair of events to a distinct pair of events.

The value analogue may be helpful here. If St Francis is a good man, then we can similarly 'transfer' that goodness to anyone who is in all natural respects just like St Francis. Suppose, for example, that St Francis is good because he is compassionate—then any person who is similarly compassionate must also be good. More likely, St Francis is good in virtue of possessing a *nature N* which embraces some more complex combination of attributes like compassion, but the point would be the same. If St Francis is good, then anybody with the same nature N is also good. One possible explanation for this transfer of goodness is that it is the *first-order property* of *being compassionate* (of or having nature N) which is, in the first instance, the bearer of goodness—that is, of a *second-order* property of goodness. We can thus distinguish the (upper-case G) Goodness of properties with the derivative (lower-case g) goodness of their instantiations.[4] First-order properties that are good are *virtues*, because they instantiate this second-order property of goodness. But if the first-order property has that second-order

---

[4] See Forrest (1988); Oddie (1991); and Forrest's reply in his (1992).

property, and the instances of the first-order property are good because of the goodness of the property, then *any* instance of a valuable property or a virtue is (derivatively) good or virtuous. This not only gels with the common-sense view that what makes an individual good is the Goodness of his nature, but it immediately explains transfer. Suppose X is good. X must have some nature or other, say N, the Goodness of which makes X good. So N must be Good. Suppose Y shares X's nature (Y is just like X in all natural respects). Then Y also has N. It follows that Y must also be good. The transfer of goodness is explained.

Now consider the causal case. Why is it that the causal *connection* between X's being P and X's being Q *transfers* to the pair Y's being P and Y's being Q? Suppose that what makes for the causal connection between the two individual events is that there is a contingent second-order relation of *nomic necessitation* holding between the first-order properties P and Q. That is to say, the fundamental connection holds between the first-order properties P and Q rather than between property instances: P *nomically necessitates* Q. Given that this connection holds at the level of the properties, any other instantiation of these two properties by an individual must also stand in the relation of causal connection. The causal connection thus transfers from one such pair to another.

Causal connections, then, are undergirded by a contingent second-order relation of nomic necessitation which holds between first-order properties. But causation comes in more than the simple iron-clad variety. There can be probabilistic causation as well. Again, the exact nature of probabilistic causation is hotly disputed, but the underlying intuition is that a cause in some way or other raises the objective chance of its effect occurring. What we have said about the relation between causation and nomic necessitation can be extended to the relation between probabilistic causation and *chance* or *propensity*. Nomic necessitation is the extreme end of a continuous magnitude, *propensity*, which takes pairs of properties as input, and delivers numbers between 0 and 1 as output. Preparing an electron in the singlet state, say, endows it with a $1/2$ chance of being spin-up or spin-down. This means that there are two properties— say *electron in the singlet state* (S) and *electron with spin up* (U)—and that the propensity for U given S is 0.5. Any electron would similarly be spin-up with a probability of 0.5 if prepared in the singlet state.

Let's accept, then, that causation is a relation, holding between event-tokens but undergirded by second-order relations of nomic necessitation and probabilification between first-order properties. Both Armstrong and Tooley espouse *sparse* theories of properties, and we have seen that convexity captures many of the property intuitions which motivate such theories—like the intuition that the operations of disjunction and negation do not necessarily preserve propertyhood. So the DTA account of the connection between causation and higher-order relations, in conjunction with the convexity account, yields the conclusion that causation is a relation between event-tokens which is undergirded by higher-order relations of nomic necessitation and probabilification between convex conditions of a quality space.

Returning to the larrikins, suppose that something about the cat bating causes your aversion. What could do that? Only a *property* if the DTA account is on the right lines. And a property is a convex condition, if the convexity account is on the right lines. (Recall that on the convexity account a conjunction of properties is itself a property, so the claim here does not lack sufficient generality.) Suppose, as now seems plausible, that there is no convex condition at the natural level, a token of which is commensurate with your aversion. It follows that the causal claim (that there is something about the cat bating that *causes* your aversion) is true only if there are causally relevant properties at work here other than the purely natural candidates in the offing. So, for the causal claim to be true, value properties (or more likely *fusions* of value and natural properties, which are themselves value properties) must stand in a higher-order relation of nomic necessitation or probabilification to your desiderative states.[5]

This would mesh nicely with the convexity constraint. For your experiences to be reliably tracking features of the world, they have to stand to those features in the right way. Small variations in a feature must be represented by small variations in the experience

---

[5] The leading idea in this section I owe to Paul Studtmann. Note that I am not claiming that a pure value property (like cruelty) will *directly* cause your aversion all by itself (just as the temperature does not *directly* cause the thermometer to output the correct reading). Clearly, there are other causally relevant conditions which, in conjunction with the cruelty (or temperature) produce your aversion (or the reading).

of that feature. Betweenness in the world must be correlated with betweenness in conceptual representation.

There is one rather interesting consequence of this causal hypothesis. How should we classify nomic relations between value and nature? They have a foot in both camps, so it would be wrong to classify them as purely natural. They seem rather to be on the evaluative side of the divide. In that case we are faced with the following rather radical possibility—that the totality of natural facts does not actually settle all the value facts. There would be some contingent facts (the causal connections between value and nature) which would not be determined by nature alone. This claim is not essential to the defence of robust realism, but if it is true, then it would be an added reason for rejecting those versions of naturalism which turn on the determination of value by nature.

7.8 Towards a Robust Value Realism

Nothing is easier than to postulate a bunch of entities. The hard task is to show that the entities postulated can earn an honest existence for themselves. Are the postulated entities anything more than redundant ontological cogs, spinning to no effect? Do they do any work? Can they explain something that would otherwise be puzzling? Can we have reasonable beliefs about them? All of these questions can be answered in the affirmative if the entities in question are causally networked with the world in general and with our experiences in particular. In the previous two chapters I have argued that values are irreducible. They are not reducible to experiences of value, nor are they reducible to anything else that is natural. In this chapter I have argued the case for causation by values—an apparently radical thesis—but in making it plausible, it has become apparent how such causation would mesh smoothly with the natural fabric of the world. In the next and final chapter I will bring the different threads of the argument together and resolve some of the problems which this robustly realist account of value brings into sharp relief.

I find this arg. unclear after 1reading

8   VALUE, JUDGEMENT, AND DESIRE: BRIDGING THE GAPS

THERE are different ways of carving up the space of possible positions on value. I opened this investigation with one such carving. I close with another.

The robust realist countenances three important, inevitable, but also somewhat troubling, logical gaps—gaps which antirealists of different stripes attempt to close or to reduce to manageable proportions. First, there is the logical gap between the way things seem and the way they are: it seems to me that the moon is larger than the sun (but in fact the sun is larger). There is the logical gap between the way things seem and what is believed: it seems to me that the moon is larger than the sun (but I believe that the sun is in fact larger). Finally, there is the logical gap between what is believed and the way things really are: I believe that the moon is larger than the sun (but in fact the sun is larger).

These gaps are inevitable, but they are also irksome. They make possible a range of phenomena that are typically taken to be cognitive shortcomings. The gap between appearance and reality is associated with the possibility of *illusion*. The gap between belief and reality is associated with the possibility of *error*. The gap between appearance and belief is associated with a possibility that has no common name, so I will call it *incongruence*. It is the possibility of such cognitive shortcomings that the idealist would prefer to expunge.

8.1   The Gappiness of Realism

It will be useful to depict the gaps in the realist's universe in a diagram (fig. 8.1).

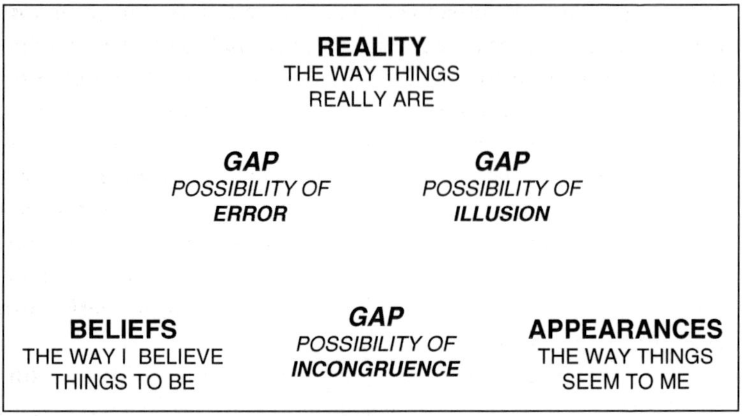

REALITY
THE WAY THINGS
REALLY ARE

GAP
POSSIBILITY OF
ERROR

GAP
POSSIBILITY OF
ILLUSION

BELIEFS
THE WAY I BELIEVE
THINGS TO BE

GAP
POSSIBILITY OF
INCONGRUENCE

APPEARANCES
THE WAY THINGS
SEEM TO ME

FIG. 8.1   *The gaps in the realist's universe*

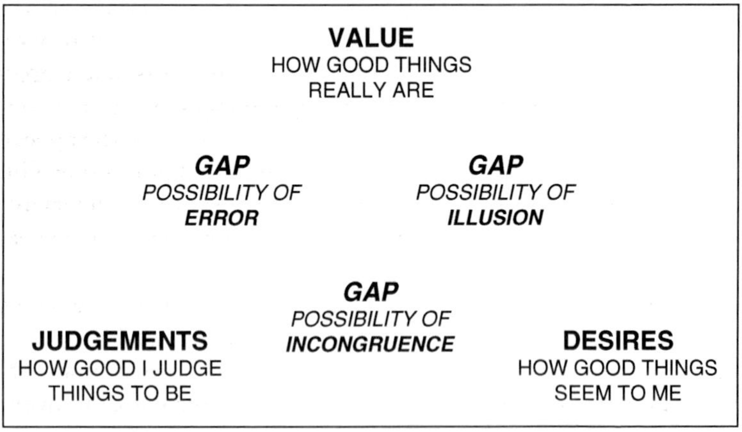

VALUE
HOW GOOD THINGS
REALLY ARE

GAP
POSSIBILITY OF
ERROR

GAP
POSSIBILITY OF
ILLUSION

JUDGEMENTS
HOW GOOD I JUDGE
THINGS TO BE

GAP
POSSIBILITY OF
INCONGRUENCE

DESIRES
HOW GOOD THINGS
SEEM TO ME

FIG. 8.2   *The gaps in the value realist's universe*

Realism about value can also be characterized by three gaps (fig. 8.2). Appearances of value are, I have argued, *desires*. Beliefs about value are *value judgements*. The reality at issue is, of course, *value*. So, corresponding to the appearance–reality gap, we have the *desire–value gap*: our desires may well not be proportional to actual value. We may desire more something which is of lesser value. (Varieties of idealism about value are characterized by attempts to reduce this gap, by reducing value to some species of desiring.) Corresponding to the belief–appearance gap, we have the *judgement–desire gap*: our desires may not be proportional to our value judgements. We may desire more something we judge to be of lesser value. (Varieties of non-cognitivism are characterized by attempts to close this gap.) Finally, corresponding to the belief–reality gap, there is the *value–judgement gap*: our judgements, perhaps even our most justified judgements, may well not be right. This makes room for *error* about value, perhaps even error at the limit of our best attempts to purge our desires and our value judgements of incoherence. (Varieties of dispositional and ideal-limit antirealism attempt to close this gap.)

That there are these gaps—providing the possibilities of illusion, error, and incongruence—is not so troubling in itself. We are familiar, for example, with the kind of systematic 'illusion' that is generated by the fact that our perceptions are perspectival, the fact that we see the world from a certain point of view, and that as objects recede from us, they appear smaller. This explains why the sun appears smaller than the moon, even though it is much larger. Once we know there are laws governing the way in which apparent size alters with distance, we can happily accommodate the appearances. But it would be troubling if there were a substantial probability that these gaps are large—that there is massive, undetectable, uncorrectable illusion, incongruence, and error. That is the realist's nightmare.

Antirealists and realists both typically want to avoid the scepticism threatened by the spectre of massive gaps. Antirealist responses tend to deny that the gaps ever existed in the first place. The realist, on the other hand, acknowledges the gaps, but avoids scepticism by showing how the gaps can be bridged. The realist invokes appropriate bridges both between appearance and reality, and between appearance and belief, thereby allowing connections between reality and belief.

Appearances are both caused by, and are presentations of, reality. If one's sensory apparatus is in good working order, then experiences constitute defeasible reasons for beliefs about the world. Beliefs may, of course, impact appearances—both for good and for ill, maybe correcting mistaken or incompatible appearances, or distorting otherwise quite accurate experiences. By virtue of the direct connections (solid arrows) between appearance and

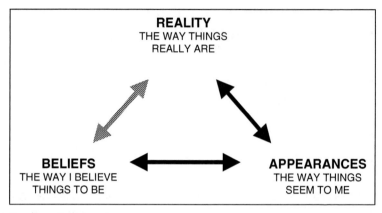

FIG. 8.3   *Bridging the gaps*

reality   and   between   appearance   and   belief,   we   have derivative connections (grey arrow) between belief and the world (fig. 8.3).

The corresponding nightmare for the value realist is not the bare possibility of the gaps between judgement and desire, between desire and value, and between value and judgement—we are all familiar enough with those—so much as the high probability that our desires will be wildly inappropriate to the values, that our judgements and our desires will be totally incongruent, and that there will be massive or undetectable error in our judgements. The value realist wants to bridge the gaps, not completely of course, but enough to make it intelligible how there could be an appropriate congruence between value and desire, between judgement and desire, and finally between judgement and value.

8.2   Bridging the Gaps

If the perceptual analogy is sound, then the value realist might avoid her nightmare in ways analogous to those that realists employ when grappling with knowledge of the external world. Experience is connected, on the one hand, to the world, and on the other, to our beliefs about the world. Analogously, desire—our

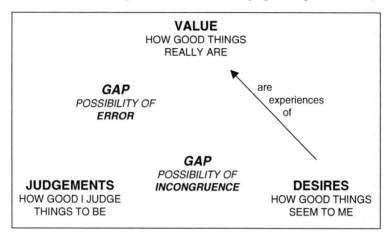

FIG. 8.4   *The experience conjecture*

experience of value—is connected, on the one hand, to value itself, and on the other, to our judgements of value.

The first connection between desire and value is given by the experience conjecture (fig. 8.4). Our desires present states to us as either good or bad.

But to secure the bridge at the reality end, we need an additional causal thesis—that desires can and do co-vary with value in the appropriate way (fig. 8.5). These are not the only two bridging connections between value and desires. We have also seen that value realists of quite different stripes can accommodate a role for desires in determining the overall shape of value—subject to objective constraints to which the pure idealist cannot appeal. They may do so by partly constituting the value of some states. Subject to the constraints, my desires make a contribution to the totality of desires, and thereby make a contribution, admittedly small, to the overall shape of value. I say that the realist *can* allow this, but the evidence that she *must* do so is not overwhelming. The relatively weak contribution made by my particular desires is indicated in fig. 8.6 by the broken arrow. But desires also make their own contribution to value, by adding to or subtracting from the overall sum of good by their appropriateness.

We also need links to bridge the desire–judgement gap. The first desire–judgement link is also provided by the experience thesis.

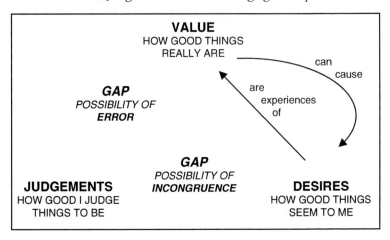

FIG. 8.5   *The causal networking thesis*

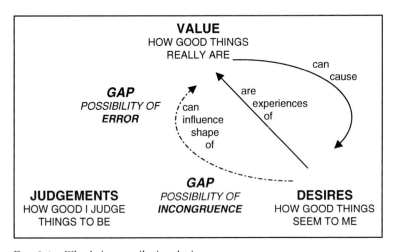

FIG. 8.6   *The desire contribution thesis*

P's *seeming good to me*—my desire that P—provides a defeasible reason for the corresponding value judgement that P actually is good (fig. 8.7).

But further, when something appears to me to be good, and there is no counteracting defeater on the horizon, then, if I am rational, I will be disposed to judge it good. Undefeated experiences of value

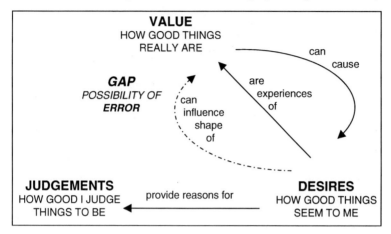

FIG. 8.7 *Desires as value data*

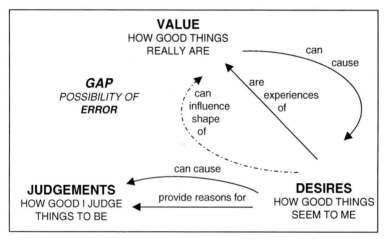

FIG. 8.8 *Desires influence value judgements*

thus raise the probability of acceptance of the corresponding judgement in a rational being. We can summarize this as the thesis that desires can influence value judgements (fig. 8.8).

Judgements are not always simply by-products of desire. A new value judgement, taken up into the web of judgement, may impact on other judgements, necessitating revisions in those.

Those judgements in turn can play an important reciprocal role in shaping and influencing desires (fig. 8.9). An accurate theory of the good may correct for, or eliminate, a wayward desire. But an inaccurate theory of the good may also distort or eliminate a perfectly appropriate desire, or induce an inappropriate desire.

This last link entails, of course, that our experiences of value—our desires—are at least to some extent theory-laden. But this is no more an impediment to the acquisition of reasonably accurate judgements than is the theory-ladenness of experience in general. In both we seek a harmonious and coherent body of beliefs, attempting to maximize the fit between theory and data, between concept and percept. Anomalies exist, and can survive our best attempts to excise them. (We are not perfect beings even as we pay homage to a regulative ideal of perfection.)

This rich network of connections between value and desire, and between desire and judgement, forges the needed connection between judgement and value. The values themselves help form our value judgements, *via* our experiences of value, and so those value judgements can and often do track value (Fig. 8.10).

8.3   Perspective, Location, and Distance in Value Space

I am typing this in the back of my van, on a sunny autumn day, in a car park in Denver, Colorado, listening to the second movement of Mozart's A major violin concerto on the radio. I have acquired some beliefs on the basis of these experiences: that it is a warm, sunny, autumn day, for example, and that the music being broadcast is really quite good. In one sense these beliefs are straightforwardly true, but only provided one interprets them as implicitly relativized to my current situation. I can render this relativization explicit by adding *around here* or *in my current position* to each claim. Interpreted as unrestricted claims about the world at large, however, they are patently false. It isn't autumn in Melbourne, let alone on Mars. It is cold and drizzly in Manchester, while it's hot and dry in New Mexico. And most of the music being broadcast these days is pretty bad—a fact that would be unpleasantly obvious if I were to hit the seek button on the radio. What I am experiencing now is

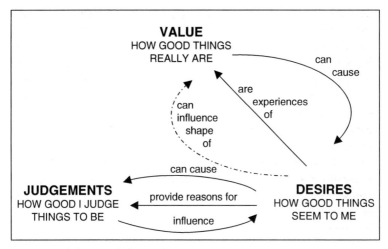

FIG. 8.9   *Judgements influence desires*

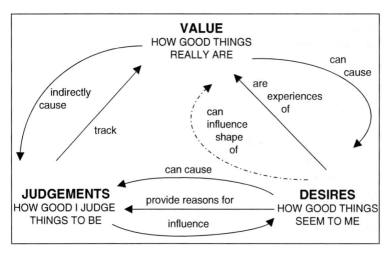

FIG. 8.10   *The gaps bridged*

a highly perspectival take on a certain fragment of the world, that bit of the world which radiates out a fairly short distance from a certain car parked in Denver, one autumn day.

A centre-piece of my argument for robust realism is the experience conjecture—the thesis that desires are experiences of the value of states of affairs, and that, as a consequence, they can and do serve as value data. Further, I have argued that they share with our perceptual experiences a perspectival quality. My desires provide me with a highly partial, agent-relative take on value. Now the perspectival nature of *perceptual* experience does not undermine its status as a source of data about the world. But this is presumably in part because we understand—intuitively, as well as mathematically—how appearances vary according to the laws of perspective. The moon's appearing larger than the sun does not undermine the epistemic worth of visual size data, because we understand why it appears larger, given our situation. The moon's appearing larger than the sun from our position on Earth is precisely what one would expect given the positions of these three heavenly bodies. In order to make the parallel between desires and perceptions plausible, we need at least a sketch of a theory of value perspective. We need some account which helps explain how the agent-relativity of desire is compatible with the agent-neutrality of value.

Many goods and evils are naturally assigned an analogue of *location*, although their co-ordinates are not typically spatial. The pain I experienced after my last ski accident is an example. The pain can be located by specifying two dimensions—a person (me) and a time (10.20 a.m. on 24 March 2003). If pain is an evil (possibly a conditional evil), it follows that some evils can be assigned a location. Persons are one dimension along which goods and evils can be located, and time is another.

Some goods and evils clearly cannot be located at person–time *points*. My pain lasted an hour. The locus of that evil is thus a two-dimensional line extending along the axis of time, rather than a mere point in time. Our fight not only lasted an hour, but involved both of us. So the locus of that evil is a region, involving a couple of people and a one-hour stretch of time. The Holocaust, one of the greatest evils of the twentieth century, clearly involved a large community of persons stretching over many years.

It's true that my pain was an evil *for me*, our fight an evil *for us*, and the Holocaust an evil *for all those who suffered in it*. But my pain was not *simply* an evil for me; our fight was not *simply* an evil for us; and the Holocaust was not *simply* an evil for those who suffered it. All these were evils, full stop. My pain was an evil, albeit a small evil; our fight was a slightly more weighty evil; and the Holocaust a vast evil. But the Holocaust was a vast evil constituted by a huge array of other, smaller evils—this man's humiliation, that woman's incarceration, this boy's torment, that child's enforced separation from her parents, this woman's being tortured and shot, that man's losing his family in the gas chambers, and countless others. These constituents of the evil that was the Holocaust are more localized than the Holocaust itself. Their regions are contained within the immense and unimaginable region of suffering which the Holocaust encompasses.

If goods and evils can be assigned locations, and one dimension is constituted by persons, then we can begin to think about the notion of distance between a person and these located goods and evils. Clearly I am very close to my own pain, an immediate consequence of the fact that I am one co-ordinate of the locus of the evil which is my pain. The other co-ordinate is time. Two distinct pains of mine may be located at different times. And it is natural to think that I am currently much closer to some pains (the one I am currently experiencing) than I am to others (one I experienced twenty years ago, or one I will experience in twenty years' time).

The merit connection says that there is just one appropriate response to each realization of value. One should experience the value *exactly as it is*. Given the experience conjecture, this means that one should desire things *precisely to the extent that they are good* (or *in direct proportion to value*). As high-minded and attractive as that might sound initially, on reflection it seems not just a tall order, but rather, a positively undesirable order. We have already mentioned two examples (Chapter 3) which throw doubt on the merit connection: the case of your pain compared with the stranger's pain, and saving your daughter from drowning compared with saving the stranger's daughter. Here is a third. Imagine that your spouse has contracted a very serious, life-threatening illness. The morning you learn of your spouse's illness, you are informed by her physician that the very same illness is afflicting hundreds of people in a village in some far-flung country. These people are total strangers to you. You know nothing about them and have no connection with them other than that they share your spouse's illness. Obviously you care about their fate, and you may well feel closer to them in their suffering because of your spouse's sharing their illness. You might well acknowledge that, objectively, the suffering and death of any one of those strangers from the same illness which afflicts your spouse is just as bad as the suffering and death of your spouse. The universalizability of value delivers that equivalence rather swiftly. But should you *long* for the recovery of each and every one of those far-flung strangers just as much as you long for the recovery of your spouse? Given that there are hundreds of people in that community, should your desire that all those unknown, distant strangers recover, really be *hundreds* of times stronger than your desire that your own spouse recover? Shouldn't your love for your spouse inform your desires at all? To say *no* here seems at best odd, and at worst, indicates a lack of fully human sensitivities (Slote 2004).[1]

These three cases suggest that the agent-neutrality of value does not demand from us complete agent-neutrality of desire. If anything, it seems that if one is to be a genuinely good person, disposed to respond appropriately to value, the strength of one's desires should *not* be *directly* proportional to value, but should rather be sensitive to one's location in value space and relation to the realization of the value at issue. Let's try to make this a little more precise.

Where $D(G)$ is short for 'the strength of a desire which is appropriate to a good of magnitude G', the original merit connection can be stated succinctly thus:

> *Original merit connection*: $D(G) \propto G$.

The idea of value location and of value distance does not mandate rejecting the merit connection entirely. Rather, it suggests that the merit connection is a first rough approximation. The experience conjecture, by drawing attention to the parallel between perception and desire, will point us in the direction of a more accurate and adequate merit connection.

Of two objects that are equidistant from you, the larger should, of course, appear larger to you. Likewise, of two goods that are equidistant from you, it is appropriate for the greater good to exert the greater motivational attraction. (That much is, of course,

---

[1] For an extraordinary account of one man's attempt to obey the merit connection and ignore his location in value space, see Parker (2004). Parker's account of Zell Kravinsky seems to bear out Slote's thesis.

endorsed by the original merit connection.) Of two objects that are the same size, the one that is closer should appear larger. Similarly, of two states of affairs that are of equal value, the one that is closer to you should exert greater motivational force on you. The motivational force exerted by a valuable state of affairs should systematically diminish with its distance from the valuer. We can spell out these ideas in a couple of constraints on appropriate desires.

First, then, equidistant goods should exert a motivational pull on a valuer in proportion to the magnitude of the good.

> *The equidistance desideratum*: For goods located at the same distance from a valuer, it is appropriate for the strength of desire to be directly proportional to the magnitude of the good.

Where $D(G, d)$ is short for 'the strength of a desire which is appropriate to a good of magnitude G at distance d from the valuer', the desideratum can be stated thus:

Where d is held fixed, $D(G, d) \propto G$.

This is, of course, close to the original merit connection.

Secondly, the strength of the desire appropriate to a certain good should decline with distance of the good from the valuer. In order to determine how it should decline, let us focus on the case of equally valuable goods at different distances from a valuer. Note that, just as with Newtonian gravitational force, motivational force should never equal zero—no matter what finite distance from the valuer the good in question is located, there should be some, possibly very weak, attractive force. So here's a first stab at such a desideratum, one which closely parallels the equidistance desideratum.

> *The equi-value desideratum (1st approximation)*: For goods of a fixed value at varying distances from a valuer, the valuer's desires are completely appropriate if the strength of desire is inversely proportional to the distance from the good.

Or:

Where G is held fixed, $D(G, d) \propto 1/d$.

So, one's desires are appropriate to value if doubling the distance of a good halves the strength of the desire.

These two desiderata together entail that a valuer's desire for a good is appropriate if the strength of desire is directly proportional to the good and inversely proportional to the distance from the valuer. Setting the constant of proportionality to 1 we have:

Revised merit connection (first approximation): $D(G, d) = G/d$.

As natural as this account might seem, there is an immediate problem. It violates the equidistance principle in one important limiting case—namely, where the goods are both at zero distance from the valuer. In that case the denominator on the right-hand side is 0, and so the strength of the appropriate desire is undefined. Note that this defect is shared, and hence ensured, by the first approximation to the equi-value principle. That approximation to the equidistance desideratum also fails to deliver the right result for the limiting case of zero distance of one of the two goods.

One might define the desire at zero distance by taking the limit of $D(G, d)$ as d tends to 0. This will certainly yield a determinate strength for the appropriate desire, but it may be the wrong strength. G/d tends to infinity as d tends to 0. But is it always the case that for any two goods, no matter what their relative magnitudes, a valuer who is at zero distance from both of them should respond to them with equal and infinitely strong desires? Suppose that you are a pure egoist and you face a choice between two immediate goods, one of which is much better for you than the other. It seems that the greater good should seem better to you, not that both should seem equally and infinitely good.

Interestingly, the original merit connection suggests a way of correcting this defect. Recall that, according to the original merit connection, something is good just to the degree that it is appropriate for it to be desired. This is tantamount to the claim that no matter how far from a valuer a good is located, the valuer's desire is appropriate if and only if the strength of his desire is directly proportional to the magnitude of the good itself. Setting the constant of proportionality at 1, this can be summarized:

Original merit connection: $D(G, d) = G$.

The original merit connection does satisfy the equidistance desideratum—even in the limiting case—although it does not satisfy the equi-value desideratum. The distance variable is, of course, completely idle here—it doesn't appear on the right-hand side—because the original merit connection ignores value distance altogether. A crucial variable is often suppressed when it is tacitly presupposed to assume a fixed value, and in such cases the formula proposed is usually correct in those cases in which the variable actually assumes that value. Suppose, then, that the original merit connection is actually right for the zero-distance case. We could formulate this in a third desideratum

> *The zero-distance desideratum*: If goods are located at zero distance from a valuer, then the valuer's desire is appropriate if the strength of desire is proportional to the magnitude of the goods.

Or, setting the constant of proportionality at 1,

$$D(G, 0) = G.$$

Clearly this is incompatible with the equi-value desideratum as stated, but it suggests a minor modification to it, one which would contain the best features of the original and deliver the zero-distance desideratum. Instead of having goods diminish in appropriate motivational force by the factor $(1/d)$, let's simply shift the curve over and satisfy the zero-distance desideratum by setting the decay factor at $(1/(d + 1))$.

> *The equi-value desideratum*: Where G is fixed, $D(G, d) \propto 1/(d + 1)$.

This, in conjunction with the first desideratum, yields:

> *Revised merit connection*: $D(G, d) = G/(d + 1)$.

This revised merit connection principle delivers all three desiderata.

This sketch of an account of the perspectival element in experiences of value gels with a number of intuitions about how our desires should be responsive to value. It explains how our desires can be agent-relative, yet still be appropriate responses to agent-neutral value. It is quite appropriate for one to have a greater desire for one's own good and the good of those closer to oneself, than for the equal good of those who are distant. It also explains how we can deduce facts about agent-neutral value from apparently inaccurate value experiences together with facts about how close we are to the locations of value. So your rather weak desire that a person distant from you not suffer a certain fate can be good evidence that that kind of fate is really rather bad. That it doesn't seem so bad to you at the moment is explained not by its insignificance but by its distance from you. And your very strong desire that you not suffer a certain fate may not be very good evidence that that fate is so bad after all.

This framework clearly provides us with an answer to Lemos's central objection to the thesis that desires constitute value data. (Recall that we deferred a fuller answer to this objection in section 3.5.)

It seems possible that someone might know that two states of affairs are of equal intrinsic value and prefer one as such to the other without having any reason to think that either is better. James might know that his being happy is as intrinsically good as John's being happy, and yet James might prefer his being happy to John's being happy. On the view under consideration this would imply that James has some reason to think that his own happiness is intrinsically better than John's. (Lemos 1994: 194)

James desires his own happiness more than he desires John's, and John desires his happiness more than he desires James's. Given the experience conjecture, we apparently face a dilemma. We must either say that the value experiences here are inappropriate to their objects (that the desires are all wrong); alternatively, if they *are* appropriate, we seem to be forced to say that James does indeed have evidence that his own happiness is more valuable than John's, and by parity that John has equally good evidence that his happiness is more valuable than James's.

Neither horn of the dilemma is particularly palatable. But the dilemma clearly rests on an underlying assumption: namely, the original merit connection—that desires are ideally directly proportional to value. Once we embrace the revised merit connection, acknowledging the perspectival nature of value experiences, the dilemma evaporates. It is entirely natural for John's happiness to *seem* more valuable to John than does James's happiness. And John can cheerfully acknowledge that it seems that way to him even while he also subscribes to the agent-neutral value of all happiness, wherever it occurs. Is this really profound?

8.4   Value Distance and Second-Order Desires

We can sharpen Lemos's criticism using the matrix model of Chapter 4. Here are the four relevant states (table 8.1).

TABLE 8.1.   *James and John*

	S_1	S_2	S_3	S_4
James	happy	happy	sad	sad
John	happy	sad	happy	sad

We imagine that James's initial first-order desires are completely self-regarding. He is indifferent between S_1 and S_2 (the two situations in which he is happy) and also between S_3 and S_4 (the two situations in which he is sad). And he strongly prefers the situation S_2, in which he is happy and John is sad, to the situation S_3, in which he is sad and John is happy. John is similarly self-regarding. He prefers S_3 to S_2, and is indifferent between S_1 and S_3, and between S_2 and S_4. James's first-order desires for each outcome are thus simply a reflection of the value of James's happiness to James himself, and likewise John's base desires are a reflection of the value of John's happiness to John. So let's assign numerical magnitudes to their desires for these states (table 8.2).

Using only their first-order desires as reasons for beliefs about the good, and the principle that what seems so (probably) is so, James and John could form the following beliefs about the ordering of the states:

James's initial judgements
S_1 has the same value as S_2;
S_2 is better than S_3;
S_3 has the same value as S_4.
(viz. James's happiness contributes to value, John's doesn't.)

John's initial judgements
S_1 has the same value as S_3;

TABLE 8.2.   *James's and John's first-order desires track their own happiness*

	S_1	S_2	S_3	S_4
James	1	1	0	0
John	1	0	1	0

S_3 is better than S_2;

S_2 has the same value as S_4.

(viz. John's happiness contributes to value, James's doesn't.)

They agree on just one fact about value: that S_1 is better than S_4.

Assume, however, that James and John do not have perverse higher-order desires. They do not hate each other; nor are they entirely self-absorbed egoists. Suppose, that is to say, that each invests some, perhaps modest, fraction of care in the other. In other words, to each it seems that the good of the other, and his happiness, is indeed worth something (table 8.3).

The data provided by their second-order desires seems to be in conflict with the data provided by their first-order desires. Now we know that if they revised their first-order desires in the light of their second-order desires, then that would alter their first-order desires—their perception of the value of states of affairs (table 8.4). In the light of these appearances, they might embrace the following sets of judgements:

James's revised judgements

S_1 is better than S_2;

S_2 is better than S_3;

S_3 is better than S_4.

(viz. James's happiness contributes a lot to value, and John's contributes a little.)

John's initial judgements

S_1 is better than S_3;

TABLE 8.3.   *Second-order desires of James and John*

	James	John
James	0.9	0.1
John	0.1	0.9

TABLE 8.4.   *First-order desires after refinement*

	S_1	S_2	S_3	S_4
James	I	0.9	0.1	0
John	I	0.1	0.9	0

S_3 is better than S_2;
S_2 is better than S_4.
(viz. John's happiness contributes a lot to value, James's contributes a little.)

So, both can apply their second-order desires to correct for the initial misperceptions and assist in the formation of more accurate experiences (and beliefs) about value on the basis of agent-relative desires. But they need not stop here. Both may recognize that they are located some value distance from the other, and, given that closer goods appear better than do more distant goods, they may deduce that the other's happiness *seeming* less good than one's own is not conclusive evidence that it is in fact less good. Given the distance, seeming less good may in fact be good evidence of being just as good.

This response to Lemos ties value distance and value perspective to the theory of higher-order desires introduced in Chapter 4. It gives that apparatus a more realist interpretation, something to which we are entitled at this stage in the light of the failure of the major antirealist arguments in general, and of value idealism in particular.

Let the initial first-order matrix reveal not how much first-order desire each individual invests in each state, but rather how much first-order *good* accrues to each individual in each state. Thus, in each state, each person is a location for good, and the entry in the matrix tells us how much good is situated at that location. This now suggests a connection between value distance and the weights in the second-order care matrix. Consider an example of a care matrix (table 8.5). Let the value distance between X and Y be d_{XY}. The weight w_{XY} that X places on Y diminishes with increasing distance. At zero distance we should have maximal weight, but if

TABLE 8.5. *Care matrix*: C_1

	Romeo	Juliet	Nurse	Lady Capulet
Romeo	0.5	0.4	0.08	0.02
Juliet	0.3	0.5	0.1	0.1
Nurse	0.1	0.1	0.6	0.2
Lady Capulet	0	0	0	1

weights are normalized, that maximum is 1. So it is natural to suppose that the weight that it is appropriate for X to place on Y's good is given by the following formula:

The inverse weight–distance connection: $d_{XY} = (1/w_{XY}) - 1$.

This converts the weight matrix into a corresponding 'distance' matrix (table 8.6).

Now that we have correlated weights (second-order desires) with distances (or perhaps perceived distances), we must turn to the revision procedure—the procedure for adjusting first-order desires by second-order weights. This procedure can be regarded as a kind of perceptual *synthesis* (in the Kantian sense) of the two kinds of data into a more coherent perceptual experience of value. How good a situation will seem to a person turns out to be a weighted average of how good the various locations within that situation strike him. So, since Juliet is close to Romeo, her happiness will seem to him, to contribute a lot to overall value. Since Lady Capulet is distant from him, her happiness seems not to contribute much at all. Perception of overall value is thus a weighted average of the value at various locations, where the weights are determined by the perceiver's value distance from those locations.

We can now frame the refinement procedure of Chapter 5 in the following way: *perceived* value distance must be distinguished from *real* value distance. Lady Capulet, for example, *errs* in her thoroughly egoistic second-order desires, by placing 0 weight on everyone save herself. She perceives herself to be infinitely removed from any other locus of good. That, I argued in Chapter 5, is an error on her part. Now we can add that it is an error in her perception of value distance.

TABLE 8.6. *Distance matrix corresponding to* C_1

	Romeo	Juliet	Nurse	Lady Capulet
Romeo	1	1.5	11.5	49
Juliet	1.5	1	9	9
Nurse	9	1	0.7	4
Lady Capulet	∞	∞	∞	0

One revision of first-order desires in the light of second-order desires is clearly mandated. We know that repeated revisions of first-order desires in the light of second-order desires will eventually lead to convergence to agent-neutral desires, provided there are no perversely distorting second-order desires (egoism, hatred, obsessive altruism), and provided the rather weak connectedness condition is satisfied. But does the demand of coherence in desiring *require* us to revise repeatedly? Do James and John, for example, have to keep revising their first-order desires in the light of their second-order desires so that eventually they will both end up desiring the happiness of all in a perfectly agent-neutral manner, neither one desiring his own happiness more than that of the other? If so, then the merit connection comes back with a vengeance. We would be obliged to continue revising until we all end up desiring the same states to the same degree, in proportion to actual value. The perspectivity of value perception would then be a flaw, a defect which ideally—in the limit of obligatory desire refinement—would be eliminated.

There is an additional premiss which would certainly deliver this result, but without it I cannot see how repeated revisions are mandatory. The premiss is this: that one's own good is identical to what one *perceives* one's own good to be. That is to say, the state S is good *for* X precisely to the extent that S *seems* good to X. Admittedly, these two notions (its *seeming to X that S is good*, and *S's being good for X*) are easy to conflate. Indeed, that principle is a common theme of value idealism, and idealists will probably be loath to admit that it is a conflation, insisting rather that it is a genuine equivalence. Grant, for the moment, that we do have a genuine equivalence here.

In their first state of desire, James and John are each a locus of value, each of which has a magnitude of o or 1, depending on whether the individual so located is happy or not. Then both revise their first-order desires in the light of their second-order desires. Now, S_2 *seems* to John to be a little less good (overall) than it was. If the equivalence holds, S_2 now *is* a little less good *for John*. The amount of value at the John locus has diminished. On the other hand, the amount of value at the James locus has risen correspondingly. For S_2 now *seems* to James to be a little better (overall) than it was, and so if the equivalence holds, S_2 now *is* a little bit better *for*

John. Should they stop there? No. Given that the values at these locations have actually *changed* as a result of this revision (even though their distances from each other have not) they should both now perceive those values *differently* from how they perceived them on the earlier occasion. They should now have different perceptions of the good of the various different states. The average value of the various locations of good in S_2 must seem less to James now, because now there is only 0.9 at one locus (the one closest to him) and 0.1 at the other. Averaging in accord with his distance from both he will arrive at a new overall assessment—0.82. If he and John both revise systematically, there will be a new distribution of first-order desires and (given the equivalence) a new distribution of value over locations (table 8.7). The same applies again, so each is obliged to synthesize a new perception of value which, in turn, by the equivalence, produces a new distribution of actual value over locations. Eventually their desires will converge, as will the values themselves, in the limiting matrix (table 8.8).

So the proposed equivalence mandates repeated revision and entails the original merit connection. Without the equivalence there does not seem to be any reason to go past the first step in the revision. Suppose, now, that how much good there is at a certain location is *not* given by how good the whole situation seems to the person located there. Then, after the first revision, the value of James's happiness does *not* diminish, and the disvalue

TABLE 8.7.   *Revised first-order desires = revised localized goods*

	S_1	S_2	S_3	S_4
James	1	0.82	0.18	0
John	1	0.18	0.82	0

TABLE 8.8.   *Limiting first-order desires = limiting localized goods*

	S_1	S_2	S_3	S_4
James	1	0.5	0.5	0
John	1	0.5	0.5	0

of John's sadness does not rise in response to their revised desires. So there is no reason for either to again revise the first-order value appearances in the light of second-order value appearances. If the values have not changed, and their *distances* from the perceivers have not changed, then the appearances should also remain stable. That is, of course, quite compatible with each perceiver drawing the correct *inference* from their agent-relative data about the relevant agent-neutral goods.

After the first revision of first-order desires in the light of second-order desires, repeated revisions are not simply adjustments to first-order desires in the light of one's perceived distance from the various goods. Rather, what they amount to is a change in *perspective*—a change in one's perceived distance from those goods. This is brought out by the fact that the procedure of repeatedly revising first-order desires is equivalent to the alternative procedure of repeatedly revising second-order desires (and applying the revised weights to the original first-order matrix). Now systematic revision of second-order desires is equivalent to systematic changes in perceived distance. In the limit we typically end up apparently equidistant from all possible goods. While there is certainly rational pressure to bring perceived distance into line with actual distance, only on the assumption that the limiting second-order matrix yields *actual* value distances does this translate into rational pressure to continue to revise one's second-order desires. There may well be a natural inclination to distort and exaggerate the nearness of our dearest—and some consequential adjustment for that may be necessary—but it certainly doesn't follow that everyone is equidistant from every possible good in the universe, or that everyone should perceive goods as though that were the case.

8.5 Knowledge of the Good by Direct Acquaintance

I began the exploration of realism about value with what is perhaps the most well-known and influential argument against it—the argument from the queerness of value. I followed one contemporary interpretation of this argument—call it the *belief–desire* interpretation—which appeals centrally to the independence of belief and desire. The mere belief that something is valuable is not intrinsically motivational because it is logically disjoint from one's desire-set. If a denial of this independence is foisted on the realist, then an antirealist conclusion is within easy reach, but the realist can easily resist the denial. In Chapter 2 I sketched how the realist can both embrace the independence of belief and desire and still explain the puzzling asymmetries which suggest internalism. The key to this explanation is the experience conjecture—that desires are experiences of the good. This conjecture was defended in greater detail in Chapter 3, and buttressed in Chapter 7 with the defence of the possibility of causal networking of value with experience. Finally, with the development of the thesis of value perspective, we can explain why the puzzling asymmetry is quite a bit less puzzling than its strict Moorean counterpart. The schema for generating puzzling pairs is shown in table 8.9. The asymmetry is explained by the experience conjecture. If desires are value-seemings, then the pair in table 8.9 is equivalent to the pair shown in table 8.10 (with *P is good* substituted for *Q*), the asymmetry of which is not puzzling at all. The phenomenon of value perspective, however, forces us to refine this rather simple point. For I can believe of something that it is good, without its seeming *that* good to me given how far from me the good is located. For example, take the value of some rather remote event like, say, the establishment of an effective world government by the year 10,000 (table 8.11).

The first-person judgement sounds no more odd to me than the third-person judgement. I can take on board and endorse the value judgement, deriving it from various well-known truths about the evils of nationalism and so on, and yet fail to be moved by the good so apprehended. Indeed, I myself endorse the value judgement here, but after introspecting I find I have no very marked desire or longing for the event in question. The event is just too far removed from me, both in time and in the identities of the participants. Of course, it is not now settled who the participants would be, but whoever they might be, they are all very distant from my current position in value space.

Interestingly, in his classic statement of the queerness argument, Mackie does not frame the case against realism in terms of beliefs and desires and their evident independence. Rather he frames the argument in terms of *knowledge* and *acquaintance.*

TABLE 8.9. *The puzzling asymmetry*

Third-person judgement	First-person judgement
P is good, but he has no desire that P.	P is good, but I have no desire that P.

TABLE 8.10. *Moore's shadow*

Third-person judgement	First-person judgement
Q, but it doesn't seem to him that Q.	Q, but it doesn't seem to me that Q.

TABLE 8.11. *A weak asymmetry*

Third-person judgement	First-person judgement
The establishment of an effective and benign world government by the year 10,000 would be a very good thing, but he has no great desire for that.	The establishment of an effective and benign world government by the year 10,000 would be a very good thing, but I have no great desire for that.

Plato's Forms give a dramatic picture of what objective values would have to be. The Form of the Good is such that knowledge of it provides the knower with both a direction and an overriding motive; something's being good tells the person who knows this to pursue it and makes him pursue it. An objective good would be sought by anyone who was acquainted with it, not because of any contingent fact that this person, or every person, is so constituted that he desires this end, but just because the end *has to-be-pursuedness* somehow built into it. (Mackie 1977: 40)

Both acquaintance and knowledge are more than mere belief or judgement. Suppose we could have both experiential acquaintance with values and knowledge by direct experiential acquaintance. Two related questions arise. Could one be *acquainted* with the good, or could one *know the good by acquaintance*, yet remain *totally unmoved*? Further, if the realist replies negatively, and affirms that both acquaintance and knowledge by acquaintance are intrinsically motivating, does it follow that values are queer entities, totally unlike anything else in the universe with which we are familiar?

Acquaintance clearly requires having experiences of the object of acquaintance, but that is not enough. The experiences which ground acquaintance have to be accurate, and they have to be accurate *because* they are reliably tracking the features of the relevant object. To be acquainted with some object is thus to have veridical experiences of it, causally grounded in, and appropriately responsive to, the actual features of the object of acquaintance. *Knowledge* involves more than acquaintance. It involves adopting correct beliefs on the basis of good reasons, some of which may involve the having of appropriate experiences. Finally, *knowledge by acquaintance* is just what it suggests: the adoption of correct beliefs on the basis of acquaintance in experience. Knowledge by acquaintance thus inherits the requirement for veridical, causally grounded experiences. Acquaintance and knowledge by acquaintance involve both an internal condition (being suitably justified by appropriate experiences) and an external condition (one's experiences being causally grounded in, and causally responsive to, the object in question).

I have argued that these elements of acquaintance, and of knowledge by acquaintance, are just as coherent for values as they are for material objects. One can be acquainted with values by experiencing them, and only by experiencing them. An experience of something as valuable is not some obscure and problematic state, the product of an otherwise mysterious faculty of value intuition. Rather, it is the perfectly familiar experience of desire. Couple this with what it takes for experience to track a property. Given the convexity constraint, to be a reliable guide to value, one's experiences of value—desires—must be sensitive to the actual shape of value by being appropriately causally networked. To be acquainted with something as valuable is to desire it appropriately in the light of your relation to the value, precisely *because* it is valuable and located where it is. Further, it is to have an *accurate* experience of it as valuable—to desire it just to the degree that it is appropriate to desire it, given the magnitude and the locus of the value in relation to you. So someone who knows the good by being genuinely acquainted with it would be moved appropriately. She would be drawn in the direction of the good, by a motivational force directly proportional to the magnitude of the good, and inversely proportional to the distance of the good from her. What we might call *acquaintance internalism* is thus quite a bit different from the *judgement internalism*, which was featured in Smith's presentation of the queerness argument.

Value judgements which are not grounded in experiential acquaintance, even those which might count as value knowledge, do not necessarily have these features. For example, I may have been indoctrinated into endorsing some true judgements about the good, and the indoctrination may leave me entirely cold. Or I might infer some true judgements about the good from value truths I do know by acquaintance. Such knowledge may not come linked to the relevant responses, and the appropriate responses may not follow in the wake of those inferences. Or I may learn about some aspect of value from a reliable and trustworthy source (perhaps one who is himself directly acquainted with the aspect of the good in question). Such knowledge may lie even further from the wellsprings of desire. So Mackie's claim that knowledge of the good would be intrinsically motivating is not generally defensible. But his thesis that a certain sort of knowledge of value would be intrinsically motivating turns out to be correct. It is correct for the kind of knowledge of value that is both close to and thoroughly informed by experiential acquaintance with the good.

We can thus affirm something rather close to the functional characterization of goodness which the passage from Mackie inspired, and which became the basis for the queerness argument:

> *Goodness = that property φ such that, necessarily, for any state P whatsoever, if one judges that P has φ, then one desires that P.*

Two modifications are in order. First, it is not the case that merely endorsing a value judgement is necessarily accompanied by desire. If, however, we restrict ourselves to value judgements known by direct experiential acquaintance of the values—that is, desires—then of course desire is necessarily involved. Second, the characterization needs to be revised to take into account the effect of both magnitude and locus of the good on desire. A suitably modified characterization of value which embodies acquaintance internalism would go something like this:

> *Value = that magnitude Γ of possible states such that, necessarily, for any state P whatsoever, if one has perfect knowledge by*

acquaintance that $\Gamma(P) = G$, and one is of Γ-distance d from P, then one's desire for P is proportional to $G/(d + 1)$.

Now, however, with this characterization of value and of knowledge of value, the premises of Mackie's queerness argument begin to look much more plausible than they did on the thinner, neo-Humean belief–desire interpretation that is currently in vogue. Mackie doubtless overstates the case by claiming that acquaintance with a value would provide one with an *overriding* motive. We only have to note the fact that one may be acquainted with two goods, one larger but further removed from one than the other. Even though I know of both by acquaintance, the closer but smaller good may well be more motivating than the larger, more distant good. But Mackie is right that acquaintance with a good necessarily provides one with both a direction and some motivation. The larger, more distant good may not finally engage the will, but it is still there, exerting some motivational attraction on me.

What follows? Does it follow that values are *queer* entities, unlike anything else in the purely natural world? Does it follow that values are entities which would make our universe inexplicably non-naturalistic? Well, yes and no.

Yes: at least some value properties are distinct from any purely natural property. The valuable cannot be reduced to the purely natural. The value realm is something over and above the purely natural realm, and without invoking values, one cannot adequately explain all that happens, even within the natural realm. Our acquaintance with the valuable is something over and above our acquaintance with the natural world, for it requires the causal networking of conditions—which are themselves not reducible to natural properties—with our experiences of those conditions. Acquaintance with value involves experiences of value, and, unlike other experiences, experiences of value are intrinsically motivating. Given these features, the realm of values must be considered inexplicable from within a purely naturalistic framework; so it is perhaps no wonder that the naturalist deems them *queer*.

But then again, no: values are not totally unlike anything in the natural world. For a start, some of them may well *be* natural properties (like the property of being in pain). Further, the way in which values, natural or non-natural, enter into the causal network, and the way in which they impact us *via* their causal relations, are both familiar and intelligible. The idea that knowledge by acquaintance with values is intrinsically motivating has a simple, appealing explanation. Knowledge by acquaintance requires acquaintance, which in turn requires veridical experiences appropriately responsive to their objects. Experiences of the value of states of affairs are mental states which, it turns out, even the Humean will grant are intrinsically motivating: they are desires. So knowledge of values by acquaintance involves having desires which are appropriately responsive to the actual shape of value, and which are correspondingly what those values merit, given their magnitude and distance from the value perceiver. That genuine acquaintance with values moves one in the direction of the good is thus unsurprising.

To have knowledge of value by acquaintance is thus to make accurate value judgements, grounded in appropriate experiences of the good—experiences which exert a motivational force in the direction of the good, and which are proportional to the magnitude of the good experienced, and inversely proportional to the distance of the good so experienced from the valuer. It's almost too good to be true.

APPENDICES

I. A Refutation of Independence

Let us say that a belief is *occurrent* if it is the belief that you are consciously attending to, and let *X's occurrent belief* = the belief of X which is occurrent. There may, of course, be no such thing as *X's occurrent belief*, because either X has more than one occurrent belief, or X has none. Ditto for *occurrent desire* and *X's occurrent desire*.

Let P be the proposition: *X's occurrent belief is false.* Let Q be the proposition: *X's occurrent desire is satisfied.* If generalized independence is true, then any belief–desire pair is logically possible. So the following must also be possible: P = X's occurrent desire, and Q = X's occurrent belief. We show that this leads to a contradiction. First, let's go with a brief proof which assumes bivalence—that every proposition is either true or false.

Suppose P is true. Then X's belief is false. But Q = X's belief. So Q is false. So it is false that X's desire is satisfied. X's desire is not satisfied. But X's desire − P. So P is false. (Contradiction.)

Suppose P is false. Then it is false that X's belief is false. But Q = X's belief. So Q is true. If Q is true, then X's desire is satisfied. But X's desire = P. So P is true. (Contradiction.)

Bivalence, however, is not compatible with the analysis of presupposition I put forward in Chapter I. There I argued for truth-valuelessness. And truth–value gaps clearly can arise when we have definite descriptions which fail to pick out an object—definite descriptions like 'the occurrent belief of X'. If there is no such thing as *X's occurrent belief*, then a *de re* claim like *X's occurrent belief is false* is *truth-valueless* rather than true or false. And since *truth* and *falsehood* are total properties of propositions, the only way that *X's occurrent belief is false* can lack a truth value is by the non-existence of *X's occurrent belief*. We can now give a proof that doesn't assume bivalence. Still, every proposition is either true, or false, or truth-valueless.

Suppose P is true. Then X's belief is false. But Q = X's belief. So Q is false. So it is false that X's desire is satisfied. X's desire is not satisfied. But X's desire = P. So P is not true—it is either false or truth-valueless. (Contradiction.)

Suppose P is false. Then it is false that X's belief is false. But Q = X's belief. So Q is true or truth-valueless. If Q is true, then X's desire is satisfied. But X's desire = P. So P is true. (Contradiction.) Suppose Q is truth-valueless. Then there is no such thing as X's desire. (Contradiction.)

Suppose P is truth-valueless. That can only be because there is no such thing as X's occurrent belief. (Contradiction.)[1]

2. Seemings as Evidence

What we want to prove is that the proposition *it seems that Q* is *prima facie* evidence for Q—that is to say, it actually raises the probability of Q—if and only if there is a non-zero probability that *it seems that Q* is a reliable indicator of the truth of Q.

Let S^Q be short for *it seems that Q*, and let Rel(P,Q) be short for *P is a reliable indicator of the truth of Q*. The *reliability thesis* says, plausibly, that the conjunction of the proposition S^Q *is a reliable indicator of the truth of Q* and the proposition *it seems that Q* raises the (subjective) probability of Q.

Reliability: $P(Q|S^Q \& \text{Rel}(S^Q,Q)) > P(Q)$.

The *non-reliability thesis* says that the conjunction of the propositions that *it seems that Q* and that S^Q *is not a reliable indicator of the truth of Q* leaves the probability of Q unchanged. Note that to say that S^Q is not a reliable indicator of the truth of Q is not to say that it is an indicator of Q's falsehood—that it is a somewhat reliable indicator of ~Q. In other words, the negation of Rel(S^Q,Q)—~Rel(S^Q,Q)—is not Rel(S^Q,~Q). Consequently, S^Q&~Rel(S^Q,Q) should not undermine your confidence in Q, and it certainly shouldn't enhance it, but simply leave it as it is. (Let's abbreviate "Rel(S^Q,Q)" to "R^Q".)

Non-reliability: $P(Q|S^Q \& {\sim}R^Q) = P(Q)$.

Clearly, whether or not *it seems that Q* is irrelevant to whether or not S^Q is a reliable indicator of the truth of Q.

Irrelevance: $P(R^Q|S^Q) = P(R^Q)$ (and $P({\sim}R^Q|S^Q) = P({\sim}R^Q)$).

Finally the following are standard properties of probability:

Additivity: $P(A|C) = P(A\&B|C) + P(A\&{\sim}B|C)$.
Chain rule: $P(A\&B|C) = P(A|B\&C) P(B|C)$.

---

[1] I am indebted to Paul Studtmann for forcing me to think about logical limitations on the generalized thesis of independence. Although this example is not one of those he suggested, it is certainly inspired by it.

To Prove: $P(Q|S^Q) > P(Q)$ iff $P(R^Q) > 0$.

1	$P(Q|S^Q) = P(Q \& R^Q|S^Q) + P(Q \& \sim R^Q|S^Q)$	(Additivity)
2	$P(Q \& R^Q|S^Q) = P(Q|S^Q \& R^Q)P(R^Q|S^Q)$	(Chain rule)
3	$P(Q \& \sim R^Q|S^Q) = P(Q|S^Q \& \sim R^Q)P(\sim R^Q|S^Q)$	(Chain rule)
4	$P(R^Q|S^Q) = P(R^Q)$	(Irrelevance)
5	$P(\sim R^Q|S^Q) = P(\sim R^Q)$	(Irrelevance)
6	$P(Q|S^Q) = P(Q|S^Q \& R^Q)P(R^Q)$ $+ P(Q|S^Q \& \sim R^Q)P(\sim R^Q)$	(1–5)
7	$P(Q|S^Q \& R^Q) = P(Q) + \delta$ (for some $\delta > 0$)	(Reliability)
8	$P(Q|S^Q \& \sim R^Q) = P(Q)$	(Non-reliability)
9	$P(Q|S^Q) = (P(Q) + \delta)P(R^Q) + P(Q)P(\sim R^Q)$	(6–8).
10	$P(Q|S^Q) = P(Q)[P(R^Q) + P(\sim R^Q)] + P(R^Q)\delta$	(9)
11	$P(Q|S^Q) = P(Q) + P(R^Q)\delta$	(10, Additivity)
12	$P(Q|S^Q) > P(Q)$ iff $P(R^Q) > 0$.	(11)

Here is a possible objection to the conclusion. (The following argument is based on one in Cohen (2003).) Suppose *it looks red* confirms *it is red*. Then if X looks red, I have evidence that X is red and, if that is my total evidence, then I may be entitled to adopt the claim that X is red. So now I embrace the conjunction: X looks red and X is red. Now that conjunction raises the probability that my senses are reliable, and since my only evidence for that conjunction is the original claim that X looks red, my original observation alone—that X looks red—confirms the reliability of my senses. But *that's* ridiculous because it's just too easy. Knowledge of the reliability of the senses cannot come so cheaply!

My proof shows that there is a *non sequitur* lurking in this argument. Suppose that $P(\text{Rel}(S^Q, Q)) > 0$. Then it follows that $P(Q|S^Q) > P(Q)$. That is, that S^Q raises the probability of the truth of Q. But that is quite compatible with S^Q leaving the probability of Rel (S^Q, Q) *exactly where it is*. Indeed, that it leave it unchanged is a *premiss* of the argument—it is the premiss I have labelled *Irrelevance*.

3. The BAD Paradox

If we combine the DAB thesis (viz. $D(A) = P(\mathring{A})$), with the principle of updating by conditionalization (viz. where E is the new evidence, updated probability $P^+(A) = P(A|E)$) we get a contradiction. Throughout the new evidence $E = (A \rightarrow \sim\mathring{A})$.

1   $D^+(A) = P^+(\mathring{A})$. Hence $D^+(A) = P(\mathring{A}|A \rightarrow \sim\mathring{A}) = P(\mathring{A} \ \& \sim A)/P(A \rightarrow \sim\mathring{A})$.

   Since $P(\mathring{A} \ \& \sim A) > 0$, and $\mathring{A} \& \sim A$ entails $(A \rightarrow \sim\mathring{A})$, $P(A \rightarrow \sim\mathring{A}) > 0$, we have $D^+(A) > 0$.

2   Let $P_B(A)$ be $P(A|B)$, and let D_B be the desiredness function based on P_B. The principle of desiredness tells us quite generally that $D(A) = D_A(A)$, and so, $D^+(A) = D^+_A(A)$. By DAB, $D^+_A(A) = P^+_A(\mathring{A})$. Hence $D^+(A) = P^+_A(\mathring{A}) = P(\mathring{A}|A \ \& (A \rightarrow \sim\mathring{A})) = P(\mathring{A} \& \sim\mathring{A} \ \& A)/P(\sim\mathring{A} \ \& A)$. Since $P(\sim\mathring{A} \ \& A) > 0$ and $P(\mathring{A} \ \& \sim\mathring{A} \ \& A) = 0$, we have $D^+(A) = 0$.

REFERENCES

ANSCOMBE, G. E. M. (1957), *Intention* (Oxford: Blackwell).

ARISTOTLE (1962), *Nichomachean Ethics*, trans. Martin Ostwald (Indianapolis: Bobbs-Merrill Co.).

ARMSTRONG, D. M. (1978), *Universals and Scientific Realism*, 2 vols. (Cambridge: Cambridge University Press).

——(1989), *Universals: An Opinionated Introduction* (Boulder, Colo.: Westview).

BEALER, G. (1982), *Quality and Concept* (Oxford: Clarendon Press).

BLACKBURN, S. (1993), *Essays in Quasi-Realism* (New York: Oxford University Press).

BRENTANO, F. (1969), *The Origin of our Knowledge of Right and Wrong*, ed. R. Chisholm, trans. R. Chisholm and E. Schneewind (London: Routledge).

BROAD, C. D. (1930), *Five Types of Ethical Theory* (New York: Harcourt Brace).

BUTCHVAROV, P. (1989), *Skepticism in Ethics* (Bloomington, Ind.: Indiana University Press).

BYRNE, A., and HAJEK, A. (1997), 'David Hume, David Lewis, and decision theory', *Mind*, 106: 411–27.

CHISHOLM, R. (1986), *Brentano on Intrinsic Value* (Cambridge: Cambridge University Press).

CHURCHLAND, P. M. (2001), 'What happens to reliabilism when it is liberated from the propositional attitudes?', *Philosophical Topics*, 29 (1&2): 91–112.

COHEN, S. (2002), 'Basic knowledge and the problem of easy knowledge', *Philosophy and Phenomenological Research*, 55 (2): 309–29.

CRESSWELL, M. (1985), *Structured Meanings* (Cambridge, Mass.: MIT Press/Bradford Books).

DANCY, J. (1993), *Moral Reasons* (Oxford: Blackwell).

DREIER, J. (1992), 'The supervenience argument against moral realism', *Southern Journal of Philosophy*, 30 (3): 13–38.

DRETSKE, F. (1977), 'Laws of nature', *Philosophy of Science*, 44: 248–68.

DUMMETT, M. (1978), *Truth and Other Enigmas* (Cambridge, Mass.: Harvard University Press).

ELLIOT, C. (2000), 'A new way to be mad', *Atlantic Monthly*, vol. 286 (6) (Dec.). Online at *http://www.theatlantic.com/issues/2000/12/elliott.htm*

FORREST, P. (1988), 'Supervenience: the grand property hypothesis', *Australasian Journal of Philosophy,* 66: 1–12.

——(1992), 'Universals and universalisability: an interpretation of Oddie's discussion of supervenience', *Australasian Journal of Philosophy,* 70 (1): 93–8.

FRANKFURT, H. G. (1971), 'Freedom of the will and the concept of a person', *Journal of Philosophy,* 68: 5–20.

——(1999), *Necessity, Volition and Love* (New York: Cambridge University Press).

FUMERTON, R. (1990), *Reason and Morality: A Defense of the Egocentric Perspective* (Ithaca, NY: Cornell University Press).

GÄRDENFORS, P. (2000), *Conceptual Spaces* (Cambridge, Mass.: MIT Press).

GIBBARD, A. (1990), *Wise Choices, Apt Feelings* (Cambridge, Mass.: Harvard University Press).

GOLDSTICK, D., and O'NEILL, B. (1987), 'Truer', *Philosophy of Science,* 31: 631–72.

HARMAN, G. (1977), *The Nature of Morality: An Introduction to Ethics* (New York: Oxford University Press).

——and THOMSON, J. (1996), *Moral Relativism and Moral Objectivity* (Oxford: Blackwell).

HOOKER, B., and LITTLE, M. (2000), (eds.), Moral Particularism (Oxford: Clarendon Press).

HUEMER, M. (2001), *Skepticism and the Veil of Perception* (Lanham, Md.: Rowman & Littlefield Publishers).

HUMBERSTONE, L. (1992), 'Direction of fit', *Mind,* 101: 59–8.

HUME, D. (1955), *A Treatise of Human Nature,* ed. L. A. Selby-Bigge (Oxford: Clarendon Press).

JAMES, W. (1884), 'What is an emotion?' *Mind,* 9: 188–205.

JOHNSTON, M. (2001), 'The authority of affect', *Philosophy and Phenomenological Research,* 63 (1): 181–214.

KELLY, C. (2003), 'A Theory of the Good' (University of Colorado, PhD dissertation).

KEMENY, J., and SNELL, J. (1967), *Finite Markov Chains* (Princeton: van Nostrand).

KIM, J. (1978), 'Supervenience and nomological incommensurables', *American Philosophical Quarterly,* 15: 149–56.

——(1993), 'Multiple realization and the metaphysics of reduction', in J. Kim, *Supervenience and Mind* (New York: Cambridge University Press), 309–35.

LEHRER, K. (1997), *Self Trust: A Study of Reason, Knowledge and Autonomy* (Oxford: Clarendon Press).

——and WAGNER, C. (1981), *Rational Consensus in Science and Society* (Dordrecht: Reidel).

LEIBNIZ, G. W. (1961), *Discourse on Metaphysics*, trans. P. G. Lucas and L. Grint (Manchester: Manchester University Press).

LEMOS, N. M. (1994), *Intrinsic Value: Concept and Warrant* (New York: Cambridge University Press).

LESLIE, J. (1979), *Value and Existence* (Totowa, NJ: Rowman and Littlefield).

LEWIS, D. K. (1972), 'General semantics', in D. Davidson and G. Harman, (eds.), *Semantics of Natural Language* (Dordrecht: Reidel), 169–218.

——(1981), 'Causal decision theory', *Australasian Journal of Philosophy*, 59: 5–30.

——(1983), 'New work for a theory of universals', *Australasian Journal of Philosophy*, 61: 343–77.

——(1986), 'A subjectivist's guide to objective chance', in D. Lewis, *Philosophical Papers*, ii (Berkeley: University of California Press), 83–132. *et al.* (eds.), *Ifs* (Dordrecht: Reidel).

——(1988), 'Desire as belief', *Mind*, 97: 323–32.

——(1989), 'Dispositional theories of value', *Proceedings of the Aristotelian Society*, supp. vol. 63.

——(1996), 'Desire as Belief II', *Mind*, 105: 303–13.

MACKIE, J. (1946), 'A refutation of morals', *Australasian Journal of Philosophy*, 24: 77–90.

——(1977), *Ethics: Inventing Right and Wrong* (New York: Penguin).

MATERNA, P. (1998), *Concepts and Objects* (Helsinki: Acta Philosophica Fennica).

MEINONG, A. (1972), *On Emotional Presentation*, trans. M. Schubert (Evanston, Ill.: Northwestern University Press).

MOORE, G. E. (1960), *Principia Ethica* (London: Cambridge University Press).

MULLIGAN, K. (1998), 'From appropriate emotions to values', *The Monist*, 81 (1): 161–88.

MURDOCH, I. (1970), *The Sovereignty of Good* (London: Routledge & Kegan Paul).

——(1993), *Metaphysics as a Guide to Morals* (New York: Penguin).

NOZICK, R. (1981), *Philosophical Explanations* (Cambridge, Mass.: Harvard University Press).

——(1989), *The Examined Life: Philosophical Meditations* (New York: Simon and Schuster).

OAKLEY, J. (1992), *Morality and the Emotions* (London: Routledge).

ODDIE, G. (1982), 'Armstrong on the eleatic principle and abstract entities', *Philosophical Studies*, 41: 285–95.

——(1986), *Likeness to Truth*, Western Ontario Series in Philosophy of Science (Dordrecht: Reidel).

——(1987), 'Truthlikeness and the convexity of propositions', in Theo Kuipers (ed.), *What is Closer-to-the-Truth?* (Amsterdam: Rodopi), 197–217.

—— (1991), 'Supervenience and higher-order universals', *Australasian Journal of Philosophy*, 69: 20–47.

—— (1992), 'The possibility and value of possibilities for value', *From the Logical Point of View*, 2: 46–62.

—— (1994), 'Harmony, purity, truth', *Mind*, 103: 452–72.

—— (2000), 'Permanent possibilities of sensation', *Philosophical Studies*, 98: 345–59.

—— (2001*a*), 'Axiological atomism', *Australasian Journal of Philosophy*, 79: 313–32.

—— (2001*b*), 'Hume, the bad paradox and value realism', *Philo*, 4: 1–30.

—— (2001*c*), 'Recombinant values', *Philosophical Studies*, 106: 259–92.

—— (2001*d*), 'Scrumptious functions', *Grazer Philosophische Studien*, 62: 137–56.

—— and MENZIES, P. (1992), 'An objectivist's guide to subjective value', *Ethics*, 102 (3): 512–34.

—— and TICHÝ, P. (1990), 'Resplicing properties in the supervenience base', *Philosophical Studies*, 58: 1–11.

PARKER, I. (2004), 'The gift', *New Yorker*, 2 Aug., 54–63.

PETTIT, P., and SMITH, M. (1990), 'Backgrounding desire', *Philosophical Review*, 99: 565–92.

PLATO (1980), *Plato: Symposium*, ed. Sir Kenneth Dover (New York: Cambridge University Press).

—— (1953), *The Dialogues of Plato*, trans. B. Jowett, 4th edn. (Oxford: Clarendon Press).

POPPER, K. (1963), *Conjectures and Refutations: The Growth of Scientific Knowledge* (London: Routledge & Kegan Paul, 1963).

ROSAN, L. J. (1955), 'Desirelessness and the good', *Philosophy East & West*, 5: 57–60.

SAYRE-McCORD, G. (1988), (ed.), *Essays on Moral Realism* (Ithaca, NY: Cornell University Press).

SCHELER, M. (1973), *Formalism in Ethics and Non-Formal Ethics of Value*, trans. M. Frings and R. Funk (Evanston, Ill.: Northwestern University Press).

SHIELDS, C. J. (2003), *Classical Philosophy: A Contemporary Introduction* (London: Routledge).

SLOTE, M. (2004), 'Famine, affluence and empathy', in G. Oddie, and D. Boonin, (eds.), *What's Wrong?* (New York: Oxford University Press), 548–56.

SMITH, M. (1987), 'The Humean theory of motivation', *Mind*, 96 (381): 36–61.

—— (1991), 'Realism', in P. Singer (ed.), *A Companion to Ethics* (Oxford: Blackwell), 399–410.

—— (1995), *The Moral Problem* (Oxford: Blackwell).

SMITH, M. (2002), 'Exploring the implications of the dispositional theory of value', *Noûs*, 36: 329–47.

SOBEL, D. (1999), 'Do the desires of rational agents converge?', *Analysis*, 59: 137–47.

SOLOMON, R. C. (1981), *Love: Emotion, Myth, and Metaphor* (New York: Anchor Press/Doubleday).

SPINOZA (1955), *Ethics*, trans. R. H. M. Elwes (New York: Dover).

STAMPE, D. W. (1987), 'The authority of desire', *The Philosophical Review*, 96 (2): 335–81.

STEIKER, V. (2001), 'Dressing for dinner (and other things my mother knew)', *The New Yorker*, 24 and 31 Dec., 64–70.

STOVE, D. C. (1972), 'Misconditionalization', *Australasian Journal of Philosophy*, 50 (2).

SWOYER, C. (2001), 'Properties', in E. Zalta (ed.), *Stanford Encyclopedia of Philosophy* URL = http://plato.stanford.edu/entries/properties/.

TENENBAUM, S. (1999), 'The Judgement of a Weak Will', *Philosophy and Phenomenological Research*, 49 (4): 875–911.

TENENBAUM, S. (2007), *Appearances of the Good*, (New York: Cambridge University Press).

TICHÝ, P. (1978*a*), 'De dicto and de re', *Philosophia*, 8: 1–16.

——(1978*b*), 'Existence and God', *Journal of Philosophy*, 76: 403–20.

——(1986), 'Constructions', *Philosophy of Science*, 53: 514–34.

——(1988), *The Foundations of Frege's Logic* (Berlin: de Gruyter).

TOLSTOY, L. (2001), *Anna Karenina*, trans. R. Pevear and L. Volokhonsky (New York: Penguin).

TOOLEY, M. (1977), 'The nature of laws', *Canadian Journal of Philosophy*, 7: 667–98.

——(forthcoming), 'Counterfactual analyses of causation', *APA Pacific Division Conference 2004*.

WEDGEWOOD, R. (2001), 'Sensing values?' *Philosophy and Phenomenological Research*, 63 (1): 215–23.

WOLF, S. (1988), 'The deep-self theory', in F. Schoema (ed.), *Responsibility, Character and the Emotions* (New York: Cambridge University Press), 46–62.

YABLO, S. (1992), 'Mental causation', *Philosophical Review*, 101: 245–80.

INDEX

absorber 109–10
acquaintance internalism 236–9
additivity of value
  see value, additivity of
altruism 113–16, 138
analysis 149–50
Anna Karenina 67–9
Anscombe, G. E. M. 33
apotemnophelia 126–31
approval 5, 17, 38, 41
Aristotle 38, 130
Armstrong, D. M. 20, 51, 147, 151, 207, 209
atheism 8, 10, 11
aversion 5, 134

BAD
  see belief as desire
balanced matrix 101
Bealer, G. 149
behaviourism 18
belief as desire 78–80, 243
Berkeley, Bishop 15, 16, 83, 142
Blackburn, S. 6
blindsight 51
Boolean closure 147, 151–2
brain in a vat 51
Brentano, F. 38, 73
Broad, C. D. 38, 48, 84
Buddhism 70–1
buyer's regret 68

callousness 144, 160, 161, 162, 198–202
Cantor 35
caring 86–102
causal exclusion argument 20, 181, 187–91
causal exclusion principle 188
causal networking 20, 21, 22, 26, 181–210
causation 191–5

by values 190, 198–206
  mental 195–8
  regularity theory of 18
Chisholm, R. 38, 73
Churchland, P. M. 206
cognitivism 5, 28–47
Cohen, S. 242
commensurateness of cause to
  effect 192–209
conceptual condition 197, 204
conceptual space 154–5, 173–5, 206
connectedness (of desires) 100–4,
  107–12, 116–18, 122, 125, 129, 137
constructions 145–6, 150
content-state distinction 52–3, 64–5,
  183
convergence in desires 85, 93–104,
  107–8, 115–25
convex closure 158, 168
convexity 26, 152–80, 203–6
convexity constraint 204–6, 209, 236
cosmological argument 21
Cresswell, M. 149
cruelty 144, 160, 161, 162, 182, 198–9,
  200–6

DAB,
  see desire as belief
Dancy, J. 19
de re, de dicto 11
decision theory 78
desire
  agent-relativity of 5–63, 81, 85, 89,
    91–3, 100–6,
  as belief, 78–80, 243
  base 88–95
  first-order 88–95
  desire, value of 70–3, 131–6
  desires, appropriateness of 131–6, 139,
    163–80

desire (*Contd.*)
  desires, coherence of 68, 81, 85,
    87–104, 125, 136–40, 230–1
  desires, ideal 98–100, 102–6, 112, 119,
    137–8
  desires, refinement of 25, 81–106,
    107–40
  desires, reflexive 96–7
  desires, second-order 84–106,
    107–40
  desire-value gap 27, 212
desire-judgement gap 27, 35, 213, 216
desirelessness 70–2
determinables and determinates 154,
  160, 161, 162, 191–204
determination 15, 19, 25, 141–3 187–9,
  202, 210
  see also supervenience
direction of fit 32–33
disappointment 67–9
disapproval
  see approval
disjointed conditions 153–66, 179, 176,
  178
disjunctive properties 151–4, 175, 178
dispositionalism
  see value (dispositional theory of)
Divine command theory 111
Dreier, J. 19, 143
Dretske, F. 207
Dummett, M. 11

egoism 106, 107–13, 138, 228, 230, 231
Einstein, A. 96
Eleatic Principle 20, 21, 181, 191
Eleatic Stranger
  see Eleatic Principle
Elliot, C. 126, 129
emotion, theories of 73–8
emotivism 5
epiphenomenalism 191
epistemic respect 96
equalizer matrix 101, 103, 115, 118
error theory 9, 10, 11, 14
Euthyphro 111
excluded middle 9, 10
experience conjecture 24, 25, 27, 40–6,
  60–80, 104, 180, 184, 215, 219–22,
  226, 234

experiences of value
  see experience conjecture
expressivism (*see also* non-
  cognitivism) 37

fictionalism 9, 12, 20
fine-grained properties 35, 148,
  149–51
Finn, Huck 65
Forrest, P. 207
Frankfurt, H. 84, 87, 97
Frege, G. 150
Fumerton, R. 59
fusion 179–90, 209

Gärdenfors, P. 154, 159, 206
gerrymandered properties 154, 177, 179,
  see also disjointed conditions;
    disjunctive properties
Gibbard, A. 6
God 2, 4, 8–12, 109–11
Goldstick, D. and Oneill, B. 156

Harman, G. 6, 181–91
hatred 120–5, 129, 138, 231
Hooker, B. and Little M. 20
Huemer, M. 51
Humberstone, L. 33
Hume, D. 31, 33, 45, 48, 76, 204
hyperintensionality 149

Iago 63–7
ideal limit theory 16, 213
ideal observer 16, 63
idealism 12, 14–18, 23–6, 51, 69, 80–1
identity theory 18, 20, 191
impartialism 117–19
independence of belief and
  desire 32–45, 76, 233–4, 240–1
infatuation 116–17
instrumentalism 4
internal realism 16
internalism 24, 28–38, 80, 234–8
intuitions of value 41–2, 57, 182, 236
irreducibility
  see reduction

James, W. 74
Johnston, M. 38, 73

judgement internalism 29, 32, 36, 38, 78, 237
judgement-desire gap 36–8, 213, 215
just deserts 177

Kant, I. 21, 51–2, 230
Kelly, C. 130, 132, 140
Kemeny, J. and Snell, J. 89, 99, 110
Kim, Jaegwon 19, 141, 175
Kravihsky, Z. 222
Kripke, S. 197

laws 206–10
Lehrer, K. 87, 89–90, 96, 120–1
Leibniz, G. W. 130
Leibniz's Principle 148, 159, 171, 172, 197
Lemos, N. 58, 59, 61, 226, 229
Leslie, J. 21
Lewis, D. 21, 78–80, 83–5, 149,
logicism 18
love 17, 38, 73, 76–7, 86–9, 102–4, 106, 116, 121–2, 124–5, 222

Mackie, J. 9, 13, 14, 31, 235–8
magnetism of the good 104–5
  see also internalism
mark of being
  see Eleatic Principle
Markov Chains 99, 109, 120
Materna, P. 150
measurement 204–6
Meinong, A. 38, 73
Menzies, P. 80
merit connection 38–9,60–3, 102–3, 133, 139, 221–6, 231–2
mind dependence 14, 15, 16, 17
misconditionalization, fallacy of 66
Moore, G. E. 19, 43, 142, 143
Moore's paradox 43–5
motivation, Humean theory of 31, 48
motivational inertness 24, 50
Mulligan, K. 38, 80
Murdoch, I. 5, 21

natural basis (of value
  property) 159–60, 162–6, 172–5, 180, 201–3
naturalism 18, 19, 23, 25, 141–3, 158–80
necessary coextension 147–8, 151

negative properties 151–2
Neoplatonism 21
nihilism 9, 12, 23, 160–1, 189
nomic necessitation 208–9
non-cognitivism 5–7, 12, 23, 24, 28–46, 213
non-conceptual content 80
Nozick, R. 87, 130

Oakley, J. 74
Oddie, G. 17, 35, 79, 83, 141, 142, 145, 148, 156, 166, 168, 177, 207
ontological dependence 17, 144–5
organic unity 26, 130–1, 138, 166, 168,

pain 35–6, 61–2, 139–40, 163–70, 177, 182–7, 198–200, 221–2, 238
Parker, I. 222
partial irreducibility 160
particularism 19
perspectivity 60–3, 69, 81, 85, 89, 105, 213, 218–26
perversity 125–31, 228, 231
Pettit, P. 56
phenomenalism 16, 25, 83
phlogiston 161
Plato 3, 13, 19–20, 70–2, 87, 191, 235
pleasure 18, 73, 88, 130, 132, 139–40, 163–79
Popper, K. 156
possible worlds 20, 21, 35, 179–80
prescriptivism 5
presupposition 3, 8, 9, 14, 22
  existential 8, 9
  presuppositional failure 11, 22, 161
Principal Principle 80
probabilistic causation 208
propensity 208
property
  purely natural property 178, 238
  purely value property 179
  theory 26, 147–80
propositional content 4, 5, 22, 31, 33,
psychological egoism
  see egoism
puzzling asymmetry 24, 28–45, 234–5

quality space 154–9, 172, 209
  see also conceptual space

quantum mechanics 15
queerness 14, 24, 30–33, 47, 81, 180, 233–9

realism 1–27
  degrees of 22–3
  scientific 4, 8
  theological 4, 8, 11
reciprocating care 101
reducibility
  see reduction
reduction 14, 15, 17, 18, 19, 20, 21, 22, 25,
    26, 38, 141–3, 144–6
refinement theory 25, 81–106, 228–31
response dependence 16
richness 130
role theory 12, 13
Rosan, L. J. 70
Russell's theory of descriptions 10–11

SAD
  see seeming as desire
Sayre-McCord, G. 4
schadenfreude 144, 161
Scheler, M. 38, 73
seeming as desire 78–80
self-hatred 129–30
Shields, C. 130
Slote, M. 222
Smith, M. 31–4, 56, 85, 104, 237
Sobel, D. 85
Solomon, R. C. 75, 87
Spinoza 18, 76
Stampe, D. W. viii
Steiker, V. 199, 205
Stove, D. C. 66
structured properties
  see fine-grained properties
Studtmann, P. 209, 241
supervenience 19, 22, 106, 141–80,
    187–204
Swoyer, C. 147

Tarski's T-schema 6
Tenenbaum, S. viii
thick value concepts 160–2
Thomson, J. J. 6
Tichý, P. 11, 35, 148, 149, 150
Tolstoy, L. 67
Tooley, M. 195, 207, 209
transcendentism 21, 26
trust 120
truth 2–14
  truth aptness 4–7
  truth value gap 10–12
  disquotational theory of 6–7
  truthvaluelessness
    see truth value gap
truthlikeness 8, 156

universalizability 19, 25, 48, 141–4, 207,
    222

value
  additivity of 26, 166, 168
  data 24, 47–78, 220
  dispositional theory of 83–6, 96, 104
  experiences of
    see experience conjecture
  idealism 24, 25, 82–104, 138, 140, 190,
      212, 229, 231
  of desire 70–3, 135–7
  residue 25, 83, 107, 138–9
  scepticism 26–7, 191
  space 144, 170–80, 199, 201, 218–22,
      235
value-convexity hypothesis 160, 162
value-judgment gap 27, 213
verificationism 12

Wagner, C. 89, 96, 120
Wolf, S. 97

Yablo, S. 191–8